Note: The author uses the term "Chinamen" in the title advisedly, fully aware that in current parlance it is considered a derogatory term. At the turn of the twentieth century, however, it was used by Chinese and non-Chinese alike as a descriptive word for "Chinese man," in the same vein as "Englishman" and "Frenchman," and did not necessarily bear any negative connotation. It is solely in this historical context that the word is employed.

THREE TOUGH CHINAMEN

Scott D. Seligman

Three Tough Chinamen

By Scott D. Seligman

ISBN-13: 978-988-8769-31-5

© 2012, Scott D. Seligman

This book has been reset in 10pt Book Antiqua. Spellings and punctuations are left as in the original edition.

HISTORY / Asia / China

EB052

All rights reserved. No part of this book may be reproduced in material form, by any means, whether graphic, electronic, mechanical or other, including photocopying or information storage, in whole or in part. May not be used to prepare other publications without written permission from the publisher except in the case of brief quotations embodied in critical articles or reviews. For information contact info@earnshawbooks.com

Published by Earnshaw Books Ltd. (Hong Kong)

CONTENTS

Author's Preface   ix

A Note on Romanization and Chinese Names   xiii

Dramatis Personae   xv

Chapter I: Tangled in a Snarl   1
In which Moy Jin Kee and his wife Chin Fung, American citizens returning after a trip to China, are detained in Tacoma, Washington by immigration authorities pending an investigation of their right to be admitted.

Chapter II: The Road to Exclusion   4
In which the confluence of events behind the great Chinese Diaspora, the conditions leading to America's exclusion of Chinese, and the practicalities of enforcing Chinese exclusion are considered.

Chapter III: Beginnings   12
In which the history of the Moy family of Duanfen and the early life of the Moy brothers is presented.

Chapter IV: California Dreaming   20
In which Jin Kee and Jin Mun make the voyage to California, meet the Leland Stanfords and return to China to marry and in which Jin Mun prospects old claims and works for the railroad.

Chapter V: Another Good Man Gone Wrong   32
In which Jin Fuey arrives in America and he and Jin Kee move to New York, where Jin Kee speaks out against the Chinese Exclusion Act, opens a mission and get arrested for larceny.

Chapter VI: He Stands High Among His Countrymen   49
In which Jin Fuey is sent to seminary and medical school, elopes, adopts a daughter, works in a Chinese hospital and takes a job with a church.

Chapter VII: Moy Jin Mun Will Furnish The Corpse   66
In which Jin Mun reports a shipment of contraband opium, gets cheated out of his reward, translates regulations requiring all Chinese to register with the government, receives death threats and smokes opium in open court.

Chapter VIII: A Thorough American   77

In which Jin Kee brings his wife from China, opens a hotel, relocates to Chicago, doggedly pursues naturalization and becomes active in a movement to secure rights for the Chinese in America.

Chapter IX: I Created Enmity Among Our Own Countrymen   92

In which Jin Fuey speaks out against an anti-Chinese bill, joins the Immigration Bureau, purchases a New Jersey farm. is accused of smuggling and is discharged from the Service.

Chapter X: Disaster and Rebuilding   99

In which Jin Mun is ill-treated by a gang of boys, is the defendant in a lawsuit for non-payment of rent, allegedly loses three sons in the San Francisco earthquake and returns to mining.

Chapter XI: Meet Me At The Fair   111

In which Jin Kee relocates to Indianapolis and obtains citizenship, receives a gift from Viceroy Li Hung Chang, hosts Prince Pu Lun and is elevated to the Chinese titled elite.

Chapter XII: Leading the Fight   120

In which Jin Kee is named to lead the struggle against the Chinese Exclusion Act, visits Washington and meets the Vice President and the President.

Chapter XIII: I Deem It To Be A Lesson   128

In which Gop Jung joins the Immigration Bureau even as his cousin Jin Fuey is discharged, succeeds in importing his wife and son from China, and accuses Jin Mun of extortion.

Chapter XIV: Less Than Savory Characters   137

In which Jin Fuey is tried in Boston for allegedly smuggling Chinese into the United States.

Chapter XV: Reversal of Fortune I   146

In which Jin Kee is ousted from his position and stripped of his rank, returns to China and is detained and nearly denied re-entry upon his return.

Chapter XVI: Reversal of Fortune II   162

In which Jin Kee opines about the future of Chinese queues, loses his citizenship, dies, is mourned and is taken back to China by his wife for burial.

Chapter XVII: Many Impeachable Practices   174
In which Gop Jung is investigated by the U.S. Immigration Bureau for violating his oath of office and Jin Fuey is interrogated and suspected of having turned him in.

Chapter XVIII: The Chinese Nightingale   182
In which Josephine Moy becomes a vaudeville and silent film star, Josephine and Hattie Moy apply for passports, and Jin Fuey's origins are investigated.

Chapter XIX: The Man Who Took the Teeth Out of the Drug Act   192
In which Jin Fuey relocates to Pittsburgh, is arrested three times for mail fraud and dealing in narcotics, is the respondent in one Supreme Court case and the petitioner in another.

Chapter XX: Prisoner #11990   204
In which Jin Fuey serves nearly two years in the Federal penitentiary, is released and dies.

Chapter XXI: Peacemaker   215
In which Jin Mun leads the Six Companies, participates in the General Peace Association, travels widely in support of efforts to quell triad violence, is ruined in the stock market crash and dies.

Epilogue   224

Moy Family Tree (Abridged)   230

Moy Jin Kee Chronology   232

Moy Jin Mun Chronology   234

Jin Fuey Moy Chronology   236

Glossary of Chinese Terms and Place Names   238

Notes   241

Acknowledgments   285

About the Author   289

Author's Preface

My acquaintance with the Moy brothers, who lived more than a century ago, is the happy result of modern technology. Digitization and optical character recognition software have made many old newspapers easily and efficiently searchable online. I found my way to the Moys by browsing turn-of-the-century editions of the *Washington Post*. Looking to learn about the history of Washington, DC's tiny Chinatown, I happened on the story of a Chinese immigrant named Moy Gop Jung, who held positions from laundryman and Sunday school teacher to detective and constable, helped the police track down Chinese troublemakers and attempted unsuccessfully to wed a Caucasian woman in the District of Columbia. The *Post* declared him "one of the most interesting men employed in Uncle Sam's service."

Moy Gop Jung *was* interesting, and he got even more so when I found, on the Ancestry.com website, a 925-page case file about him from the U.S. Immigration Bureau's Chinese Exclusion Act collection. He worked as an interpreter for the Bureau until being accused of a litany of offenses, including perjury, smuggling illegal immigrants into the United States and selling classified information. He was also, as it turned out, a bigamist.

In perusing the file about his investigation – which unfolded like a Perry Mason mystery – I was introduced to several of his relatives, and discovered that as remarkable as Moy Gop Jung's story was, those of three brothers he called his uncles were even more so. There was Moy Jin Kee (1847-1914), who spoke out eloquently against the Chinese Exclusion Act, opened a Methodist mission in the heart of New York's Chinatown and became a key figure in the American Chinese community's efforts to lobby for the rights of citizenship. Jin Kee's brother, Moy Jin

AUTHOR'S PREFACE

Mun (1851-1936) was a protégé of Leland Stanford, a prospector in the California Gold Rush, a dabbler in the opium trade and for a time the leader of the Six Companies, the most powerful Chinese organization in America. And most interesting of all was Jin Fuey Moy (1862-1924), a physician who was arrested several times for drug-related offenses, was the subject of two Supreme Court cases that helped shape early federal efforts to regulate narcotics and are cited frequently to this day, and who served two years in the Atlanta Penitentiary for his crimes.

And so while Moy Gop Jung will make a couple of appearances in this work, it is principally a book about his uncles – or more precisely, his first cousins, once removed.

When my grandfather, Abraham Seligman, emigrated to the United States from Byelorussia (now Belarus) in 1905, the Moy brothers had already been in America for at least a quarter of a century; in the case of Moy Jin Kee, it had been nearly twice that length of time. They spoke better English than he did. But as soon as Abe had cleared Immigration at Ellis Island, he enjoyed far more freedoms than the Moys ever were permitted in their many decades in the same country.

Abe endured his share of hardships, to be sure, but he wasn't required to carry a residence permit that proved his right to be in the United States, and didn't risk prison or deportation if he failed to produce valid identification. He was free to return to Europe if he wished and then turn around and come back to America, and would face no intensive grilling from an Immigration official demanding to know how many rows of houses there were in his native village, or the names and birth order of his father's brothers. He could pick a wife from an already large population of Jewish women in America or, if he preferred, from among the many who continued to flow into New York harbor every day. Congress had passed no law that effectively barred the entry of women from Europe on the presumption that they probably intended to work as prostitutes, as it had done with Asian women.

AUTHOR'S PREFACE

True, the Moys and their fellow Chinese-Americans had arrived uninvited, as guests in somebody else's country, and as such arguably had no legal basis on which to demand civil rights. But immigrants like my grandfather, who had come under similar circumstances from dozens of other countries, were afforded such liberties automatically, and were free to become citizens. Apart from Africans, who had by and large arrived involuntarily and under very different circumstances, only the Chinese were singled out for shabby treatment based solely on bigotry by a nation that, for the most part, saw alarmingly little contradiction between such intolerance and its proud democratic and egalitarian ideals.

Hemmed in by prejudice and restrictive laws, the Chinese in America did what they had to do to succeed and prosper. Most kept their heads down and tried to amass a little capital to provide for their families and support themselves in retirement upon their return to China. But the Moy brothers, scrappy and ambitious, crossed lines and broke barriers. They spoke out about the injustices perpetrated against their countrymen, decried the Exclusion Act and railed about the pernicious effects of the Geary Act, its malicious successor. And they were leaders in the fight for the betterment of their compatriots, promoting Chinese unity, mediating conflict among Chinatown's triads and pushing for equality under the law for all of America's Chinese.

They also used all available means to get ahead and to defend their prerogatives and interests, up to and including committing petty crimes and, in the case of one brother, heinous ones. At a time when the vast majority of Chinese in the United States were living in a perpetual defensive crouch, these men were making waves, taking names and filing suits. And unlike many of their compatriots who eventually headed home when their adventure was over, they were also putting down roots. The Moys were in America to stay.

The brothers' stories are compelling in their own right, but there is also much in them that transcends the conflicts in their

AUTHOR'S PREFACE

own lives. Nearly all of the problems experienced by Chinese people living in America during the exclusion period are evident in them. They are stories that offer a window into the lives of Chinese men in America – for the overwhelming majority were men, their women having been effectively excluded – at the turn of the 20th century. They are stories of outwitting laws that were patently unfair and that ordained that they accept third-class status if they desired even a small share in the American dream. And they are stories of a clash of cultures: how Western notions of rule of law and oaths of office fared among Asian immigrants when they went head to head, as they inevitably had to, against more ancient values like clan loyalty, and against personal interests and greed.

It was my good fortune to stumble onto the Moy brothers, each of whom, in his own way, deserves to be rescued from obscurity. I share their stories in the hope that the reader finds them as compelling as I have.

Scott D. Seligman
Washington, DC,
September 1, 2012

A Note on Romanization and Chinese Names

No standard Romanization for Chinese names was used a century ago in the original documents consulted in the preparation of this book. While the venerable Wade-Giles system was available for the Mandarin dialect of northern China, no comparable, widely used system has ever existed for Cantonese, less still the Taishan dialect spoken in the home villages of the Moy brothers in Guangdong Province.

This matter was irrelevant while the Chinese remained in China, where written communication was accomplished entirely in characters. But when Chinese immigrants reached America's shores, some form of Romanized spelling of their names was required. If the immigrants themselves didn't know how to render their names in letters – and most surely did not, at least initially – this was done for them by ship captains, immigration officers, court clerks or journalists, few of whom spoke any Chinese at all.

The result is a hodgepodge of spellings, some more, some less true to the various Chinese pronunciations, the consequence of different people spelling personal and place names as they sounded to them. Making matters more difficult, many Chinese immigrants went by more than one name. Moy Jin Kee, for example, was called by his full name in New York, but became Moy Ah Kee once he went to Chicago and was known simply as Moy Kee by the time he got to Indianapolis. And then there is the Chinese convention of placing the surname first and the given name after, which was not universally understood by those who kept track of Chinese in America, so surnames were sometimes taken for given names and *vice versa*. In some cases, the Chinese

A NOTE ON ROMANIZATION AND CHINESE NAMES

themselves reversed the order of their names once they crossed the ocean, adopting the American convention. Thus, Moy Jin Fuey was known as Jin Fuey Moy, but Moy was no less his surname for this arrangement.

For purposes of clarity, I have adopted one, consistent rendering and spelling for each name in this book. Because I cannot change how the names appear in the historic documents or the quotations from them that appear in these pages, I have used the same spellings the Moy brothers and their contemporaries used during their lifetimes. In the table that begins on the following page, I have listed the names of important characters in the story, including "aliases" for each who was known by more than one name, or whose name was generally spelled in more than one way. For the Chinese names, I have included their equivalents, where known, in the modern *pinyin* system.

For Chinese place names, I have generally relied on the *pinyin* system. In the few instances in which traditional spellings appear, such as in quotes from historic documents, I have indicated the *pinyin* spellings in italics immediately after the first mention of them. Please consult the glossary at the end of this work for the standard characters (simplified characters were not yet in use during the period covered in the book) associated with the Chinese names and terms.

DRAMATIS PERSONAE

MOY FAMILY	
Moy Jin Kee (梅振基; *Mei Zhenji*) (1847-1914)	Preacher who opened a Christian mission in New York's Chinatown and was arrested for theft shortly thereafter. Merchant who lived in Chicago and then Indianapolis and who led a national effort to secure rights for Chinese-Americans. For a time a fifth-degree Mandarin and a United States citizen. *Aliases: Moy Kee* (梅基), *Moy Ah Kee* (梅阿基), *Moy You Yin* (梅耀彥).
Moy Jin Mun (梅振文; *Mei Zhenwen*) (1851-1936)	Protégé of Leland Stanford who worked as a miner, an interpreter and a merchant. Prominent figure in San Francisco's Chinatown who led the powerful Six Companies and helped to stop triad wars through the General Peace Association. *Aliases: Moy Ki Choo* (梅岐佐), *Moy You Mun* (梅耀文).
Jin Fuey Moy* (梅振魁; *Mei Zhenkui*) (1862-1924)	Physician who worked in Christian missions and as an interpreter for the U.S. Immigration Bureau. Arrested for smuggling Chinese laborers and trafficking in narcotics. Party to two Supreme Court cases concerning the distribution of narcotics by physicians. Lived in New York, New Jersey and Pennsylvania. *Alias: Moy Siu Yun* (梅紹元).
Moy Kye Hin (梅岐?; *Mei Qi ?*) (1854-ca. 1919)	Brother of Jin Fuey, Jin Kee and Jin Mun who lived in San Francisco and Philadelphia and returned to China in 1918. *Alias: Moy You Lim* (梅耀廉).
Moy Yuen Bong (梅遠邦; *Mei Yuanbang*) (?-1879)	Father of Jin Fuey, Jin Kee, Jin Mun and Kye Hin. Lived in Taishan and probably never left China.
Moy Gop Jung (梅甲長; *Mei Jiachang*) (1864-1918)	First cousin once removed of Jin Fuey and his brothers who rose from laundryman to interpreter for the U.S. Immigration Bureau. Lived in Peoria, New York, Washington, Baltimore and Pittsburgh. *Alias: Moy Nai Tow* (梅迺澡).

*Unlike virtually all of his relatives in the United States, Jin Fuey Moy reversed the traditional order of his names and followed the American custom of placing his surname last.

DRAMATIS PERSONAE

Chin Fung (1856-aft. 1915)	Wife of Jin Kee. *Aliases: Toy Fong, Chin Fung Kee.*
Gong Shee (江氏; *Jiang Shi*) (1856-1906)	First wife of Jin Mun and mother of his four eldest children. Born in China, she emigrated to San Francisco in 1875 but returned to China in 1886 and never came back to America.
Wong Shee (黃氏; *Huang Shi*) (1871-1953)	American-born second wife of Jin Mun and mother of at least six of his children. *Alias: Wong Ngoy Jin.*
Hatita Alice Dolbow Moy (1869-aft. 1930)	Delaware-born wife of Jin Fuey and adoptive mother of Josephine Moy. *Alias: Hattie Moy.*
Josephine Augusta Moy (1888-1985)	Adopted daughter of Jin Fuey and Hattie Moy. Vaudevillian and motion picture actress who performed under the name of the Lady Tsen Mei. *Aliases: Lady Tsen Mei, Lady Sen Mei, Josephine Chong Moy.*
Hu Shee (胡氏; *Hu Shi*) (1872-aft. 1922)	Chinese wife of Moy Gop Jung. Emigrated to the United States with Moy Sher Park in 1914.
Moy Sher Park (梅社柏; *Mei Shebai*) (1901-1964)	Son, or possibly "paper son," of Moy Gop Jung and Hu Shee. Emigrated to the United States with Hu Shee in 1914. *Aliases: Moy Shere Park, Moy Shu Park, Ah Park, Henry DeMaire.*
Moy Shoo Chong (1858-1943)	Philadelphia laundryman and biological father of Josephine Moy. *Aliases: Moy Chong* (梅長), *Moy Oy Nai* (梅?迺).
Jessie Whitehurst (1858-1889)	Wife of Moy Shoo Chong and biological mother of Josephine Moy. *Aliases: Jersey Whitehurst, Jersey Chong.*
Moy Hee (梅禧; *Mei Xi*) (1873-?)	First cousin of Jin Kee and his brothers who lived in Indianapolis and took over Jin Kee's restaurant, together with two others, when Jin Kee returned to China in 1907. *Alias: Moy Bing Hee.*

DRAMATIS PERSONAE

Moy Hun (1870-?)	First cousin of Jin Kee and his brothers who lived in Indianapolis and took over Jin Kee's restaurant, together with two others, when Jin Kee returned to China in 1907. *Alias: Moy You Hun.*
Dong Gum Hong (1878-?)	Relative of Jin Kee and his brothers who lived in Indianapolis and took over Jin Kee's restaurant, together with two others, when Jin Kee returned to China in 1907. *Aliases: Charlie Hong, Charlie Moy.*
Ning Tong (1883-?)	One of two "paper sons" claimed by Jin Kee and Chin Fung. *Aliases: Say Fong, Moy Ning Tong.*
Ning Yip (1883-?)	One of two "paper sons" claimed by Jin Kee and Chin Fung. *Aliases: Hai Gim, Moy Ning Yip.*
Moy Chow Heung (1877-?)	Adopted daughter of Jin Mun and Gong Shee. *Aliases: Josephine Moy, Josie C. Hung.*

OTHERS	
Aisin-Gioro Pu Lun (愛新覺羅 · 蒲倫; *Aixin Jueluo Pulun*) (1869-1925)	Manchu Prince and cousin of the Guangxu Emperor. Represented China at the 1904 St. Louis World's Fair and visited Indianapolis for 10 days. Instrumental in elevating Jin Kee to the titled elite.
Aisin-Gioro Tsai Tao (愛新覺羅 · 載濤; *Aixin Jueluo Zaitao*) (1857-1925)	Brother of the Prince Regent of China and uncle of child Emperor Pu Yi. Visited the United States in 1910 to study the American military and announced China's plans to do away with the hair queue.
Rev. Charles S. Brown (1835-1880)	Superintendent of the Methodist Church's Five Points Mission in Manhattan who baptized Jin Fuey and presided over the Mott Street Mission that employed Jin Kee.
Kate Burton Lake (1846-1928)	Schoolteacher who met Jin Mun through the Chinese Mission of the Methodist Episcopal Church's Women's Home Missionary Society in San Francisco.

DRAMATIS PERSONAE

Li Hung Chang (李鴻章; *Li Hongzhang*) (1823-1901)	Leading figure in the Imperial court of the late Qing Dynasty and one of China's key diplomats of the period.
Sir Cheng-Tung Liang Cheng (梁誠; *Liang Cheng*) (1864-1917)	American-educated Chinese minister to the United States who supervised Jin Kee's lobbying effort to repeal the Chinese Exclusion Act. *Alias: Liang Pi Yuk* (梁丕旭).
Mei Lan Fang (梅蘭芳; *Mei Lanfang*) (1894-1961)	Famous Beijing Opera star who traveled to the United States in 1930 and met Jin Mun and his family in San Francisco.
Pang Wah Jung (1865-?)	So-called "vice mayor" of Indianapolis' Chinatown who traveled to Washington with Jin Kee and was later ousted from his position at the same time as Jin Kee. *Alias: Pang Gawk Yuen.*
Henry C. Parke (1824-1901)	New York-based importer of Chinese and Japanese goods who employed Jin Kee and later accused him of theft.
George Washington Reed (1817-1889)	Publisher of the *Brooklyn Daily Eagle* and employer of Jin Fuey at his residence in Brooklyn, New York.
Leland Stanford, Sr. (1824-1893)	Governor of California, Central Pacific Railroad magnate, U.S. Senator. Employer, for a short time, of Jin Kee and Jin Mun, and ostensibly a lifelong friend of Jin Mun.
Joseph Chak Thoms (1861-1929)	Chinese-born, American-educated physician who employed Jin Fuey at New York's first Chinese hospital. *Alias: Tom Ah Jo.*
Jane Lathrop Stanford (1828-1905)	Wife of Leland Stanford, who developed affection for Jin Mun and offered to adopt him.
Wong Kai Kah (黃開甲; *Huang Kaijia*) (1860-1906)	Yale-educated Chinese diplomat who accompanied Prince Pu Lun to America and arranged his visit to Indianapolis.
Wu Ting Fang (伍廷芳; *Wu Tingfang*) (1842-1922)	Chinese Minister to Washington in the early 20th century who cut off his hair queue in 1911, causing a trend among Chinese-Americans.

Chapter I
Tangled in a Snarl

As 62 year-old Moy Jin Kee and his wife of 36 years disembarked from the S. S. *Suveric* at the Port of Tacoma, Washington on March 11, 1909, they were immediately taken into custody by U.S. Immigration officers. Despite the fact that Jin Kee had lived in the United States for more than half a century, had been granted full citizenship in 1897 by the Circuit Court of Marion County, Indiana and spoke English fluently, the officers felt impelled to undertake a comprehensive investigation of the couple's right to be admitted, lest they be derelict in their duty to enforce America's Chinese exclusion laws.

Only three years earlier, the diminutive Jin Kee – he stood not quite five foot three in his fine silk Mandarin robes – had been received by Theodore Roosevelt at the White House. He probably lobbied the President against those very laws, which were widely hated by America's Chinese, having caused them incalculable difficulty and anguish during the more than a quarter century they had been in effect. Jin Kee was able to secure audiences in Washington with the President and with Vice President Charles W. Fairbanks, whom he knew personally, in his capacity as the unofficial "mayor" of Indianapolis' Chinatown, the head of a nationwide movement organized to fight for the rights of Chinese in America and a Mandarin of the Fifth Degree. Jin Kee was a *somebody*. But any Chinese seeking entry into the United States at the turn of the twentieth century was presumed to be something less than a nobody unless he could prove otherwise.

Jin Kee and his wife Chin Fung, a slightly built, delicate creature with rosy lips and feet only three inches in length as a consequence of tight binding during her childhood, had been gone less than a year and a half on a trip to their native land. When they boarded the steamer in Hong Kong to return to their adopted country, however, they had no idea how difficult and humiliating the process of getting back to Indiana would prove. But neither Jin Kee's certificate of citizenship, nor his long tenure in the United States, nor his acquaintance with high-ranking government officials, nor his alleged fathering of two American-born sons counted for much as far as the Immigration officials were concerned.

Accommodations at the detention center were miserable. Husband and wife were quartered on different floors in the two-story firetrap, which had been built only two years earlier to accommodate 125 people, but was already severely overcrowded. The building lacked indoor plumbing – forcing Chinese, Japanese, Indian and European inmates to share wash basins as they performed their daily ablutions according to their various customs – and ventilation was poor. Criticized by local authorities as one of the most unsanitary buildings in the city, it was nonetheless the best the United States government was prepared to do for the couple while they were incarcerated in the state of Washington. By contrast, no expense seems to have been spared in mobilizing the vast bureaucracy to investigate their case. That process that took nearly six weeks, involved personnel in four cities and cost American taxpayers a tidy sum of money.

The couple ought to have been given a much easier time. Although Jin Kee was born in China, he was a *bona fide* American citizen, a rarity among Chinese in America. As such, he presumably had an inalienable right to land. But the Chinese Exclusion Act and subsequent legislation had plunged the status of even naturalized Chinese into limbo, despite the fact that the restriction on citizenship had been phrased, in the original legislation, in the future tense: "*hereafter* no State court or court of the United States shall admit Chinese to citizenship." The ambiguity, unfortunately, worked to the couple's distinct disadvantage.

The *Seattle Daily Times*, declaring Jin Kee "tangled in a snarl of the exclusion law," ran a large photo of him across two columns on its front page and observed that his case "has excited attention in this country and China." He was, after all, a fairly well-known figure in the United States, and many efforts were made by influential friends of his to lobby the Immigration Bureau for the couple's immediate discharge. But instead of boarding the next train for Indiana, he and his wife were shown to separate, squalid quarters and compelled to languish in them for an interminable month and a half.

The tedium and the depressing surroundings took their toll. Questioned about his case by the *Seattle Daily Times* a month into his incarceration, a distraught Jin Kee pleaded that "all I want is to have it decided and my wife and I allowed either to go to Indianapolis . . . or back to China." But which direction they would ultimately take would be determined not by their citizenship status, but by how much property was still in their name, and how much money was owed to them back in Indianapolis.

CHAPTER II
THE ROAD TO EXCLUSION

The tepid welcome Jin Kee received in America in 1909 was quite a departure from his experience half a century earlier, when he initially landed in San Francisco as part of the first wave of Chinese immigrants to America's shores. Between the onset of the California Gold Rush in 1848 and the passage of the Chinese Exclusion Act in 1882, tens of thousands of them – the vast majority, like him, southern Chinese men from Guangdong Province – left their homeland to seek their fortunes in America. They were by no means China's first economic emigrants, nor were they her largest wave. Chinese had been putting down roots in Southeast Asia for centuries, and the Straits Settlements of Singapore, Penang and Malacca alone were home to several times the number who went to the United States. Those who chose America made up only a fraction of the estimated two million Chinese who left their country in search of wealth or a better life during this unhappy period.

A confluence of events conspired to create this great Chinese Diaspora. First were China's humiliating defeats in the Opium Wars of 1839-1842 and 1856-1860. Under treaties the empire had been forced to sign with Britain and other powers, its domestic market was pried open to foreign goods. This, in turn, brought about dislocations in the agricultural sector that impoverished peasants and caused many to lose their land. Between the Opium Wars, the Taiping rebellion broke out against the Qing, or Manchu, Dynasty. Instigated by a Christian convert emboldened by the regime's international humiliations, the rebellion was a civil war with some social reformist goals that began in 1851.

Fourteen years passed before Taiping rebels, who eventually took control of a large swath of southern China, were suppressed by Qing forces, and the conflict caused the deaths of millions. It is unlikely the Moy clan was spared.

Then, between 1855 and 1867, there was violent conflict between the local Cantonese and the Hakka (*Kejia*) people, northerners who had relocated to the south much earlier and who competed for scarce land. Finally, during this period the Taishan region, where Jin Kee and his brothers were born, experienced more than its usual share of droughts, storms, typhoons, blights, earthquakes and plagues. These natural disasters were exacerbated by overpopulation – Guangdong's 1787 population of 16 million had ballooned to 28 million by 1850 – and a finite amount of arable land insufficient to support so many people.

All these factors combined to make the already hardscrabble life of the region insufferable. Together they made the unthinkable – pulling up roots and heading for a far-off land – seem reasonable, even though emigration was explicitly forbidden. Among those who saw the sense in it were one of Jin Kee's uncles – his name is now lost – who made the long voyage to America some time in the early 1850s, and Jin Kee and his brothers as well, who left somewhat later.

Two principal magnets attracted Chinese immigrants to America: the Gold Rush of 1848, which had brought the uncle to California; and the building of the transcontinental railroad, which began in 1865 and brought many thousands more. By 1851, three years after news of the discovery of gold at Sutter's Mill had reached China, an estimated 25,000 Chinese had left for California, most of them from Guangdong, whose people had easy access to the sea, some familiarity with Westerners and a tradition of emigration. By 1860, the immigrant Chinese population in America had reached nearly 35,000, a figure that grew to just over 63,000 in 1870 and more than 105,000 in 1880, two years before the Exclusion Act, which effectively ended large-scale immigration, was passed.

THREE TOUGH CHINAMEN

Although the Chinese had not initially been unwelcome in America, there had always been some prejudice against them, and as early as 1852 agitation began in California for a state law to prohibit further immigration from China. Things got much worse after the completion of the railroad in 1869, however. Large numbers of Chinese were put out of work just as the country experienced an economic depression, and they began to look for other employment. Some went east, but the majority remained in the West. Most gravitated to Chinatowns in the larger cities, where they often lived cheek by jowl with unemployed or underemployed Americans. Their willingness to work for low wages put them at odds with these laborers, and the result was often violent confrontation. The hapless Chinese frequently got the worst of the battles.

As attitudes toward Chinese laborers hardened, Americans predisposed to resent them found many other things about them to dislike. They were said to be odd-looking and strangely dressed; they were clannish and resisted assimilation; they lived in crowded and unsanitary conditions that spread disease; they were heathens, mentally and morally inferior to whites; they ate rats and other disgusting creatures and they were leeches who sent their gold back to China rather than spending it in the United States, where it would benefit Americans.

Another complaint was that the Chinese were immoral, with Chinese women in particular considered especially lascivious. Prostitutes of all nationalities serviced California's working men, but those from China attracted particular attention. Early Chinese immigrants were nearly all male, and those who had married generally did not bring their wives to America. The relatively few Chinese women who did make the journey were, for the most part, brought over for the express purpose of serving in brothels. The common impression was that all Chinese women were degenerate and that Chinese prostitutes were seducing white men into depraved behavior and exposing them to disease. It was thus a short leap to the conclusion that they should all be kept out entirely.

Accordingly, in 1875, the U.S. government enacted legislation to restrict the entry of Asian women coming to work as prostitutes. In practice, however, the bill, called the Page Act after Rep. Horace F. Page, the California Republican who introduced it, served to slow the immigration of *all* Asian women to a trickle. Chin Fung, who first arrived in the company of her husband Jin Kee in 1883, was very much an exception. She became one of a handful of Chinese women in Chicago in the 1890s, and until 1907 was the only Chinese female in Indianapolis.

The ultimate result of the growing anti-Chinese sentiment – despite efforts by Jin Kee and others to defuse it – was the Chinese Exclusion Act of 1882, which prohibited Chinese laborers from entering the United States for 10 years and rendered Chinese living in America ineligible for citizenship. Those already in the United States would not be expelled and were free to travel abroad, but only after obtaining pre-departure certification from the government of their right to reside in America would they be guaranteed re-entry. Chinese who were merchants, diplomats, teachers, students and travelers, or who were born in America, were exempt: only they were permitted to bring in family members.

For all practical purposes, the Exclusion Act froze the approximately 110,000-member Chinese-American community in place when it took effect in the spring of 1882. The majority could no longer hope to be reunited with family members legally unless they returned to China. Many eventually did just that, and America's Chinese population slowly began to dwindle. This coincided with some eastward migration, however, so even as the nationwide numbers declined, the Chinatowns of the Midwest and the East actually grew for years after the Exclusion Act was passed. Jin Kee and his brother Jin Fuey rode the leading edge of that wave, moving to New York in the late 1870s.

Enforcing the Exclusion Act required organization and resources, and the federal government established an elaborate bureaucracy to track, identify and share information about Chinese residents and would-be immigrants. Authority was vested initially in the Customs Service, then transferred, in turn, to the Treasury and the Commerce and Labor Departments. Chinese bureaus were set up in Baltimore, Boston, Chicago, El Paso, Los Angeles, Honolulu, New York, Philadelphia, Portland (Oregon), San Francisco, Seattle and even Montreal, with headquarters in Washington, DC. Jin Fuey and his cousin Gop Jung found employment as interpreters in several of these bureaus. Although the basic goal of the Chinese bureaus was to keep out those whose entry was forbidden, bureaucrats also kept tabs on resident Chinese, maintaining dossiers on many, particularly when they applied for re-entry permits in advance of trips home. This was especially true after the passage in 1892 of the Geary Act, which not only extended the Exclusion Act for another decade, but also mandated registration of all Chinese in the United States under penalty of imprisonment or deportation.

In the early years of the Chinese Bureau, documentation was generally available to prove or disprove claims. Those who professed American birth were asked to show birth certificates, and Immigration officers could consult ship passenger records to verify arrivals of those who had entered legally. In 1906, however, all that changed for San Francisco residents and for those who had entered through the Port of San Francisco – a high proportion of the Chinese in America. The earthquake and subsequent fire in that year destroyed the city's vital records and incoming ship manifests. But the loss of records actually proved a boon for many Chinese: it rendered claims of American birth far more difficult to disprove.

Most Chinese in the United States at this time were not American-born; indeed, they hardly could have been, since there were so few Chinese women in America as a consequence of the Page Act, and intermarriage between Chinese men and women of other races was rare. But an 1898 Supreme Court case had established that Chinese born in America were indeed eligible for citizenship under the Fourteenth Amendment, and with citizenship came a cherished right: the ability to bring in children fathered abroad. After the earthquake, therefore, many Chinese came forward with fraudulent claims of American birth. The number who claimed citizenship by virtue of American birth or familial relationships with those born in the United States rose from 634 in 1905 to 4,754 in 1924, even as the overall Chinese population was declining. And the government, lacking evidence to disprove their claims, saw little alternative but to grant full citizenship to many.

The possibility of importing sons brought with it ample opportunity for corruption, since it was a highly prized privilege for which some were prepared to pay handsomely. It became common for the newly minted American citizens – or for Chinese who qualified as merchants – to go back to China and report the birth of a son upon their return, whether or not a son had actually been born. This practice secured a slot for a child of the same approximate age to emigrate at some future date which could be sold to another family or given away to relatives. The illegal immigrant boys who filled these slots came to be known as "paper sons," and two allegedly American-born children whom Jin Kee had imported probably fell into this category, which would account for why he did not press this argument in his case for readmission. Jin Kee's brother Jin Mun and their cousin Gop Jung probably both brought in boys in this way as well.

As time went on, the Immigration Bureau and the Chinese community became increasingly sophisticated in their efforts to foil each other's devices. Immigration officials learned to set traps to expose imposters, and the Chinese, in turn, formulated strategies to outwit the inspectors. Immigration kept photographs and copious records of departing Chinese so as to verify their identities if they sought re-entry, and to confirm those of others who claimed to be related to them. In lengthy interviews before departure, officials asked not only basic questions about places and dates of birth and lineage, but also demanded arcane details such as the number of rows of houses in the person's home village in China, the location of the family's home or the village well, the names of neighbors and relatives and their ages, the birth order of siblings and children and whether the women referred to – mothers, aunts or wives – had natural or bound feet. When these topics were broached with the same individual upon re-entry or with alleged relatives seeking admission, the answers could be compared and inconsistencies analyzed to help determine eligibility.

For their part, the Chinese became proficient at anticipating the questions inspectors were likely to ask and the traps set for them, and they made sure that those seeking entry were thoroughly briefed on what to say – and, just as importantly, what not to say. A common practice was to prepare "coaching papers" containing information the would-be immigrant needed to know: the answers to questions that had already been asked of other family members and those likely to be asked. Gop Jung did precisely this when he imported his ostensible son in 1914. Sometimes these cheat sheets were hefty documents that included annotated maps of the home village. "Paper sons" had to master a great deal of basic family information of which a true relative would already be well aware.

Sometimes Immigration officials called on Chinese already living in America to ask about others pursuing admission or re-admission, or seeking a certain status under the law (*e.g.*, that of merchant). They might be summoned to the Immigration office or an officer might appear at their place of business. There was no time to prepare for such interrogations, so one had to be nimble. One unwritten rule was never to imply that someone who professed to be American-born had actually been born in China. This kind of testimony could change someone's status overnight and could result in deportation of someone already in the United States. The threat of prosecution, detention, incarceration or deportation was ever-present, because if Chinese wished to remain in America, the Exclusion Act made it criminal

SCOTT D. SELIGMAN

> If asked whether you or your mother know anybody in the United States, you both must reply affirmatively. I know one distant uncle named Nai Dung, who was born in the United States; he came back home from the United States in S.T. 2 (1910) and he was at that time entrusted with a letter from my father, for delivery to my mother. We are very closely related to him. He lives in Hoy Hong Village, which is close by our village. For these reasons we often saw each other, and in that way know him. He left home to return to the United States about May or June, S.T. 3 (1911), where he makes his living. If asked whose son he is you are to reply that he is the second son of Ding Yiu; his boyhood name is Ah Toy. If further asked as to his family affairs, say that you dont know much about them, as you have never heard your older relatives discuss such matters; that you are too young to personally know; that you only knew his mother once came back to China from the United States to live, and is still living (in China).

A 1916 translation by the Immigration Service of a fragment of a "coaching paper" prepared by Moy Gop Jung, a cousin of the Moy brothers, for use by Moy Sher Park, who emigrated to the United States in 1914 as his son, but who may, in fact, have been a "paper son" brought in on behalf of someone else. The original Chinese document is lost. Source: National Archives and Records Administration, Philadelphia, PA.

for most of them to reunite with their spouses and children. Such restrictions were imposed on no other Americans, including new immigrants from other parts of the world. Citizenship was unobtainable, and racism made assimilation nearly impossible.

These restrictions were put in place only in the final decades of the 19th century, however. Times were simpler when the Moy brothers first reached America. The Chinese were not yet considered undesirable; that would all come later.

Chapter III
Beginnings

Moy Yuen Bong was a Chinese tea merchant who traveled to England, learned about Jesus Christ and acquired a Bible that he brought back to China and shared with his son. Or he was part-owner of a shipping line and was aboard one of its vessels moored in San Francisco harbor when one of his sons was born on board in 1862. Or he was born in California. Or he was a Mandarin who lived in a village in north China, 87 miles from Beijing, a Methodist minister and leader of the Freemasons in Guangzhou, or a schoolteacher who lived quietly with his wife in a small village in Xinning County of China's southern Guangdong Province. The stories were plentiful; it was truth that was in short supply.

Who he was depended on who was asking, on which of his sons was answering and on the situation in which the son found himself. It was advantageous for son Jin Kee to have had a converted Christian father when he himself was preaching the gospel on Mott Street in New York's Chinatown and when he was playing for sympathy after being charged with stealing. The family's ostensible residence in the Beijing area lent credence to the same son's later claim – surely bogus - to distant kinship with a prominent figure in the Imperial Court of the late Qing Dynasty. And for Moy Yuen Bong to have been born in California would have meant that all of his sons – including Jin Fuey, who made the claim – would automatically be eligible for American citizenship, and not subject to the burdensome restrictions imposed on Chinese in the United States by the Chinese Exclusion Act and successor legislation.

Of all of the stories, by far the most likely is the one that places him in Xinning – called Taishan since 1914, following the founding of the Chinese Republic – a county that lies along the southern coast of Guangdong. Located in the southwest corner of the Pearl River delta, Taishan, home to the Moy clan since the 14th century, is about 90 miles west of Hong Kong and 60 miles southwest of Guangzhou. Its climate is tropical, with short, relatively mild winters and long, sweltering summers. An estimated 80 percent of the Chinese who came to America between the mid-19th and mid-20th centuries could trace their origins to this 1,300 sq. mile county.

The ancestors of most members of the vast Moy clan lived in a township in Taishan called Duanfen, where Moy is by far and away the dominant surname. The name is associated with 123 different villages in Taishan County, all but one located in

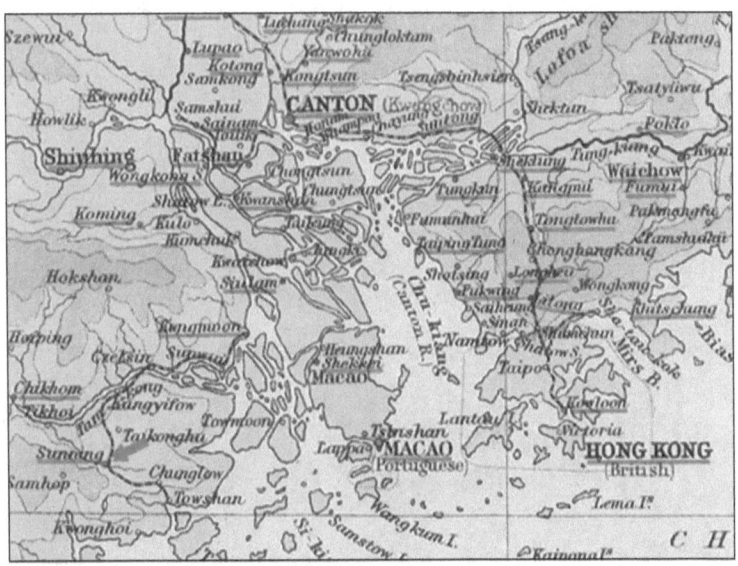

Detail from a Protestant missionary map of Guangdong Province. An arrow in the lower left-hand corner of the map points to Sunning (Xinning; later Taishan) County, where the Moys' native village of Hai Yang is located. Source: Institute of Social and Religious Research, World Missionary Atlas (New York Institute of Social and Religious Research, 1925).

that township. According to a family history written in 1664, the progenitor of the Moys, originally from Anhui Province, settled in Duanfen in 1371. He is said to have chosen the area because of its beautiful beaches and islands. He certainly could not have been attracted by more pragmatic features like an abundance of rich farmland, as the region is hilly and has historically lacked sufficient arable land to sustain its inhabitants.

Moy Yuen Bong was probably born in the 1820s or 1830s and was a member of the 15th generation of the clan, a fact discernible from his name. To keep track of all-important familial relationships, families throughout China had embraced a practice in which all members of the same generation would share one of the two Chinese characters in their given names. Males in the 15th generation of the Moy family adopted the character Yuen (遠; *Yuan*) as part of their names at the time of marriage. And when all the generation names were arranged in order, from eldest to youngest, the characters could be read as a sort of acrostic

Fragment from Clan Genealogy of the Moys of Duanfen (端芬梅氏族譜), *a family history written by Moy Min Kui* (梅明蘷) *of the eleventh generation in the third year of the reign of the Kangxi Emperor, or 1664. Courtesy of Tow H. Moy.*

poem. Read as a poem, the verse set lofty life goals for future generations; read as a list of names, it made the pecking order clear, signaling the level of deference expected from any one family member to any other. Someone from an earlier generation would deserve, and expect, to be addressed with the respect due an elder by someone from a later generation, even if he was actually younger than his relative.

The Moy family poem was preachy and not particularly elegant, but it did its job of exhorting descendants to honor and follow in the footsteps of their forebears. Written in classical Chinese, it began with the 11th generation – the generation of its author – and read as follows:

元錫德瑞
遠耀迺宗
友恭忠良
萬福攸同
崇禮尚仁
克繩祖武
開基創業
貽厥孫謀

Heaven-bestowed virtue and good fortune
Shone from afar on your ancestors.
Be friendly, respectful, loyal and honest,
And a myriad of blessings will long be yours.
If you revere propriety and elevate humanity,
You will carry on the cause of your forebears.
By establishing a foundation and creating an enterprise,
You can ensure a bright future for your descendants.

Comparable poems existed for females only occasionally, although it was not unknown for sisters to share a character in their names. Like women themselves, however, their given names were generally not considered significant by the establishment, and outside of her family, a female – married or not - would generally be known only by her own surname plus the character shee (氏; *shi*), which can be translated as "née" or "Ms." The unfortunate result is that the given names of many were not recorded and have therefore been irretrievably lost. This is the case with Moy Yuen Bong's two wives.

The village of Hai Yang, in which Moy Yuen Bong lived with his family, was a small, rural community, all of whose men – then as now – belonged to the Moy clan and shared the surname. Since marriages between spouses bearing the same family name were taboo – they were considered incestuous – brides were recruited from other families in neighboring towns and villages, but never from among the Moys. And similarly, Moy girls married out and generally left their native villages after they wed.

Hai Yang residents farmed rice in the paddies adjacent to the village – never-ending, backbreaking work that followed the cycle of the seasons. They also raised vegetables. The community amounted to little more than a couple of dozen single-story, brick and earth buildings arranged in rows along dirt paths, their gray, clay-tiled roofs curling gently upward at the eaves to ward off malevolent spirits, which were believed to travel in straight lines. Houses had dirt floors and their occupants slept on straw mats. They revered their Moy forebears in ancestral halls and prayed for abundant harvests to earth gods housed in small shrines on their property.

Moy Yuen Bong was one of at least five brothers, and his two wives both came from the Chin family. Between them they bore him four sons and a daughter, the latter of whom undoubtedly left the village at the time of her marriage. The eldest son, Jin Kee, was born in Hai Yang in about 1847. He was followed by Jin Mun, born in about 1851; Kye Hin in 1854 and Jin Fuey in 1862. Jin Fuey was a son of the second wife, as possibly was Kye Hin. These were their boyhood names. The family poem assigns the character You (耀; *Yao*) to the 16th generation, and all four brothers would eventually have adopted that name had they remained in

China through adulthood. Three of them did so anyway; only Jin Fuey, who married a white woman and never returned to China after leaving for America, never used the generation name.

Boys in the village began their studies at age six or seven and continued for a few years – long enough to become literate. Moy Yuen Bong, who by one account was a teacher, gave his sons a head start. As soon as Jin Mun could talk, his father taught him to recite the *Three Character Classic*, a 13th century Chinese text based on Confucian thought that was often used to begin a child's formal education. Fewer than 1,200 characters in all, the text was divided into lines of three characters each – hence its name. It was read aloud by boys, their bodies swaying rhythmically with the meter. Jin Mun memorized the entire book and never forgot the words or the moral teachings embodied in them.

There was no free public education, but the fact that Moy Yuen Bong's sons were able to go to school does not necessarily mean he was well-to-do. Schooling for Moy boys was paid for, thanks to the generosity of a fourth generation ancestor who had passed the Imperial examination and become a government official. He bought about 115 acres of land and directed that the income from the property be earmarked for future activities of overall benefit to the clan. These included the veneration of ancestors and the education of sons.

The boys began formal schooling at age seven. All of their teachers were male. Students sat on stools, learned by rote and recited their lessons in unison. Occasionally a teacher would strike a boy on the hand or the bottom if he misbehaved, but this did not happen often. "There are no bad boys in China as there are here in this country," Jin Kee once observed. "The boys are respectful and polite to all who are older than themselves, and while they have their plays and their fun, they do not think it fun to hurt anyone." This was in marked contrast, he implied, to some of the youngsters he had seen in American cities who found sport in vandalizing laundries and taunting the Chinese immigrants who operated them. Those youngsters had been taught to regard the Chinese as an inferior race, and their mischief often went unpunished.

School days, like work days, were long and arduous. Classes began before dawn and lasted until after dinner, so by age 10 the boys could write quite well. Vacations were scheduled around the rice harvests – one in the spring and one in the fall – so they could work in the fields. Recreation, when time permitted, included kite-flying, walking on stilts, shooting sparrows with a bow and arrow and training beetles to fight, laying wagers on the results. Firecrackers were set off at Chinese New Year. A favorite prank was to place a package on a footpath with a string attached; when someone stooped to pick it up, a boy hiding behind a nearby fence would pull the other end of the string and make it jump.

Gop Jung, a cousin who also made the journey to America, recalled the beatings in school as somewhat less benign affairs. Born in Hai Yang two years after Jin Fuey, he had begun studying at age six. "I might have stayed at school and hammered away," he once declared, "had it not been for the dreadful custom of whipping a child so brutally in that country . . . I stood the chastising as long as I could and then I decided to run away." At about age 12 he stowed away on a ship bound for San Francisco.

Village life was oppressive. The imperative of the harvest virtually guaranteed that most of those who stayed could expect to farm the nearby lands for the rest of their working lives. Thus, when the opportunity to go abroad and seek their fortunes came – quite early in life in the case of the Moy brothers – they all seized it. But unlike most of the early Chinese immigrants to America who left to mine for gold with every intention of returning, the Moys (or three of them, anyway; Kye Hin returned to China for good in 1918) opted to build their lives in their adopted country. Each, in his own way, achieved success in America, and surely did not believe that returning would offer him more of it. In this, they were probably not wrong. Although Hai Yang today boasts paved roads, multi-story buildings, cement floors, running water and power and telecom cables, it otherwise looks much as it probably did a century ago. Chickens and dogs still run free, and village life still marches to the unremitting rhythm of the harvest.

For Jin Fuey, the trip to America would be the first and last time he would cross the Pacific. He would take an American wife and would never return to China. Jin Kee and Jin Mun both did go back, long enough to be married to wives who eventually joined them in America. Jin Kee, in fact, returned four times in all: once to marry, once to retrieve his wife, once on the trip that landed him in the detention center in Washington state on his return and a final time to be laid to rest. Taishan would remain a factor in the lives of all three brothers, but not one of them would ever call it home again.

Chapter IV
California Dreaming

Jin Kee, the eldest, was the first of his brothers to travel to America. Some time in the late 1850s, he and an uncle made the 90-mile journey to Hong Kong, probably by junk from the Taishan coast, as most emigrants did. From there they boarded a sailing ship that took nearly eight weeks to reach San Francisco. Steamships were just beginning to sail that route and were capable of cutting the time in half, but scheduled transpacific steamship service would not begin for another decade.

Emigration was technically an illegal act. Out of a fear that Ming Dynasty loyalists might build power bases outside of China from which to challenge their rule, the Manchus had, from the start of their reign, made it a criminal offense for Chinese to leave, and threatened to punish any who attempted to do so. As a practical matter, however, this rule was no longer enforced by the mid-19th century, and it certainly was not viewed as a significant impediment by the Moys or other men of Taishan intent on seeking their fortunes abroad. By the 1860s, through the treaties China was forced to sign with foreign powers, the restriction was essentially rendered moot.

The Chinese on board ship were quartered below deck, in steerage. Passage cost $40 and included all meals. For Jin Kee and the other Chinese passengers, this meant soup, meat and vegetables, served up in large, earthen bowls, as well as rice and tea. Passengers brought their own chopsticks and their own bedding. The two-month voyage was a thoroughly unpleasant ordeal. Packed tightly in the holds of ships not originally intended for human cargo, passengers suffered from dim light, insufficient ventilation and poor sanitation. The stench was awful; disease spread quickly and not a few perished from illness or other hazards. In the fall of 1859, Chinese laborers on another ship, the clipper ship *Mastiff*, were smoking opium below deck and accidentally caused a serious fire. Terrified, the 181 passengers rushed to the lifeboats. Fortunately, only one died; the rest were rescued by a nearby ship and taken to Honolulu.

Since the money required for passage was a king's ransom for most would-be travelers, many signed indenture agreements before they left Hong Kong, committing themselves to work for a fixed wage for three years in exchange for the price of the ticket. The Moy brothers, however, were exceptions. Jin Mun, who arrived a year or so after Jin Kee, had his passage underwritten by an uncle who had returned from California with a bag of gold dust, and Jin Kee's fare was likely also paid by the same uncle, probably the very one with whom he was traveling.

None of these newly arrived Chinese boys could have found San Francisco anything other than endlessly fascinating and bewildering. The discovery of gold at Sutter's Mill in 1848 had brought a motley collection of people to California, and most came by way of San Francisco before fanning out to the mines. The Forty-Niners included Indians, Mexicans, Pacific Islanders, Spaniards, Englishmen, Irishmen, Germans and Frenchmen as well as Peruvians, Chileans, and, of course, Chinese, and Jin Kee and Jin Mun had to live among them and learn to communicate with them. Fortunately, both boys had a gift for language, and it did not take long before they became fairly proficient in English.

The appearance of all these immigrants caused rapid growth in the polyglot settlement – both in people and in land. San Francisco's population, estimated at about 25,000 in 1849, more than doubled by 1860 to nearly 57,000, and ballooned to just short of 150,000 by 1870. To accommodate the growing number of inhabitants, the town had to expand – literally. Hills were leveled to create flat land suitable for building, their sandy soil dumped unceremoniously into the bay, and the reclaimed land pushed the waterfront further east, where new wharves were constructed. Streets were graded and tents and shanties steadily gave way to more solid structures as a proper city rose on the peninsula.

The Chinese had their piece of this boomtown's action. By the mid-1850s, "Little China" - the term "Chinatown" was not yet in use - was emerging on the upper part of Sacramento Street, the length of Dupont Street and on several adjoining avenues. Chinese shopkeepers and merchants set up businesses dealing mostly in wares from the old country, the aromas emanating from their groceries, cigar stores, wash houses, butcher shops, opium dens and brothels co-mingling in alleyways packed so tightly that every bit of space was utilized. By official count, there were about 2,700 Chinese in San Francisco when the Moy boys arrived, and about 12 times that number in the rest of California. The actual figures, however, were surely substantially higher, since census takers were hard pressed to conduct an accurate count. Most of the Chinese immigrants were out mining gold, with those in the city more likely to be working as merchants or laborers, principally as porters and laundrymen. The latter washed clothes in local lagoons and wells and ironed them by drawing them over pans filled with burning coals until the creases disappeared.

From the very beginning, Chinese people organized mutual aid societies for cultural, charitable, economic, social and political purposes. These groups fell into three general categories: region-based (dependent on the part of China – usually the part of Guangdong Province - from which an immigrant had come); clan-based (groups organized around a single Chinese surname); and secret societies, or triads, generally known by the term "tong" (*tang*). Not only San Francisco, but all Chinatowns in America featured networks of such organizations, which levied dues, provided social services, mediated disputes, enforced discipline, dispensed justice and offered some measure of protection and security. The six most important regional associations sat at the top of the pyramid, and cooperated through an umbrella group called the "Six Companies." It was the most powerful of all the organizations, and the *de facto* government of the Chinese community.

The Chinese brought along not only their cultural institutions, but also their vices. A Chinese language newspaper, the *Gold Hills News*, was already being published by 1854 and a couple of Chinese theaters had opened. A part of Dupont Street was also given over to gambling establishments, which were frequented principally by Chinese, although whites occasionally dropped by as well. Opium dens did brisk business, and many of the Chinese women in the town worked in brothels, which lined Dupont and portions of Pacific Avenue. Over time, secret societies became heavily involved in managing many of these enterprises, and conflicts among them often got violent, giving rise to the widespread conception that Chinatowns were dangerous places where bloody tong wars were fought daily on the streets.

The Chinese were not only living in America; they were also dying in America, and in San Francisco those whose bodies were not able to be sent home to China immediately were being buried in Yerba Buena Cemetery, a 13-acre, triangular site bounded by Larkin, McAllister and Market Streets about where the present day Main Public Library stands. Once a year, in the spring, the Chinese community would form a grand procession to the graveyard, which they shared with other ethnic groups, and bring along roast pigs and goats, firecrackers and paper money to appease the spirits of their departed. If funds could be raised, the bones of those interred would eventually be exhumed, returned to China and reburied in their home villages. If not, America was where they would spend eternity, but it would probably not be at Yerba Buena. The brisk growth of the city required that the graveyard be evacuated and the land used to serve the living, so beginning in 1866, most of the bodies were disinterred and transferred to Golden Gate Cemetery in modern-day Lincoln Park. It was not a scrupulous process, however, and body parts were continually unearthed during excavations on the former site of Yerba Buena throughout the 20th century.

Jin Kee found work selling newspapers and remained in the city for a while, but soon moved on, leaving Jin Mun, who had enrolled in school to study English, in the care of cousins. Jin Kee set off to seek his fortune not in the gold mines, but in Sacramento, the new state capital, about 90 miles away. If San Francisco was the main focus of Chinese life in California – indeed, of all of America – Sacramento definitely came in second during this era. The former was known by several names in Taishan dialect, one of which was Dai Fow (*Dafu*), or "big city," and the latter, correspondingly, was colloquially styled Yee Fow (*Erfu*), or "second city." A total of 814 Chinese lived there in 1852, of whom only 10 were women. The count doubled to more than 1,700 by 1860, and doubled again to about 3,600 in 1870. As in San Francisco, these city-dwellers were more likely to be shopkeepers and laborers than miners. Most settled on I Street between Second and Sixth, an undesirable, low-lying part of town prone to flooding, and began setting up institutions like mutual aid societies, a social hall and a theater.

Sacramento was much closer to the mines, but prospecting was not Jin Kee's focus. In about 1864, when he was 17, he found a job not in the Chinese quarter, but rather in the tony downtown area in which ground had already been broken on a new Capitol building. He had the good fortune to get hired as a servant in the home of one of the titans of California history: Governor Leland Stanford.

Originally from New York, Stanford had married in 1850 and followed his brothers to California to seek his fortune. An attorney by training, he had moved with his wife Jane in 1856 to Sacramento, where he started a business and went into politics. One of the organizers of California's Republican Party, he became the state's first Republican governor in 1861, but held the office for only one two-year term. Rather than seek re-election, he accepted an offer to become president of the Central Pacific

Railroad, which had been organized in 1861 and which, the following year, had been granted the franchise for construction of the western portion of the new transcontinental railroad. Stanford knew something about railroads; his father had been one of the principal contractors on a rail line constructed between Albany and Schenectady in the 1830s. As a youth he had watched it being built, and had found the project enthralling.

The Chinese boy had never seen such opulence as he did when he entered the Stanford mansion for the first time. It stood at the corner of 8th and N Streets in downtown Sacramento, two blocks west of the Capitol. Leland had bought the 4,000 square-foot, two-story Renaissance revival structure for $8,000 in 1861 and would expand it substantially years later. The couple kept three servants, a bookkeeper and a coachman in residence. Jin Kee was engaged as a cook, and the Stanfords were kind to him. He credited them with being partially responsible for giving him a solid English education. A year or so after he was hired, he sent for Jin Mun, who had turned 15 and was ready for the working world. He introduced the boy to the Stanfords, who generously invited him to join their household as a gardener.

Jane Stanford became very fond of the youngster and eventually offered to adopt him, according to Jin Mun's descendants. Jane had married at the age of 22, was

Leland and Jane Lathrop Stanford at the time of their marriage in 1850. Source: Days of a Man, the autobiography of David Starr Jordan, World Book Company, 1922.

The Stanford mansion at the corner of 8th and N Streets in Sacramento, California, as it appeared in the 1860s before it was substantially enlarged. Jin Kee is said to have worked as a cook there, and Jin Mun as a garden boy. Source: Library of Congress.

already in her late 30s at this time and remained childless. In 1868 she would, in fact, bear a son, but by the mid-1860s it was beginning to look as if the couple would be forever barren. An attractive, 15 year-old Chinese boy without parents in America might well have caught her eye at that stage of her life. Jin Kee, however, objected to the adoption on the grounds of racial and social differences, and there was also the fact that Jin Mun's parents were still very much alive in China. The adoption never took place, but Jane is said to have given Jin Mun a gold ring with his name engraved on the inside, a memento he treasured for the rest of his life. However, there is no mention of Jin Mun in the extensive collection of her papers housed today at Stanford University, including her will, which did list several of her Chinese servants as heirs. Nor does any documentary evidence of Jin Mun's relationship with Leland appear to survive.

Stanford was a shrewd man; detractors called him a robber baron and an opportunist. He was fickle when it came to the Chinese, and his attitude was one that truly mattered. In the inaugural speech he delivered upon assuming the office of Governor on January 10, 1862, he referred to Chinese in decidedly derogatory terms and committed himself to restricting their continued immigration. "Asia, with her numberless millions, sends to our shores the dregs of her population," he declared. "There could be no doubt . . . that the presence of numbers of that degraded and distinct people would exercise a deleterious influence upon the superior race."

Within three years, however, having changed his governor's hat for a railroad man's cap, Stanford changed his tune as well. The Central Pacific had been having problems with its largely Irish workforce. Persuaded of their indispensability, the laborers often staged strikes for higher pay and were notoriously unreliable; many would disappear immediately after payday. After a fresh infusion of funds in early 1865, the railroad needed 5,000 additional laborers to work on the stretch of track in the foothills of the Sierra Nevadas between Newcastle and Colfax, California and its recruiters were having difficulty finding enough workers for the job.

A solution to both problems could potentially be found in the engagement of Chinese laborers, who were plentiful and willing, but it was a controversial idea, even within the ranks of Central Pacific's management. Eventually, 50 Chinese were hired for an initial trial, followed by an additional 50. They proved able and well-disciplined, they did not strike, and they were willing to accept less money than the railroad had to pay whites. By the end of 1865 3,000 had been recruited. Stanford, writing in that year, now found the Chinese workers to be "quiet, peaceable, industrious, economical – ready and apt to learn all the different kinds of work required in railroad building."

After the railroad was finished, however – Stanford himself

helped drive in the final, golden spike at Promontory Point, Utah on May 10, 1869 – many Chinese laborers were suddenly idled, and the former governor eventually turned on them again. During his successful 1884 campaign for the U.S. Senate, he allied himself with supporters of anti-Chinese bills, and even spoke out in the early 1890s in favor of a plan to bring 50,000 blacks to California to work as farmers as a device to drive out the Chinese.

This second change of heart, like his first, appears to have been less a principled stance than one based on utility and self-interest. Yet his public pronouncements aside, Stanford seems to have had close and enduring relationships with individual Chinese he had come to know personally. He must have had true affection for Jin Mun; if his wife had gone so far as to offer the boy the possibility of adoption, her husband would surely have given his assent, and Stanford is said to have been helpful to Jin Mun at other points in his life as well.

By 1870, both brothers had left the couple's employ to seek their fortunes elsewhere and as something other than domestic servants. Jin Mun, lured by the promise of riches in the gold mines, left Sacramento in about 1866 to work as a prospector. For the next three years, he took to reworking claims that other miners had abandoned, panning for gold that might have been overlooked. He was not alone. For years after the Gold Rush, many Chinese turned to mining "placer deposits" – accumulations of gravel and sand containing minerals and precious metals – that white miners had decided were "worked out," meaning they did not offer sufficient return for labor expended. Searching for gold in this way required little investment, and the fact that white miners had given up on these claims minimized the danger of violent confrontation with them in which the Chinese were often the losers. Still, it was a tough way to make a living.

Jin Mun did well enough at placer mining to afford a trip back to China to marry in 1869 or 1870, when he was about 20 years old. Jin Kee went back, too, and also wed on this trip. As was the custom, neither chose his own bride. Jin Kee's father and stepmother had found a woman, Chin Fung, for him. She was probably from a nearby town, and judging from her surname was from the same clan as both of his father's wives. He had not known Chin Fung before his departure, however, and in fact did not see her until the ceremony, common practice in China at the time. The two wed in 1873 in what proved to be a stable marriage that lasted until his death.

For Jin Mun, the parents turned to the Gong family, and he was wed to a woman named Gong Shee. But about a year later, he returned to America without her. He spent a good portion of the subsequent decade reworking old mines in California and Nevada, and these places were not considered fit for Chinese women. Life was rough, and Jin Mun told stories of being held up while riding on a stagecoach and of massacres by Indians. He added, however, that the Chinese had felt much safer than the whites in these confrontations, because the Indians, assuming from their Mongolian features and long, queued hair that the Chinese were simply members of another Indian tribe, did not molest them.

Mining was Jin Mun's first love, but he also dabbled in agriculture. In the 1870s and 1880s, Chinese were recruited to build levees to reclaim the swamplands of the Sacramento River delta. Many then stayed on to farm the land, which was very fertile. In 1876, together with two other San Francisco Chinese, Jin Mun leased 196 acres on Andrus Island for five years at a cost of $10 per acre. According to the terms of the lease, the tenants were to plant 3,000 eucalyptus trees and fence in the property at the landlord's expense.

Jin Mun is also said to have found work with the Central Pacific during this period, due to his ability to speak English well and likely to the intervention of Stanford. According to his grandson, he got a job as head foreman for the railroad, although no independent evidence for this appears to survive. After 1869, most of the Chinese employed by the Central Pacific were idled, but there was still work to be had straightening and maintaining tracks, which kept many Chinese laborers employed in the general vicinity.

Within weeks of the driving in of the golden spike, about 1,400 Chinese railroad workers moved west to Truckee, a mill town in eastern California just 30 miles from Reno. During the Gold Rush, the settlement had developed as a gateway to California mining country, and it later served as a camp for railroad construction crews. With the sudden influx of these Chinese, the population became one-third Asian overnight, and Truckee's Chinatown suddenly became the second-largest in the West, smaller only than that of San Francisco.

The Chinese lived apart from the other residents, although they mingled with them often in the course of doing business. There was work for many in Truckee, for some in railroad construction and maintenance and for others in the timber industry, plus the usual complement of laundries and groceries that served these other laborers. State law prohibited Chinese from owning real estate and from obtaining business licenses, so these were among the few vocations open to them. But there was also growing racial tension in the town, and there as elsewhere, anti-Chinese feeling was on the rise. The friction had many causes, but the most explosive was a growing number of unemployed white working men on the one hand, and, on the other, an industrious Chinese population more than willing to undercut them by accepting lower wages for whatever work was available.

Jin Mun was in Truckee in the mid-1870s, just at the point that bad blood began to explode into bloodshed. For much of the latter half of the 1870s and into the 1880s, Truckee saw riots against its Chinese residents and suspicious fires in its Chinatown. Jin Mun later told his children that he had been caught in an anti-Chinese riot in Truckee in 1874 in which Irish union members went after the Chinese. He may have had the date slightly wrong, though. Truckee's Chinatown did experience a series of four fires in a 10-day period in 1874, but there were more in the years that followed, and a white laborer's group was not actually organized until two years later. He was saved from harm when an Irish police officer he had befriended took him into his home until the violence had subsided. But bloodshed in Truckee was to ebb and flow for many more years. An 1878 fire destroyed its Chinatown, and the Chinese, prohibited from rebuilding on the same site, were forced to cross to the other side of the Truckee River and set up camp in a new location.

In the same year, it was the *Truckee Republican* newspaper that first printed the slogan, "The Chinese Must Go," which became the rallying cry of the California nativist Workingman's Party headed by Irish-American demagogue Denis Kearney. Pro-labor and deeply anti-Chinese, Kearney agitated against wealthy capitalists and had a special grievance against those who employed Chinese. On October 29, 1877, he led an angry mob to the summit of San Francisco's Nob Hill, the site of the mansions of several railroad barons, including that of Stanford, who had moved there in 1874. Addressing the crowd, he threatened to lynch "railroad magnates, thieving millionaires, and scoundrelly officials."

Truckee's torment finally subsided well after Jin Mun's departure, when the white population adopted a new strategy that was as effective as it was non-violent: a boycott. The white labor club mounted a successful economic embargo of all enterprises in the town that employed Chinese workers. The boycott reached its zenith between 1885 and 1886, and within a matter of weeks, Truckee's entire Chinese population had departed, as the remaining townspeople celebrated the occasion with a torchlight parade.

Chapter V
Another Good Man Gone Wrong

In February of 1875, Jin Kee returned to America without his new wife, but with his youngest brother, Jin Fuey, in tow. They sailed aboard the S.S. *City of Pekin*, a Pacific Mail Line steamship, in half the time it had taken Jin Kee to travel from Hong Kong more than a dozen years earlier. The fare was $50, but passage was considerably more bearable. The middle deck of the *Pekin* had been fitted out with a frame upon which canvas stretchers were placed, allowing the passengers to sleep on comfortable bunks. A month or so after they set out, the two landed in San Francisco, where Jin Kee would remain for the next three years. Jin Fuey, however, had the good fortune, five months after their arrival, to meet up with a man named George Washington Reed, publisher of New York's *Brooklyn Daily Eagle*, who was visiting California. It was a pivotal encounter that would change his life forever.

The 58 year-old Reed had moved to Brooklyn from his native Pennsylvania eight years earlier, taken a job with the *Eagle* as manager of its advertising business and joined the Marcy Avenue Baptist Church. Exactly how Reed met Jin Fuey is not recorded, but he took to the 12 year-old boy immediately and offered to bring him back to New York to work as a servant in his home. With his elder brother's assent – this was, after all, the exact same path Jin Kee had traveled himself when he was engaged by the Stanfords - Jin Fuey agreed and went east to live with Reed and his wife, Harriet. He probably traveled there with the Reeds on the transcontinental railroad, in whose construction his fellow

Chinese had recently played such a major role.

New York's Chinese numbered only in the hundreds in 1875. Fewer than a dozen were recorded in the state in the 1870 census, and while that number grew steadily, there were still fewer than 1,200 in 1880. The vast majority lived in the New York City area, and more particularly in lower Manhattan and Brooklyn. Those who had made it to the east coast were working primarily as laundrymen, cigar makers and cooks, with the occasional shopkeeper or sailor among them. Many, like Jin Fuey, were from Xinning, and in the 1870s a critical mass was beginning to congregate in the Five Points neighborhood. Named for the intersection of Manhattan's Anthony (now Worth), Orange (now Baxter) and Cross (now Mosco) Streets, the area was famous for vice, disease and violence. Irish, Italian, Jewish, German and African immigrants had populated it earlier in the century. It remains part of Chinatown to this day.

It was becoming fashionable to employ Chinese servants in wealthy American homes. An article in the *New York Times* published at the time of Jin Fuey's arrival in the city asked, "Is the Chinaman to be the domestic servant of the future? Will another census show him stealthily supplanting the European in our households, and setting up his gods on the kitchen mantels of this Christian land?" In Jin Fuey's case, it was precisely the other way around. The boy soon began to profess an interest in Christianity. Whether the attraction was more a case of true conviction or perceived path to personal advancement is unclear, but Jin Fuey would, on March 7, 1880, be baptized a Christian, and not by Reed's Baptists, but by the Rev. Charles S. Brown, superintendent of the Methodists' Five Points Mission in lower Manhattan.

The diminutive Jin Kee, short, stout and with deep-set eyes, had also become a Methodist. He had enrolled in a mission school set up in Chinatown in 1868 by the Rev. Dr. Otis Gibson, who had spent a decade as a missionary in Fuzhou, China and spoke both the Fuzhou and Cantonese dialects. Under Gibson's tutelage, the young man was also baptized. Then, in September 1878, Jin Kee, too, made his way east, and when he arrived in New York, he presented Reed with letters of introduction from several prominent San Francisco clergymen. Reed graciously invited him to stay at his home until he could get established and introduced the young man, who had by this time become quite capable in English, to Henry C. Parke, a friend who owned a business that sold imported Chinese and Japanese goods.

Parke needed an assistant, and he offered Jin Kee six dollars a month to help out in the store as a combination salesman, designer, silk painter and mender of porcelain and lacquer ware. It was not a great deal of money, but during the seven months the young Chinese worked for him, Parke introduced him to some of New York's more prominent Methodists. Jin Kee joined Brooklyn's First Place Methodist Church, began making the circuit of other local houses of worship and appeared to have a promising career as a preacher before him. Within a few months he had spoken at Reed's Marcy Avenue Baptist Church, St. James Methodist Episcopal Church, Grace Methodist Episcopal Church and at a Sunday school in Harlem. The Methodist elders, recognizing his potential value as a missionary among his fellow Chinese, began to hatch plans to sponsor him for further education at Drew Theological Seminary in New Jersey after a preparatory course at Pennington Seminary.

Jin Kee. Source: Louis J. Beck, New York's Chinatown: An Historical Presentation of Its People and Places. *(New York: Bohemia Publishing Company, 1898).*

In addition to preaching the gospel, Jin Kee began to speak out on the issues of the day, and no topic was as combustible or as critical to the welfare of the Chinese community as the sentiment brewing in Congress and the country at large to restrict further Chinese arrivals into the United States. Chinese immigration had been more or less a regional issue until the 1870s because so few Chinese lived east of the Rocky Mountains. In 1870, more than 99 percent of America's 63,000-plus "Celestials," as they were sometimes called, lived in the West, fully 78 percent in California alone.

But others outside the West had a stake in the matter as well. Missionaries throughout the country believed the Chinese in America could play a major role in efforts to convert their fellow countrymen in Chinatowns as well as in China. Then too, merchants had an interest in the developing China trade, which was inseparable from the immigration issue by virtue of the 1868 Burlingame Treaty with China. Negotiated on China's behalf by Anson Burlingame, whom President Abraham Lincoln had named U.S. envoy to China in 1861 and who was trusted by the Manchu government, the treaty protected American commerce in China, encouraged free emigration of Chinese into the United States and set out protections for Chinese already living in America, among other things.

The immigration issue heated up in California during the bad economic times of the 1870s, and both political parties, their eyes on California's electoral votes, took up the cause of Chinese

> ST. JAMES' METHODIST EPISCOPAL CHURCH,
> 128th st. and Madison av.
> Missionary sermon at 10½ A. M., by
> Rev. Dr. T. M. Reid.
> Anniversary Sunday School Missionary Society,
> at 7½ P. M. Addresses by
> General Clinton B. Fisk,
> the pastor, Rev. W. R Davis, and
> Moy Jin Kee, from Canton.
> Very interesting exercises by the school.

Notice of sermons at Manhattan's St. James' Methodist Episcopal Church, March 15, 1879. Source: New York Herald.

exclusion in their 1876 platforms. Republican Rutherford B. Hayes, who won the presidency in that year, favored renegotiating the Burlingame Treaty as a means to accomplish this end. In early 1879, however, an impatient Congress began considering legislation that would have abrogated it unilaterally. A bill to forbid the entry of any vessel carrying more than 15 Chinese, whether visitors or immigrants, passed the House of Representatives in January, and was on its way to passage in the Senate.

Debate over the issue played out, among other places, on the editorial page of the *New York Tribune*. The opening salvo was a February 15 letter from no less a light than the great abolitionist William Lloyd Garrison, who was reacting to reports of the previous day's deliberations in the Senate. Garrison, his eloquence undimmed by age despite the fact that he was ailing and would live only another three months, offered this view:

> It is difficult to decide in this case which is the greater, its absurdity or its injustice. We have allowed all other peoples to take up their abode with us, notwithstanding their ignorance, destitution, unfortunate training and difference of race; and they have come by the millions – Englishmen, Irishmen, Scotchmen, Frenchmen, Germans, Scandinavians, Italians, Africans, *etc., etc.* . . . We must either drive out these, or prevent any more of them seeking a refuge here, or else keep the barrier down and let the Chinese find an equal entrance, and be protected in the enjoyment of equal rights and privileges.

Garrison singled out Senator James G. Blaine, the Senate bill's most prominent sponsor, for withering criticism. Blaine was a Maine Republican and, at the time, the leading contender for the 1880 Republican presidential nomination, Hayes having pledged not to run for a second term. In response, Blaine defended the legislation in the *Tribune* several days later, and framed his arguments in decidedly racist terms. He asserted that Chinese emigration had not been voluntary, but rather bore the "worst and most demoralized features of coolyism" – a reference to human slavery – and that many of the Chinese women who had come were prostitutes, "impure and lewd far beyond the Anglo-Saxon conception of impurity and lewdness." He raised the specter of epidemic diseases resulting from further immigration, quoting a San Francisco government health officer's testimony that the Chinese lived in "tenement houses, large numbers crowded into individual rooms, without proper ventilation, with bad drainage . . . with a great deal of filth, the odors from which are horrible." And he observed that "cheap, servile labor pulls down the more manly toil to its level," warning finally that if the Chinese felt they "had a firm footing in California, they would come in enormous numbers."

The February 27 edition of the *Tribune* carried a stinging rebuttal from Garrison, who likened Blaine's "specious, vehement, race-despising speech" on the Senate floor to Daniel Webster's famous "seventh of March" speech in support of the Fugitive Slave Law of 1850. But the *Tribune's* editors had also made a laudable effort to hear from a representative of the Chinese themselves, and for this purpose they turned to Jin Kee, who, however, they condescendingly dubbed an "intelligent Chinaman," as if to imply that most of his compatriots were not so. In an interview that appeared immediately adjacent to the Garrison letter, Jin Kee expressed disillusionment with the treatment Chinese had received in America:

> We expected more from this country than any other because it was a 'nation of freemen,' but we have got less. The treatment we have received here has been shameful, and if the good people of the United States could only realize how we have been hunted and hounded about, our property taken from us by force, our poor homes burned over our heads and we stoned and driven from place to place subject to the gibes and insults of every loafer of an 'Irish fellow-citizen,' I am sure we would not have been so misrepresented by Mr. Blaine and others, and would find greater protection than we

now receive. The Chinamen are patient, and they bear a great deal, but they cannot bear everything.

He continued, comparing the Chinese experience in America to that of other immigrant groups, even that of black slaves:

> We are charged with all offenses because we have no vote, and because we have to work for our living. We are clean, don't get drunk, mind our own affairs, and do our duty. Can you say so much for the Irish, German, or any other foreigners? We are proscribed in California, and when a contract under which the Chinaman works runs out, he is unable to get work. They work cheaply rather than strike or starve. If they succeed in any occupation they are immediately set upon by the hoodlums and driven out of it. They are taxed to death, but pay without grumbling . . . the slaves of the South were never treated like the Chinese are now being treated in California.

Jin Kee acknowledged that many Chinese women in the United States *had* been brought for immoral purposes, but explained that "the better classes of Chinese women do not come here, because they are subject to insults and all the other hardships we have to undergo here." He asserted that he could not, for example, bring his own wife to America, and cited a story of two of his friends who had felt compelled to disguise their wives in men's clothing to save them from the insults of hoodlums. But surely he was overstating the case, because just a few years later, in 1883, Jin Kee did indeed bring his wife, and she remained in America for more than 30 years.

After the bill passed the Senate, President Hayes, insisting on a mutually agreeable solution rather than unilateral abrogation of the Treaty, vetoed it. Renegotiation eventually occurred under his successor, Republican James A. Garfield, and in 1882 the Chinese Exclusion Act was passed and signed into law by Chester A. Arthur, who had assumed the presidency after Garfield was assassinated.

In part as a result of the *Tribune* column, Jin Kee's notoriety in New York began to grow, and a reporter who interviewed him less than two months later found him not shy about speaking about himself. The writer, who visited Jin Kee in the basement apartment at 135 Canal Street that he shared with several other Chinese men, described him as "quite fat for a Chinaman, rather effeminate in the face, pleasing, intelligent looking . . . His voice is soft and low – an excellent thing in a man or woman. His eyes are oval, and big for a Chinese, innocent looking, yet keen . . . his mouth is large, his lips full and his smile sweet."

The reporter portrayed the 32 year-old Jin Kee as a Renaissance man – or, as he put it, a "Chinese Admirable Crichton," a reference to a multitalented 16th century Scot who was an accomplished horseman, fencer, musician and orator fluent in 12 languages. The writer exaggerated Jin Kee's talents, praising him as a doctor ("not only of medicine, but of art, literature, science and theology") a translator, a musician and a missionary. Jin Kee the doctor was said to be working on a cure for hydrophobia (a "vegetable remedy" applied to the dog bite). As a translator, he had done some Chinese-to-English translations for Abiel Abbot Low, an American shipping magnate who had made his fortune in China. And as a "doctor of religion" he was portrayed as able to expound on all creeds, but partial to Methodism. Jin Kee's strongest suit, however, was said to be music. "He can play on every musical and unmusical instrument known to mortal Chinamen," the reporter declared, including a Chinese cornet, a banjo, a guitar, a fiddle, and a "curious-looking affair which he called 'the cheesebox'" capable of producing "not unpleasing" sounds.

The flat Jin Kee shared was decorated with Chinese calligraphy, which he explained disingenuously to the gullible reporter spelled out "passages from the sacred writings of Confucius referring to Christ," as if there were such a thing. He confided that while he enjoyed a little drink now and then, he abhorred opium. He also announced that he intended to settle in the United States – the first public indication he had ever given of this desire, and added that he spent his spare time preaching and addressing Sunday schools and was seeking money to establish a Chinese Methodist mission in New York.

That dream was soon realized. The young Chinese firebrand who had argued so eloquently on behalf of his countrymen in the *Tribune* and who had already demonstrated his ability to preach the gospel seemed a made-to-order choice to carry out the Methodists' plans for outreach to New York's growing Chinese community. Morris H. Smith, a prominent parishioner at Jin Kee's Brooklyn church, suggested that he organize a night school under the auspices of the Methodists' Five Points Mission, which had been established in 1850. Jin Kee made it clear that he was amenable to doing so, and may in fact have put Smith up to making the suggestion. Estimating the number of Chinese in New York at about 1,000, he proposed locating the new school in the heart of the Chinese quarter, and premises were rented at 14 Mott Street, but only after another location fell through because the agent feared that if he leased it to Chinese, he would not be able to rent anything in the neighborhood to anyone else. The plan called for preaching every Sunday morning and evening, with an afternoon Sunday school session. Instruction in English was to take place daily, a prayer meeting to be held every Wednesday evening and a Bible class every Saturday evening.

The Mott Street mission occupied the second floor of an old tenement house. Some laundrymen lived in the basement, and on the first floor was a Chinese grocery. A German family that took in sewing to make ends meet lived above the mission. The grand opening on May 4, 1879 was well-attended by both Chinese and Americans, including several church dignitaries and Jin Kee's younger brother, Jin Fuey. Bits of red paper with Chinese inscriptions festively decorated the lintels of what had once been a parlor. A few benches and several pine boards placed on trunks were pressed into service as pews, and the pulpit was

Mott Street Sunday School, drawn by W. P. Snyder, from a sketch by C. A. Keetels. The Chinese characters on the wall mean "Methodist Church." Source: Harper's Weekly, July 19, 1879.

fashioned from an old bureau, the *New York Times* observed. Curious musical instruments, hymn-books and bibles printed in both English and Chinese were in evidence.

The *Eagle* noted helpfully that Chinese bibles were arranged "the same as the Hebrew, beginning at the last page and ending with the first." The *New York Herald* joked that it "read backward to a reader of English," and reported that Jin Kee looked puzzled when he was asked if "the book was to be inspected while the reader stood on his head, and whether the fact that Chinamen stood upside down at home (being on the underside of the globe) had anything to do with the puzzle."

Rev. Brown, superintendent of the mission, read aloud from the Sermon on the Mount, and remarked that if sending men and money to China to convert the Chinese to Christianity was the right thing to do, then the work of the Mott Street mission to convert those already in America must surely meet with the approval of good Christians. Then Jin Kee addressed the gathering in English. Dressed in full Chinese regalia, his head completely shaved except for a round patch at the crown about six inches in diameter from which his queue, neatly braided, emerged, he announced:

> I came here to get an education and go back to teach my countrymen Christianity. Some of the Chinamen here in New York wanted to get an education and went to the public schools, but the children would not let them study. I wanted to do something for them, and so hired this room, where they can come and be taught . . . Now we want all to come in, whether they are black, white or yellow.

That was the *New York Tribune's* version. The *Herald* had a somewhat different take on Jin Kee's remarks, and on his command of English. It quoted him this way:

> I come this place, open school, teach my countrymen 'ligion Jesus Christ. Hope evelly brother sistel come teach my countrymen lead, teach them love save you I do. I need be same way. I come here look round. See my people want learn. No think Melican flients . . . This place 'taint belly gleat. Work for Lord. No seats here belly good. No matter. Can stand up for Lord Jesus Christ. Want all people come. Black, yellow, white everybody.

By most accounts Jin Kee had acquired a fairly impressive command of English by this time, and in his interview in the *Tribune* a month earlier he had been nothing short of eloquent. The same paper commented later that he spoke English with "marvelous fluency and distinctness." It is hard to imagine that the same person who spoke of "how we have been hunted and hounded about, our property taken from us by force, our poor homes burned over our heads" would also have used phrases like "see my people want learn." and "no think Melican fliends" the following month. The *Tribune* might have been editing or the *Herald* stereotyping; probably there was a bit of both going on. The *Eagle's* view seems the most balanced: it reported that he spoke English "with comparative fluency, although of course, his grammar is not perfect nor all his accentuation correct. His sentences, too, are necessarily abrupt and jerky, but he made his meaning clear to all, and his ideas were expressed with a plain, though ungrammatical, force that many speakers cannot command."

Grammar aside, Jin Kee had been making a few choice racist comments of his own in his interviews, and these eventually filtered down to the Chinese community and got him into some trouble. "There are three classes in China," he opined to a reporter, "all of whom have different ancestors. They are the Chinese, the Tartars and the coolies. Most of those who come here are coolies and Tartars. Out of the 1,800 Chinamen in this city, not more than 20 are Chinamen, properly called. The better class do not come here because they do not get that "kind treatment" which the Treaty guarantees them; and more particularly because they cannot bring their wives with them and settle here, as the Irish and others are allowed to do."

His unfortunate - and, needless to say, bizarre and wholly erroneous- racial characterizations aside, Jin Kee was trying to make the point - in terms he thought white Americans might appreciate, and in a way that distinguished *him* from the average Chinese worker - that America ought not to be lumping all of the Chinese into one category. He went on to argue that instead of blanket legislation aimed at stopping *all* Chinese immigration, Congress ought to pass a law to suppress the slave trade carried on by "coolie-importing" companies in San Francisco that were actively engaged in importing indentured Chinese laborers - mostly for employers in Latin America - during this period.

Jin Kee's inflammatory portrayal of his compatriots came to their attention and caused a minor firestorm. As word of his insult spread, Chinese began to boycott the mission school, and he was forced to hide out until the affair blew over. He confessed to Rev. Brown that he feared for his life, and Brown did what he could to pacify the students. Far more disastrous for Jin Kee, however, was a Sunday dinner that took place in Brooklyn on May 11, 1879, just a week after the opening of the Mott Street mission. It would spell not only the end of his brief career as a Methodist minister, but also the conclusion of his sojourn in New York.

The episode began with an invitation from the *Brooklyn Daily Eagle's* George Washington Reed to his merchant friend Henry C. Parke, Jin Kee's erstwhile employer. The Reeds invited the Parkes to dinner at their home that Sunday, and shortly after the couple arrived, Reed proudly showed off an elegant silk handkerchief he had been given by Jin Kee, which the latter had told him he had brought from China. It was not the only such gift members of Reed's household had received from Jin Kee; some of the servant girls had accepted remembrances from him as well.

Parke immediately recognized the handkerchief and the other items as merchandise from his own store. Several months earlier, he said later, he had noticed that goods had begun to disappear, but he had been unable to determine who was responsible. The police were summoned and in a search of Jin Kee's apartment, they discovered three trunks' worth of Chinese silks and porcelains valued at $170. They also found on his person a roll of $112 in bills and $30 in gold.

Jin Kee was arrested forthwith and taken to "The Tombs," lower Manhattan's jail, but before being remanded to a cell, was brought before Charles W. Caffrey, captain of the first precinct, and made the butt of a bigoted joke. "Oh, if only we had Denis Kearney here now!" Caffrey said in the presence of a *New York Herald* reporter, making a reference to California's anti-Chinese demagogue. "I tell you ... there would be fun, for that Chinaman is no fool, as you will see by and by."

The jail keeper told a reporter that Jin Kee was the first Chinese ever arrested for larceny in New York, a fact confirmed by the *New York Sun*. The few who had been detained in Manhattan before that time had all been charged with gambling. It was an unusual enough occurrence to put the jailer in a quandary as to how to record the "color" of the prisoner, and he wondered whether to put him down as "white," "black" or "red." The warden solved the problem by ordering him simply to "put him down as Chinaman – that describes everything."

Jin Kee was indicted on May 19, 1879 for receiving goods stolen from Henry C. Parke. The entry appears at the bottom of this page from the Minutes of the Court of General Sessions in Manhattan. There is no record of either a trial or of dismissal of the indictment. Source: New York City Municipal Archives.

The next morning, when the court came into session, Jin Kee, dressed in Chinese garb and brandishing a Bible under each arm – one in English, the other Chinese – was hauled up before Judge Charles Flammer. He appeared penitent, his head hung low, as Parke leveled his accusations. Jin Kee admitted only to taking two small pieces of silk, however, and claimed the rest of the goods discovered had not belonged to Parke. He told the judge tearfully that the devil had gotten into him and that he had been unable to resist temptation. He was held on $1,000 bail. Later in the day, he spoke with a *New York Tribune* reporter, and offered his own account of the story, playing up his Christian *bona fides* to maximum effect:

> I came to this city ... about nine months ago. Before that I had lived about three years in California. I am married, but my wife lives in China. My father also lives there, and devotes much of his time to teaching Christianity to his countrymen. My mother died a believer in Christianity. I came to this country to be instructed in the English language and in the teachings of the Bible. It was my intention to return to China when I had accomplished these objects, and preach Christ crucified.

He did not admit guilt, but he did play for sympathy:

> [Mr. Parke] only paid me six dollars a week, and I had to work until 11 o'clock some evenings. I couldn't save any money or pursue my studies ... I supported myself lately by mending Chinese goods, and made about twenty dollars a week. Just as I was getting along with the school, Mr. Parke comes and has me arrested. I have no influence here and can't do anything. All of the Chinese goods he finds in my house he says belong to him. Some of them I brought from China. Moreover, his son made me presents, and a few of the articles I picked up myself.

Interviewed by a *Herald* reporter, Jin Kee also couldn't resist taking a few shots at Reed, whom he accused of bearing a grudge against him. He complained that Reed had brought his younger brother, Jin Fuey, to New York from California on the promise of giving him a college education, but that instead he had been keeping him as a servant in his home and paying him nothing. The ill will, he explained, was due to the fact that Jin Kee wished to liberate his brother from those circumstances.

The press was quick to condemn Jin Kee. The *New Haven Register*, for example, branded him "a regular wolf in sheep's clothing." Only the editors of the *Eagle* – Reed's own newspaper, ironically – spoke up in his defense, asserting his right to the presumption of innocence. In a May 13 editorial, they argued:

The strongest proof against him in the popular mind is that he is a Chinaman . . . The lawmakers of the nation insisted that every Chinaman is a thief . . . hence, in spite of the fact that no proof has been presented against Moy Jin Kee, the worthy people who have listened to his preaching are ready to accept the statement that he is a thief, without waiting to hear what he has to say.

But then, in the very same column, they did exactly what they criticized others for doing: they rushed to a judgment of their own. Chalking the entire affair up to the near certainty that Jin Kee was, in fact, nothing more than a "pious fraud," they asserted:

The worst feature of Moy Jin Kee's case seems to be his sudden conversion in California. The sincere believer in any religion is the slowest to be converted to another, and though Moy Jin Kee has worked exceedingly well for the benefit of other Chinamen, he still clings in his heart, as is only natural, to the superstitious regard which his compatriots feel for the pigtail . . . there is no really good reason to suppose that Moy Jin Kee has been sincerely converted. In fact, we should feel little inclined to blame him for assuming a religious belief which he did not entertain, when he saw how much worldly good it did him . . . Why should not Moy Jin Kee exchange contempt for social distinction, poverty for comfort and no prospects at all for the brightest prospects, when all he had to do was make certain professions?

The *Eagle* had little basis for determining what was going on in Jin Kee's heart, or in concluding that his profession of Christianity was anything other than genuine, but it was not entirely unjustified in raising the latter issue in general terms. There was little question that, coupled with his English ability, Christianity did offer Jin Kee – and Jin Fuey – a convenient and accelerated path to higher social status and material advancement in a country that for the most part offered its

Chinese immigrants neither. It was at least plausible that they, like other Asian converts, might have been what came by the end of the 19th century to be called "rice Christians" – people who converted less for the spiritual than for the worldly benefits that publicly accepting Jesus Christ could confer.

In an article entitled "Another Good Man Gone Wrong," the *Chicago Tribune* drew its own cynical – and bigoted – conclusion. "The evident lesson to be learned from Moy Jin Kee's transactions," it declared, "is to beware of the Heathen Chinee when he is childlike and bland, and especially when he puts on a long face and announces himself as one of 'Christ's boys.' It is not well for any church to accept him," it concluded, "until they have looked up his sleeves." It was a reference to a popular Bret Harte poem, "Plain Language from Truthful James" (also published under the name "The Heathen Chinee") in which a Chinese named Ah Sin turns the tables on a card shark out to fleece him in a game of Euchre. Ah Sin, who professes not to know the rules of the game, nonetheless fares exceptionally well, until he plays a card that had earlier been dealt to another player and is found to have secreted 24 jacks up his sleeve.

Rev. Brown posted bail for Jin Kee on May 27, and there are no press reports of the outcome of the case, nor are there any entries about it in the *Minutes of the Court of General Sessions* for 1879 beyond the initial indictment. Oddly, no record of either a trial or a dismissed indictment exists. The *New Haven Register* predicted the affair would spell the end of his tenure as a "moral reformer of his almond-eyed brethren," and this turned out to be substantially true. Following an aborted attempt to resume his ministry – he spoke at a Methodist Sunday School meeting in Harlem the following month – Jin Kee never again worked as a preacher. But he was still destined to play an important role in the effort to improve the lives of those "almond-eyed brethren," and he would eventually play it on the national stage.

Chapter VI
He Stands High Among His Countrymen

Jin Fuey's advancement in Methodist circles was not noticeably compromised by his brother Jin Kee's fall from grace. After the young man's baptism in March, 1880, an anonymous donor underwrote his education at New Jersey's Pennington Seminary. He began his studies the following month, in the spring term. He was the only Chinese among the 92 students enrolled in the school that year. Most were from the east coast, but a handful came from foreign countries, including four from Cuba, five from Ireland and one each from five other countries. At about 20 years old, Jin Fuey was in the mid-range of the boys, whose ages ran from 13 to 27.

Pennington, founded in 1838 by the New Jersey Conference of the Methodist Church, was charged with preparing young men for college, business and the ministry. Set in a quiet borough in central New Jersey, the school boasted teachers with degrees from Harvard, Princeton and Yale. Its staccato recruitment advertisements read, "first-class work; discipline good; moral and religious tone high; good home; very healthful; access easy; rates moderate; catalogues free." The seminary was run by the Rev. Thomas O'Hanlon, an 1866 graduate of nearby Princeton who was already an ordained Methodist minister before he got to college. O'Hanlon had made a career out of revivals and taught popular Bible classes in Ocean Grove, a Jersey shore Christian camp meeting community. In the course of his professional life, he converted more than 2,000 people and taught 6,000 students, of whom a tenth served in the ministry and as missionaries in foreign countries.

The school, which had also begun to admit young women in 1854, provided Jin Fuey with an unusual opportunity unavailable to other Chinese immigrants, and he wisely made the most of it. Despite the fact that he was not a native English speaker, he joined the Alpha Omega Society, the oldest of three literary societies on campus, which had been established in 1852. Alpha Omega was known for lively debates at its weekly meetings, and its activities must surely have helped him not only master idiomatic English, but also hone the argumentation skills that would serve this crafty man well for his entire life.

Five feet seven, thin and well-favored, Jin Fuey was being groomed to return to China to preach the gospel. He therefore naturally took an active interest in the topic of ministering to the

Page from the autograph book of Arthur B. Curtis, one of Jin Fuey's schoolmates at Pennington, which he inscribed on January 9, 1881 with a quote from the Chinese sage Mencius: "Though a man may be wicked, yet if he adjust his thought, fast and bathe, he may sacrifice to God." He uncharacteristically used Chinese word order for his English signature - Moy Jin Fuey - and signed in Chinese with a pen name, Moy Siu Yun (Mei Shaoyuan), a moniker he does not seem to have employed elsewhere. On the facing page (not pictured), he wrote out the entire 23rd Psalm in Chinese. Courtesy of Kathy Ramanauskas.

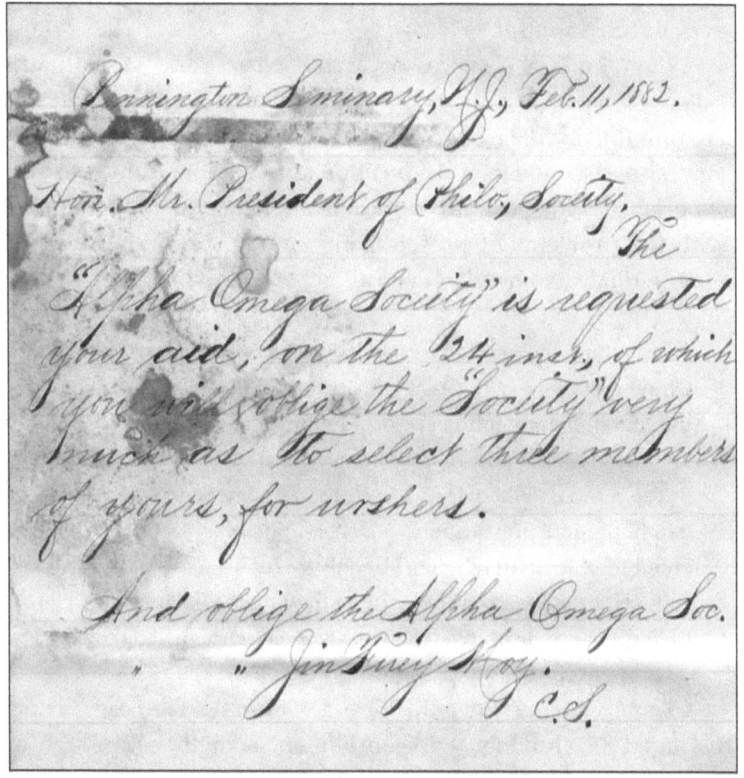

A letter handwritten by Jin Fuey in 1882 on behalf of Pennington's Alpha Omega Society, a literary group known for its lively debates. Courtesy of the Pennington School.

Chinese. While at Pennington, he participated in a discussion on that subject at the Warren Street Methodist Church in nearby Trenton, and he never lost his connection to New York's Mott Street mission which, after his brother's departure, had been relocated to the Seventh Street Methodist Church. Jin Fuey was part of a belated Christmas program held there on December 31, 1882. He led the singing of "Rock of Ages" and "Jesus Loves Me" in Cantonese, the others joining in for the chorus. The *New York Sun* reported that his intention, after finishing his English education, was to return to his native land as a missionary. But whether, in his heart of hearts, he ever really shared such an objective is doubtful.

When Jin Kee's successor at the New York Mission was called to work in China, Jin Fuey, who had graduated from Pennington in 1883, was asked to become the organization's new superintendent. This position offered him some real-life experience with pastoral work and a chance to deal firsthand with the problems of proselytizing among the Chinese. As he observed later, somewhat cynically:

> I don't think the missionaries will ever succeed in Christianizing the Chinese of this city until they first root out the evils of Chinatown – the contaminating influences of gambling and prostitution. As things are now, the Chinese go from houses of prostitution and gambling to the Sunday Schools, and from the Sunday Schools to houses of gambling and prostitution . . . The Chinese do not care anything about the Christian religion, but only go to the missions and Sunday Schools for the purpose of learning the English language . . . Here is their great opportunity – and it costs them nothing.

Classes at the Seventh Street Church's Chinese School averaged 14 students, with enrollment sometimes as high as 28, and the school was visited often by ministers for whom Jin Fuey provided interpretation. He was well-suited to the work; so much so, in fact, that during an October 1884 trip to Philadelphia, he was offered another, similar job. The position was with the newly established Chinese-American Union, an association set up to protect, instruct and Christianize the 600-odd Chinese living in the city. The group had set up a home and school at 924 Walnut Street and offered English classes, recreation programs and non-sectarian worship. The young preacher was asked to become superintendent of the organization and readily accepted.

It was a good job, but the income was modest, and to make ends meet he had to moonlight. He already had experience interpreting in church, and in 1886, he began to do the same in court. He was asked to go to Trenton, New Jersey to translate in the trial of two immigrants accused of assaulting and robbing another Chinese. He also began teaching a class at Philadelphia's Oxford Presbyterian Church. Throughout his adult life, Jin Fuey made the most of his fluency in both tongues.

That same year, with financial support from well-heeled members of his congregation, he entered Jefferson Medical College in Philadelphia, becoming what the *Philadelphia Inquirer* described as "the first Chinaman who has ever taken this course of study in the United States." Though perhaps not strictly true, this was not much of an exaggeration. As a Chinese medical student in the United States in the 19th century he was a rarity, and he was the first Chinese to enroll at Jefferson. Jin Fuey studied there until he earned his M.D. degree in April, 1890.

A year before graduation, however, he suddenly eloped with Hatita Alice Dolbow, a 19 year-old white girl originally from Wilmington, Delaware. The two were married on April 3, 1889 by a Methodist preacher just across the river from Philadelphia in Camden, New Jersey after Hattie, as she was known, lied about her age. How the two met is not clear. The girl had been missing since the previous August, and her life up to that point had been, in the words of her guardian, "a strange story of incorrigibility."

Hattie's mother, Annie Lyon, born into a prominent Wilmington, Delaware family, had married beneath herself and had been deserted by her husband, a butcher named William Henry Dolbow, when the child was just two years old. In 1887, the poor woman, who had been living hand-to-mouth, had been found dead of consumption – tuberculosis – in her Philadelphia tenement apartment at the age of 51. Her daughter was placed in Philadelphia's House of Refuge, a reform school for juvenile delinquents, until a friend of her family, a Mrs. R. B. G. Gardner, took custody of her to "rear the dead mother's child in righteous ways." Discontented with those "righteous ways," Hattie had run away, and the police had been looking for her for nine months.

Intermarriage between a Chinese and a Caucasian in this era

Record of the marriage of Jin Fuey and Hatita Alice Dolbow in Camden, New Jersey on April 3, 1889. They both misstated their ages on the marriage license. Source: New Jersey State Archives.

was not always easy. When Jin Fuey's cousin Gop Jung attempted to wed a white girl in Washington in early 1900, the District of Columbia government refused to perform the ceremony because of his ethnicity, and the couple had to cross the Potomac to Alexandria, Virginia before they could find a court willing to marry them. Even then, the court clerk had to consult with several attorneys before he was confident a marriage between the races would, in fact, be legal. Even if it was not unlawful, however, marrying a Chinese was still considered somewhat scandalous. It was simply not something young ladies of high station did, and press reports about it, when it did occur, were at once voyeuristic and bemused. A newspaper in her home town of Antwerp, New York ran a story about Gop Jung's bride with the subhead "Miss Lillian B. Patton Makes a Queer Choice." Hattie Dolbow's marriage to Jin Fuey drew headlines, too – in both the *Philadelphia Inquirer* and the *Baltimore Sun*.

"The white wives of Chinamen do not come from the highest walks of life," the *Chicago Tribune* proclaimed in 1889. "They have not had the benefits of a home and education, nor the luxuries that riches give. But in every case," it had to admit, "they seem to be contented." This was certainly true of Hattie and Jin Fuey, who sought refuge in a Chinese laundry at 445 North 9th Street after their hasty wedding. The next day, when the authorities broke in, they found the newlyweds on the third floor and arrested them both. The marriage was not annulled, however, and Hattie was surely far better off with Jin Fuey than she would have been otherwise. She was well cared for, and the two would remain married – and very closely allied – throughout the rest of Jin Fuey's life.

After graduation, Jin Fuey, who unlike his brothers and most other Chinese embraced the American custom of placing his surname after his given name (and was thus known throughout his adult life in America as Jin Fuey Moy), opened an office on Sansom Street in Philadelphia and began to build a medical practice, catering to both Chinese and Caucasians. The following year he and Hattie more or less adopted a baby girl. They took into their home a 21 month-old named Josephine, the daughter of a Germantown, Pennsylvania laundryman named Moy Shoo Chong – presumably one of Jin Fuey's kinsmen – and his wife, Jessie Whitehurst, a mulatto woman. Like Hattie's mother, Jessie had recently died of consumption. On a laundryman's earnings, Moy Chong, as her husband was known, could not care for all three of his children.

THREE TOUGH CHINAMEN

George W. Cliffe, a Caucasian banker who had patronized the laundry and befriended Moy Chong, urged him to put the children into foster care, and went so far as to apply on their behalf to the local Methodist orphanage. Cliffe lobbied hard for the children, and was able to get support for taking them from all the members of the orphanage's board save the president – the widow of a Methodist bishop – who refused absolutely to admit "colored" children. Moy Chong wasn't interested anyway; he feared his offspring would be taken from him permanently, and that he would be unable to bring them back to China if he ever decided to return.

His solution was to keep the son and place the two daughters elsewhere, where they could be raised by others but not lose their connection to their father entirely. The son was eventually sent back to China, where he lived for 18 years until returning in 1913. The other daughter, Edith, was taken in by a black woman, and Josephine, the youngest, was given to Jin Fuey and Hattie, though the couple never went through any legal procedures to formalize her adoption. Josephine would grow up to become a well-known vaudevillian and silent movie star. And she would, many years later, have some difficulty proving the circumstances of her birth.

In 1892, Jin Fuey took on a new project. He undertook to edit and publish a weekly newspaper, which he dubbed the *Chinese-American Advocate*. The bilingual publication was aimed not only at Chinese in the United States, but also at "many an American or English-speaking friend of the Chinese race," into whose hands it might fall. The English articles were drawn from other publications and were typeset; their Chinese translations appeared after them in handwritten characters. Also included was a Bible lesson and a few advertisements. The *Advocate* sold for 10 cents a copy, though an annual subscription could be had for $2.50, or $3.00 outside the United States. The initial print run was 5,000 copies, which seems excessively optimistic, given that Philadelphia's Chinese population numbered fewer than 1,000.

SCOTT D. SELIGMAN

The premier edition of the Chinese-American Advocate (華美字報), a bilingual weekly published in Philadelphia by Jin Fuey, dated June 30, 1892. Only two editions survive, and these may be the only ones that were ever published.

"The Chinaman arriving upon these shores wants to know many things personal to him, and many more which as deeply interest those with whom or among whom he is to dwell," Jin Fuey explained a bit awkwardly in an editorial in the inaugural issue. "To be useful to himself, he must acquire some knowledge of the English language . . . he needs to know something of his legal rights and the obligations under which he rests to his neighbor, according to the advanced views of the new civilization under which he now is to live."

The first issue contained 16 pages, and included domestic and foreign news of interest to local Chinese. It covered the trial of seven Philadelphia Chinese men who pleaded guilty to selling opium as well as the death of China's consul and the escape of a Chinese girl from a house of "questionable repute," both in San Francisco. This last story gave Jin Fuey an opportunity to opine passionately on collusion between purveyors of vice and the government officials who received bribes from them. On the international front, the paper reported on a conference between the Chinese and Russian governments about a telegraph line to connect Finland and Beijing and an English firm that planned to build a modern iron and steel plant near Hankou.

The big news, however, was the passage by Congress of the Geary Act the previous month. Named for its sponsor, Representative Thomas J. Geary, a Democrat from California, the bill served in part to renew the Chinese Exclusion Act, which had been valid for only 10 years and had been due to expire. But it went well beyond the scope of the previous law and levied new burdens on America's Chinese. All would now be required to carry residence permits – internal passports that had to be kept on their person at all times, under penalty of deportation or a year of hard labor. And Chinese would no longer be permitted to testify as witnesses in court or be eligible for bail in *habeas corpus* proceedings. Jin Fuey included in his newspaper the full text and a synopsis of the Act, a report on the members of Congress who had opposed it, an item on possible retaliation against

Americans then living in China, a rebuttal to some of the charges the bill's proponents had leveled against America's Chinese and some criticisms of the measure by a former American missionary in China.

Only two editions of the *Chinese-American Advocate* survive, and these may well be the only ones ever published, because another opportunity soon presented itself in the form of an offer for Jin Fuey to return to New York. It came from Dr. Joseph Chak Thoms, another Chinese physician, who had graduated from Long Island College Hospital and who, like Jin Fuey, spoke excellent English and had married a white woman. Thoms had been recruited as the superintendent of a new hospital located in a town house at 45 Hicks Street in Brooklyn. The only Chinese hospital on the east coast, it was established in January, 1891 by the "King's Daughters for China," a non-sectarian group representing several churches in Brooklyn, Manhattan and Jersey City that had been sponsoring missionary work among the Chinese. Organized exclusively for the treatment of Chinese patients suffering from bodily injury or disease, the hospital was funded by contributions, including $1,300 from Mott Street Chinese merchants. It was intended as a solution to a real problem: Many of New York's Chinese did not generally receive quality healthcare.

A youthful Jin Fuey in full Chinese regalia. Source: Louis J. Beck, New York's Chinatown: An Historical Presentation of Its People and Places. (New York: Bohemia Publishing Company, 1898).

"Sufficient reason for it," the *New York Times* explained, "is found in the fact that Chinese patients cannot understand nor make themselves understood in the ordinary hospital, where all their surroundings are strange." But language was not the only problem. Many Chinese who might have wished to eschew traditional herbal remedies in favor of Western medicine were reluctant to seek out American doctors, whom they feared wanted to secure their eyes, livers and other organs for the manufacture of drugs. Besides that, they also didn't particularly care for the food at American hospitals.

The obvious solution was an institution in which everybody spoke Chinese and ate Chinese food, and although the officers of the "King's Daughters for China" were all white – the president, Edward Braislin, was pastor of Brooklyn's Washington Avenue Baptist Church – Thoms and a Chinese nurse were the face of the hospital as far as the clients were concerned. By August, 1892, the doctor had already treated 80 patients, about half of them consumptives, and the three-ward, six-bed facility in which he and his wife had an apartment was fully occupied. Thoms felt he had his hands full. If the hospital were to serve more patients, he would need some help.

Jin Fuey – Chinese, Christian and an M.D. – filled the bill perfectly, except for one problem. New York, like many other states, required citizenship of professionals as a condition of granting licenses for them to practice their vocations. But the Chinese Exclusion Act, in expressly denying citizenship to Chinese immigrants, had made naturalization impossible, and neither Jin Fuey nor Thoms had become a citizen before the legislation was passed. A solution had been devised in New York in the early 1880s when the legislature voted to "waive alienage" of a newly arrived British attorney who sought to practice law prior to being admitted to citizenship. A Yale-educated Chinese attorney named Hong Yen Chang who applied for similar dispensation in 1887 had had a harder time; although the legislature empowered the state Supreme Court to waive his alien status, the Court initially denied him admission to the bar, and relented only after he was naturalized later that year in a court proceeding that, paradoxically, some considered illegal because it violated the Exclusion Act.

Alienage was waived in New York in Jin Fuey's case and that of Dr. Thoms, perhaps because of the urgency of their cause. But there was a catch. They were permitted to practice, but only on Chinese patients. This restriction did not pose a huge problem, because their hospital did not have any other clientele. But the venture did not prove successful, in part because of insufficient funding and in part because the Chinese remained deeply suspicious of Western medicine and still largely preferred the traditional remedies offered by the 15-20 herbalists in Chinatown. Within two months, Jin Fuey, who now had a small family to support, found himself looking for another job.

It did not take long. In 1893, he was invited to supervise the Chinese Guild of St. Bartholomew's Protestant Episcopal Church in New York City. The Guild was an effort by St. Bart's, a midtown church with Bowery origins and a strong commitment to social welfare, to address the mundane, and not merely the spiritual, needs of the residents of the Chinese quarter. Established in 1889 at 23 St. Mark's Place under the leadership of an American, it soon fell under the stewardship of Chinese Christians. The Guild helped Chinese deal with the local government and the courts and assisted with such matters as writing letters and negotiating leases. It also ran a night school, and Jin Fuey soon found himself teaching in both Chinese and English: spelling and arithmetic every night, and occasionally reading and writing as well. A small supper was provided to students, who numbered 275 in all – average attendance was 53 men – to encourage them to stay on for the evening service. In 1896, 14 of them joined St. Bart's as congregants.

Much of the work of the Chinese Guild, whose members paid annual dues of $2 and numbered nearly 500 in the organization's first year of operation, involved providing legal aid. In his annual report to the rector, Jin Fuey recounted that the Guild had helped Chinese obtain justice in 4,898 cases the previous year. The examples he cited underscore the vulnerability of Chinese laborers to harassment and the difficulties they faced in obtaining redress. One case involved the theft of all valuables from a Chinese laundry by an American teenager who had been arrested and committed to a reformatory, only to be released the next day after his mother made a $30 payment to an alderman. Another involved a young boy who broke the window of a laundry as often as three times a week, but who, after being arrested, was sent to the Society for the Prevention of Cruelty to Children and discharged the following morning with a new pair of shoes. These offenses were relatively minor, but Chinese were also targets of beatings, shootings and even, occasionally, murder.

Jin Fuey attempted to energize the police precinct captains to step up enforcement by hiring a detective to lobby them, but he did not get far. "If we arrest all these boys every time when they annoy a Chinaman," one captain observed, "we would have our hands full. Besides, what's the use? The magistrate would reprimand and discharge them on the following morning and the defendant would return home and repeat the same thing over. You cannot secure a conviction to save your life." This frustrating inability to get justice probably contributed to Jin Fuey's cynicism about law enforcement and jurisprudence in America, and to his later life decisions to operate on the other side of the law.

The St. Bart's position gave Jin Fuey a pulpit from which to speak out on broader issues, just as his brother Jin Kee had done more than a dozen years earlier. In 1896, he was asked by the Brooklyn Ethical Association, a group dedicated to the scientific study of ethics, politics, economics, religion and the natural sciences that had been established five years earlier, to attend a lecture on Chinese ethics by the Rev. Francis Huberty James, a British Baptist missionary who had spent 16 years in China, and to participate in a discussion on the topic. James opined on the commonalities between the views of the Chinese sages and Christianity, maintaining that all the Chinese lacked was the hope of immortal life and the concept of the nearness of God.

Jin Fuey did not disagree, though he felt James had not placed enough emphasis on the importance of propriety - "one of the cardinal virtues of Chinese ethics" - and of filial piety. "If any Chinaman who has committed or intends to commit any wrongful act is asked how his parents or ancestors would regard it, he is, in the majority of cases, brought to reason," he declared. It was a principle that he found easy to articulate, but that he would consistently fail to apply to himself in the years ahead.

The *Brooklyn Daily Eagle* was lavish in its praise of Jin Fuey: "He stands high among his countrymen who are living among us," it declared, "and is diligent in his efforts for the betterment of their social and moral conditions." For this reason, and because his proficiency in English made him very quotable, Jin Fuey was occasionally sought out by the press for his point of view. An opportunity presented itself with the issuance of rules for the implementation of the Geary Act.

The Secretary of the Treasury was charged with enforcing the Act, and in 1893 he had made some minor concessions to a vocal pro-Chinese lobby - which had announced its intention to test the constitutionality of the new law - as to how it was to be enforced. Photos would not be required on applications for certificates of residence, and Chinese would need to provide only one credible witness as to their residence and legal status in the United States, rather than two. When the *New York Times* sought to assess Chinese reaction to these relatively minor compromises, one of the people to whom it turned was Jin Fuey, who asserted:

> Certain men who are established and making perhaps $100 or $200 a week are not going to be arrested. They will get the certificate and be registered; but it is the poorer classes who will suffer. However, I think the abolition of the photographic clause is a good move and

will make my countrymen less restive and more easy of control.

Few Chinese initially heeded the registration requirement imposed by the Geary Act. The "Six Companies," the San Francisco umbrella group that wielded considerable influence over America's Chinese during this era, actually instructed them to disobey the law in the hope that it would be struck down by the Supreme Court as unconstitutional. But when the Court upheld the conviction of three Chinese laborers who had been found guilty of lacking residence papers, it essentially laid to rest questions about the constitutionality of the exclusion laws. The Chinese remained deeply dissatisfied, however, and became more cautious in their dealings with Americans.

For example, Christian Chinese in New York, Brooklyn and Jersey City, who for 10 years had treated their American Sunday school teachers to a summer picnic to show their appreciation for their efforts, summarily called it off in 1893 at the suggestion of the new Chinese Consul General in New York. The official had called the organizers to the Consulate on West Ninth Street and warned that with public opinion aroused by the Court's decision, "too much mingling with Americans, especially with American women, might easily lead to trouble." The local Chinese read the hint as a direct order, and, despite the fact that invitations had already been sent out, they decided, at a meeting at St. Bart's, to call off the event. It meant forfeiting $300 already spent for refreshments and chartering a steamboat to ferry them all to Cold Spring Grove on Long Island for the day.

Reaction to the cancellation among the Chinese was divided, and mirrored the complexity of their attitudes toward the overall situation, and their dilemma over the proper response. On the one hand there was righteous indignation and an inclination toward civil disobedience, which had expressed itself in the failure to register as the law had demanded. On the other, the instinct for self-preservation suggested that keeping their heads down was probably the best strategy for avoiding further trouble.

"How can we be friends of the daughters of the men who helped to pass the Geary law?" the *New York Times* quoted a merchant named Wong I. Gong as asking. And Dr. Thoms, the physician who had briefly been Jin Fuey's employer and whom the *Times* described as "the most prominent and intelligent Chinese in this city," took the opportunity to denounce American Christians as hypocrites and declare his intention to leave his church.

Jin Fuey, as supervisor of the Chinese Guild, was also quoted, but was more measured in his remarks:

> Our Consul never did a wiser thing than when he stopped this picnic, and I think the $300 is well lost . . . There are two reasons, both most judicious ones, which influenced his action. The first, and the most obvious is, of course, the advisability of our Chinese people 'lying low," to use your American phrase, until the fury of the Geary law is spent and the feeling aroused by it has subsided. The second reason, and, to my mind, far the most important in connection with the recent attacks upon the relations between the Chinese pupils and their American teachers, is the handle any accident or any mismanagement occurring on the excursion would afford the Chinese haters. In short, this stopping of the picnic is a piece of caution and praiseworthy diplomacy on the part of our Consul, who evidently believes that when you are in a field with a savage bull it is better policy to hide than to wave a red flag in his place.

Jin Fuey was not the only Moy brother concerned about the Geary Act. Across the country in San Francisco it appeared that the new law had nearly cost his elder brother Jin Mun his life.

Chapter VII
Moy Jin Mun Will Furnish The Corpse

By 1880, nearly one out of every ten San Franciscans was Chinese, and in the economically depressed decade that followed the completion of the transcontinental railroad, public attitudes toward them had grown progressively more hostile. The Workingmen's Party, a political movement led by Denis Kearney, the agitator who personified the anti-Chinese movement, was championing new restrictions that would prevent Chinese from voting, bar them from participating in public works projects and even prohibit them from working for companies incorporated in the state. Yet still they came. More than 5,500 Chinese entered the United States in 1880, nearly 12,000 in 1881 and almost 40,000 in 1882 before the Exclusion Act took effect.

After his ordeal in Truckee, Jin Mun had taken a second trip back to China in the mid-1870s, this time to fetch his wife, Gong Shee, and by 1880 had returned and taken up residence in San Francisco. According to the census, Gong Shee was 22 years old to his 28. This meant she had been about 12 years old at the time of their marriage, which would not have been considered too young in China at the time. The couple had already started a family: a two year-old daughter and a two month-old son were listed in the census as having been born in California. The son surely had been, because notice of his birth appeared in the *Daily Alta California* two days after it occurred. As for the daughter, she, too may well have been American-born, but this is impossible to verify, as early immigration and birth records for San Francisco did not survive the 1906 fire.

The Moys took a room in a Chinese lodging house at 724 Jackson Street, where their neighbors were grocers, waiters, porters, seamstresses, tailors, shoemakers, laundrymen and prostitutes. If their accommodations were typical, the family of four occupied a tiny room shared with others. A reporter describing lodging in San Francisco's Chinese quarter in 1876 wrote of a dormitory less than eight feet square, "filthy and unventilated, where perhaps a dozen human beings are packed like sardines in a box." But Jin Mun's quarters may have been somewhat more comfortable, because he had secured a good job. Having studied at a mission school, worked for the Stanfords, panned for gold and served as a go-between for the Union Pacific Railroad, he had developed a first-rate command of English, and by 1879 was hired as Chinese interpreter for the U.S. District Court in California.

A photo of Gong Shee mounted on a stone at Jin Mun's gravesite in Daly City, California. She is not buried there, however, but rather in China. Photograph courtesy of David Abelmann.

This was an appointive position; newly installed U.S. marshals were empowered to select their own staff. Jin Mun was chosen initially by Marshal Alonzo W. Poole, who assumed office in 1878 under commission from President Rutherford B. Hayes, and he was reappointed in 1882 by Moses M. Drew, who had been named by President Chester A. Arthur. As all were Republicans, it is entirely possible that Leland Stanford was partially responsible for the appointments. Jin Mun earned $75 per month in the job and soon added the title of Chinese Interpreter for the Internal Revenue Collection District of the

State of California to his resumé.

Interpreters enjoyed some latitude in the courtroom during this era, and sometimes even carried out duties considered the exclusive province of attorneys today. In the 1883 trial of Ah Jim, accused of attempting to smuggle 22 packages of tobacco from a Chinese steamer into the United States, for example, Jin Mun conducted the cross-examination of the only witness, the Inspector of Customs. "The accused was defended by Moy Jim [sic] Mun, who has a wonderful aptness in cross-examining witnesses," the *San Francisco Bulletin* declared admiringly. This ability seems to have failed him in Ah Jim's case, however, because the jury delivered a guilty verdict without leaving their seats. The prisoner was assessed a $50 fine that he could not afford to pay, which meant a 30-day jail sentence.

The role of Chinese court interpreter was a dicey one. After the Exclusion Act took effect in 1882, only those new Chinese immigrants who were not laborers could land in the United States legally, and San Francisco was, by a wide margin, the port of entry that handled the most Chinese arrivals. Those denied entry by Immigration officials did have recourse, however: they could assert that they were being detained unlawfully because they had been classified improperly, and seek entry from the courts through writs of *habeas corpus*. From 1882 to 1905, fully 9,600 Chinese *habeas corpus* cases were heard by the Federal District Court for Northern California and the California State Circuit Court.

Those who wished to appeal unfavorable decisions generally needed interpretation, and the rule was that they had to pay for such services. In such cases, Jin Mun received compensation directly from the plaintiffs. At $5 per case this added a significant increment to his government salary of $75 per month, and it may not even have been the sum total of his take. The justification for permitting such double-dipping was that the United States was not technically an "interested party" in *habeas corpus* cases, and hence no conflict of interest theoretically existed.

In practice, however, this arrangement lent itself to many possible abuses, a subject that was raised in open court by District Attorney Samuel G. Hilborn on December 17, 1883, a particularly busy day for the U.S. District Court. The S.S. *Oceanic*, in from Hong Kong, was moored in San Francisco harbor, and the *habeas corpus* applications filed by would-be traders and students on the ship who were attempting to land were coming at the court fast and furiously. A special Saturday afternoon session was scheduled to accommodate the volume of cases. By sheer coincidence, Jin Mun's brother Jin Kee, who had returned to China, was on board the Oceanic with his wife, Chin Fung. They were cleared on Saturday without incident and permitted to land, but many others were not so fortunate. By mid-day Monday the court had already heard 125 cases.

The *Bulletin* summarized the exchange between Hilborn and Judge Ogden Hoffman, Jr. this way:

> District Attorney Hilborn called the attention of the Court to the fact that Moy Jin Mun, the official interpreter of the Court, is paid a fee of $5 by each petitioner examined, in addition to the $75 per month allowed him by the government. He should be paid entirely by the government, as all the information derived from the petitioners on the witness stand by the Court comes through an interpreter paid by the petitioners . . . Judge Hoffman replied that he could see no reason why Moy could not interpret for both sides and be paid by petitioners for services rendered thereto.

The *Bulletin*, for its part, could see plenty of reasons. Jin Mun had absolute power over the petitioners, for one thing, since he was their sole conduit to the Court for translation of testimony and of any Chinese-language documents. For another, he had a strong financial incentive to encourage additional appeals, since each one resulted in the payment of a fee.

Indeed, Jin Mun was obliquely accused of abusing his office more than once. In November 1885, the *San Francisco Chronicle* declared: "it is whispered about that Moy Jin Mun had been informed against by another Chinese who testified before the jury. The witness said that Moy, while interpreter, did a land office business in assessing the Chinese attempting to land. He assessed them $250 to $500 each, excusing the high figure with the explanation that he had to divide with a great many officials."

No further evidence was presented, but the accusation was credible, even if not verifiable. The decision to shut America's doors to Chinese laborers had been a political one. Economics, however, remained a powerful magnet for Chinese seeking their fortunes and for businesses in need of cheap labor. The situation after the passage of the Chinese Exclusion Act thus offered many lucrative opportunities for personal enrichment. Bribing government officials to admit illegal aliens would not have seemed at all extraordinary to an immigrant from China, where such gratuities were the rule. Smuggling aliens was another way to skin the cat, as Jin Mun's brother Jin Fuey would discover some years later. He would be accused on two separate occasions of participating in schemes to do precisely that.

Immigrants, however, were not the only commodity that could fetch a tidy profit if smuggled into the United States. The other lucrative one was opium, which was very much associated in the popular press with the Chinese, as many of them used the narcotic in America as they had in China, and some were actively involved in importing it. There had been no restrictions on the purchase or consumption of opium in the United States prior to 1875, when San Francisco's Board of Supervisors, worried that this imported Chinese vice was spreading among respectable whites, and especially among young white girls, made it a misdemeanor to frequent opium dens, although it did not prohibit the sale or use of the drug. Other bans followed, probably motivated as much by racism as by any serious interest in drug interdiction. A state-level ban was passed in California in 1881, and the federal government got into the act by assessing tariffs on imported opium, setting the rate first at $6 per pound and then, in 1883, at $10. In 1887, Congress made importing the substance illegal, but only if the importer were Chinese. Finally, in 1890, the federal government decided to levy a tax of $10 per pound on domestically produced opium as well.

Prohibitions always create opportunities, and Jin Mun, who in addition to working as an interpreter was running a fancy goods business on Dupont Street, saw opportunity in opium. In 1891, shortly before the arrival of the S.S. *China*, a steamer from Hong Kong owned by the Pacific Mail Steamship Company, he heard a rumor that a large quantity of opium was aboard. The federal government's reward for information leading to the seizure of smuggled opium in a previous case had been $5,000, a substantial sum, and a similar payment could be expected in this case if the rumor proved true. Jin Mun wanted the money, but he knew anyone who came forward to report the shipment and claim the reward risked retribution – even assassination – by the importers.

The solution was to do it all indirectly. Shortly before the arrival of the steamer, Jin Mun approached United States Marshal William G. Long with his dilemma, and the latter brought in Collector Timothy Guy Phelps, who was willing to help out. Phelps, in turn, drew in Deputy Port Surveyor Varney W. Gaskill, who arranged for two Pacific Mail company clerks, C. H. Bailey and J. J. O'Connor, to inspect the cargo when the ship docked. Under the scenario envisioned in the plan, if opium were found, they would claim the reward money and give half of it to Gaskill to pay, secretly, to Jin Mun. Gaskill even signed a document to this effect:

> I hereby agree to pay to Moy Jin Mun $2,500, less legal expenses, to be agreed on by Collector [Phelps] and Special Agent [Evans] when the same shall have been paid to me by Bailey and O'Connor. The said $2,500 is half of informer's fees allowed by the court in the case of Marks' opium case. I have a guaranty in writing from Bailey and O'Connor that they would pay same.

THREE TOUGH CHINAMEN

The rumor turned out to be true. When the ship arrived and was searched, 18 of 40 cases that ostensibly contained chinaware were found to be filled with opium, which was seized and subsequently sold at auction by the government for $16,945. And Bailey and O'Connor, true to the plan, filed a petition in District Court asserting that they had been the informants and claiming the reward.

Two checks, each for $2,500, arrived from Washington on August 16, 1892, and shortly afterwards, Gaskill called on Bailey and O'Connor to pay Jin Mun his share. The pair reportedly just laughed at him, however, and announced they "did not propose to divide with any accursed Chinaman." They eventually did pay Gaskill $500 with a promise of $500 more. But when this sum was, in turn, proffered to Jin Mun, he rebuffed it, insisting on the full $2,500 he was due. Thwarted, he filed a lawsuit against Gaskill for the money, and eventually recovered $500 of it.

In the meantime, San Francisco-based Collector of Internal Revenue John C. Quinn called on Jin Mun – together with a dozen other bilingual Chinese – to help him translate a notice to all Chinese in the city concerning the Geary Act, the very bill that his brother Jin Fuey was denouncing in New York. The new law was slated to go into effect on May 5, 1893, a year after its passage. Because of its registration requirement, Quinn had to inform local Chinese of the deadline for registration and the attendant penalties for failure to do so, and he obviously had to issue this notice in Chinese. After Jin Mun's version was judged best, the circulars were printed and distributed. And Jin Mun thought nothing more about the matter until September 17, when a friend warned him that a campaign had begun against him. As he told a reporter from the *San Francisco Morning Call*:

> One of my friends rushed in and told me that on the bulletin boards of Chinatown were placarded copies of a letter to me in which the writer cursed me as being the man who had advised Collector Quinn

to compel the Chinese to register; who had written to Washington and urged the passage of the Geary law and he called me all the names he could think of, and wound up the letter by saying he had received $1,500 to kill me.

Although there is no evidence any of these accusations were true, Jin Mun took the death threat seriously, especially after receiving a frightening letter the next day announcing that the reward for his life had been raised to $1,800 and including a drawing of a man with a hatchet through his vitals. A *San Francisco Call* reporter who visited Quong Yick Wah, Jin Mun's shop at 901 Dupont, reported that he had acquired a rifle and two double-action revolvers, and quoted him as vowing, "I'm going to give the hoodlums a fight before they kill me . . . I am preparing for war and I propose to sell my life as dearly as possible." The police, too, were persuaded that Jin Mun's life was in danger, and lent assistance by watching the store carefully.

The vigil went on for several days. On September 26, the *Call* reported that the police were expecting a murder any day by highbinders – a term that meant Chinese gangsters – and thought that "Moy Jin Mun will in all probability furnish the corpse." It described Jin Mun as "in a state of terror bordering on frenzy" following the posting of yet another circular threatening his life. In addition to repeating the charges of cooperating with the authorities in the registering of Chinese, however, this one hinted at an entirely different transgression:

> Moy Jin Mun is selfish. Let him beware. His time is not long. Maybe in the present month. He wants all the opium business to himself. For this he tells the Custom House on his countrymen. Moy Jin Mun is a sneak.

Indeed, the *Call* quoted an unnamed source as asserting that "the truth is that these men are not after Moy Jin Mun on account of the Geary Bill or his translations, but because he gave information about smuggled opium. Moy Jin Mun has been out of favor with most of the Chinese for some five years now and has always had more or less trouble." For the time being, it was more, rather than less. In April 1893, the *Call* reported that Jin Mun had not left the back room of 901 Dupont for more than three months, except in the company of a white man. The highbinders had also organized a successful boycott of his store, which was by then close to ruin, as sales were averaging less than two dollars per week.

As the investigation of the opium smuggling progressed – it was now being referred to in the press as a "Custom House scandal" – it became clear that the facts were not as they had initially appeared. The *Chronicle* reported that "it is now generally known that Moy Jin Mun was not the informer, for he himself had admitted that he told the story concerning opium on the steamer *China* merely as the agent of a Chinese who was a member of an opium smuggling syndicate in Chinatown. If a careful investigation be made, it will probably be shown that this

> **MOY JIN WUN'S WOES.**
>
> **He Registered, but Is Doubtful Whether He Was Wise in Doing So.**
>
> One of the most uneviable of the Chinese residents is Moy Jin Wun, the much-abused and apparently unfortunate merchant who keeps a store at 901 Dupont street. Moy Jin Wun has for some time tried to carry water on both shoulders; that is, he has tried to be a good Chinese and at the same time a loyal American. This attempt has evidently proved a lamentable failure, for Moy finds himself now in a most serious predicament.
>
> Pouring his tale of woe into the ears of a CHRONICLE reporter Moy said that he would willingly talk if he were sure that his name would not appear in the paper, which apprehensive request was prompted, he said, by the fact that past newspaper notoriety had caused him much trouble.

Moy Jin Wun, the merchant, drops a few tears.

An article in the May 16, 1893, edition of the San Francisco Chronicle *included a caricature of Jin Mun, even though it got his name, and the reason his store was being boycotted, all wrong. Copyright San Francisco Chronicle. Used with permission.*

suit is commenced by Moy Jin Mun as a cloak for certain dissatisfied officials who failed to participate in the divide."

Opium was far more likely the cause of Jin Mun's troubles than translation, because the allegations that he had supported passage of the Geary law were ridiculous, and because the evidence suggests that he was very much involved in the opium trade. In late 1893, the *Chronicle* reported the existence of an opium ring in San Francisco,

"The United States Government's Official Smoker." A sketch of Moy Jin Mun from the San Francisco Chronicle, 12 May 1894. Copyright San Francisco Chronicle. Used with permission.

an assortment of Chinese and whites engaged in buying at auction quantities of the drug confiscated by the government and reselling it to Chinese men at a higher price. Apparently the auctioneers, Spear & Company, were in on the arrangement, which involved selling to certain dealers at below-market prices and shutting out others. The paper quoted William Gilchrist, who had been an Internal Revenue Service investigator for three years, as saying that the only bidders in such auctions are about 25 Chinese, and he specifically named "Moy Jim [sic] Mun, the interpreter, on Washington and Dupont" as one of them.

In a follow-up article two days later, the *Chronicle* suggested that the true reason for the vendetta against Jin Mun had been that he had interfered with this sweetheart arrangement:

THREE TOUGH CHINAMEN

It was given out that threats to kill him had been made because he did not please the Chinese while acting as a Federal interpreter. It has since been said that Moy Jim [sic] Mun got himself into disfavor because he helped to spoil the plans of the syndicate . . . Fear of bodily harm made Moy cease this traffic. He is an opium dealer as well as an interpreter.

Any doubt about Jin Mun's involvement with opium would have been erased when he was called over the next couple of years by the government to testify in cases against alleged opium smugglers. The most famous one involved the arrest of seamen aboard the yacht *Emerald* for possessing unstamped opium that allegedly had been manufactured in Victoria, British Columbia.

Possessing opium *per se* was not yet a crime in the United States, unless the drug had been smuggled into the country. The only chance the government had of securing conviction, therefore, was if the drug were found to be of foreign origin. In the *Emerald* case, Jin Mun, whom the *Chronicle* wryly labeled the "official pipe-smoker of the United States at this port," was called in to provide expert testimony. "This instrument of Celestial solace has absorbed the quintessence of many a five-tael can of poppy juice," the newspaper snickered. Jin Mun cooked the substance over a small spirit lamp and "sucked away with apparently great enjoyment, as his little eyes blinked and glistened through the wreaths of smoke. 'Him velly good,' said the expert opium smoker. 'Him Victoria opium all light.'"

The *Emerald* smugglers were convicted because of Jin Mun's verdict, and he continued to be called to opine in similar cases. Asked by an attorney how he was able to tell Victoria opium from Hong Kong opium, the connoisseur replied, "By the taste. There is as much difference between Hong Kong and Victoria opium as there is between champagne and cider, or between whiskey and salt water," he added.

Chapter VIII
A Thorough American

After the opening of the Mott Street Mission and his subsequent arrest for larceny, Jin Kee decided to return to China for a while. Before he left New York, however, he did one final deed: He filed a Declaration of Intention to become a U.S. citizen. It was a very significant move, and would prove to be a prescient one.

Declarations were the initial step in the naturalization process, and were accordingly referred to as "first papers." To file one, an alien went to court to affirm his intention to become a citizen and renounce allegiance to any foreign potentate or state. During this era, it was generally males who applied for naturalization; wives and minor children became citizens automatically when they did. Citizenship was not granted, however, unless the applicant could prove he had lived in the United States for five years and could produce acceptable witnesses who would testify as to the length of time he had lived in America and to his good moral character.

Most applicants for citizenship at this time were European immigrants. It was highly unusual for a Chinese to apply because most Chinese did not consider themselves in America to stay, and, more importantly, because the law did not seem to permit them to naturalize. In 1875, Congress had added the words "aliens of African nativity and to persons of African descent" to the description of those eligible for citizenship originally set out in the Naturalization Act of 1790, and this was understood to signal not only that citizenship would be granted to freed slaves, but that it pointedly would be *denied* to Asian immigrants. Jin Kee, who had declared his intention to make America his permanent home to a reporter the previous year, nonetheless filed his Declaration before the New York State Supreme Court on August 31, 1880, and his papers were accepted.

Soon after that, he returned to Taishan to rejoin his wife, Chin Fung, and remained there for three years. His next appearance in America would not take place until the two disembarked in San Francisco from the S.S. *Oceanic* on December 15, 1883. They probably stayed with Jin Mun and his family for a short time, but soon headed back East, and just over a year later, in early 1885, Jin Kee resurfaced in the press, having embarked on an entirely new – if short-lived – venture. He opened a hotel. And he did it in an odd location: Newark, New Jersey.

Newark was a peculiar choice because it did not have much of a Chinatown in the early 1880s. The census recorded just over a dozen Chinese in the city in 1880, remnants of a group of 150 laborers who had been brought to nearby Belleville to work in a laundry a decade earlier. The model for Jin Kee's new enterprise was Wo Kee's, a New York Chinatown establishment

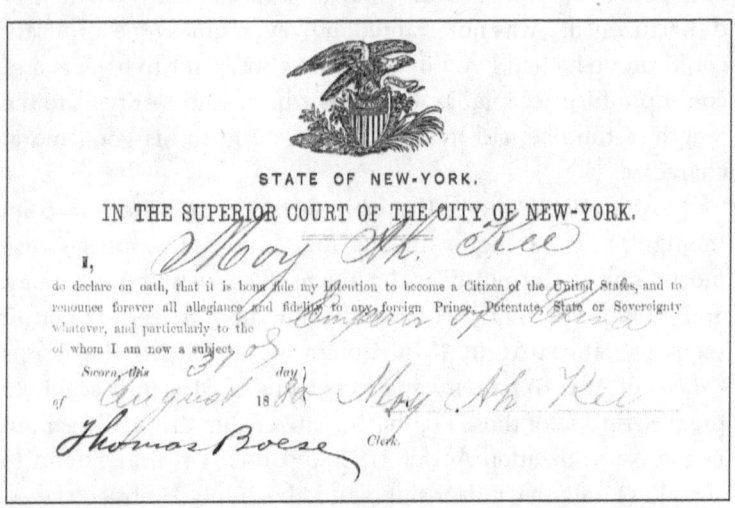

Jin Kee, a.k.a. "Moy Ah Kee," filed this Declaration of Intention to become a U.S. citizen with the New York State Supreme Court in August, 1880. Source: National Archives and Records Administration, New York, NY.

Jin Kee. Although he was dressed in full Chinese regalia, the medals were American - one was of a U.S. flag - perhaps symbolic of his desire for citizenship. He would eventually cut off his queue and adopt American dress. Source: National Archives and Records Administration, Chicago, IL. Courtesy of Soo Lon Moy and Andrea Stamm.

on Mott Street that was as much grocery and general store as it was boarding house. Jin Kee's specialties were foodstuffs of various sorts and restaurant fare, and in the rear of the store he had constructed several berths for use by lodgers. His business plan called for the addition of more bunks and berths, with several apartments, each of which could accommodate eight to ten people.

Never shy about publicity, Jin Kee invited an American reporter for a meal in order to spread the word about his new establishment, the first of its kind in New Jersey. He gave the reporter a tour and let him sample some of the wares, which included seafood, dried fruit, noodles and dried meat products. Among those the reporter found especially curious were:

- "Low-Wee," (*youyu*) a "dried mollusk with a diamond-shaped body and tentacles," *i.e.*, squid;
- "Haer-mai," (*xiami*) the meat of a small shellfish which "looked like a handful of desiccated maggots or meal-worms," but which were nevertheless "quite palatable";
- "Lai-chee," (*lizhi*) a "singularly formed and really delicious fruit, the meat of which is something like the raisin"; and
- "Yin-wa," (*yanwo*) or "bird's nests," a "gelatinous substance gathered from nests in which a brood of swallows has been reared."

When the reporter was shown several "lap chong" (*la chang*) – Chinese pork sausages – and asked what they contained, Jin Kee decided to have some fun with him. He delivered a short polemic on American culinary narrow-mindedness:

> You Americans, who call yourselves civilized, are the most foolishly prejudiced of beings on earth. You won't even let reason counteract your set notions. Suppose I tell you that it is the meat of a horse? You would turn away disgusted. Why should you do so? The horse is one of the cleanest animals existing. Did you ever see a horse eat anything dirty? He won't even eat musty grain. You cannot make him drink dirty water. A cow swallows swill and all the scrapings of your table, yet cow's meat – beef – is the staple food with you Americans.

"Lap chong" did not contain horse meat after all, Jin Kee went on to explain, still enjoying himself, but rather a delicate, fine-grained kind of meat that was sweeter and more nutritious, delicate and tender:

> I won't keep you in suspense. That's mainly cat-meat. Now, have you ever noticed that you cannot find a cat around a Chinese

laundry, except perhaps for breeding purposes? People don't know what delicious food is left undevoured when cats are permitted to die of old age . . . I can cook you a six months' old cat so that you cannot distinguish it from rabbit, and yet you would eat the latter and turn away from the other . . . It is possible that the "lap chong" of some Chinamen in catless localities may be composed of rat and even mouse-meat. I say it's possible. But not here, Mr. Reporter, not here. We've arranged for other supplies.

If Jin Kee were looking for non-Chinese customers, he might have done a better sales job, and if he were looking for a Chinese clientele, he might have chosen a location with more of his countrymen. It's difficult to see how Newark could have supported a restaurant or a hotel that catered to Chinese customers, and indeed, one must assume the venture did not last long and was a commercial failure. It never appeared in the Newark City Directory and there was no further mention of it in the press. By 1886, Jin Kee and his wife had pulled up stakes and relocated to Chicago.

Unlike Newark, Chicago had a well-established Chinatown by this time. Settled by Chinese who came east seeking their fortunes after the transcontinental railroad was completed in 1869, it was already more than 15 years old. Census takers enumerated about 180 Chinese in the city in 1880, most of them in the vicinity of South Clark Street, just south of the central business area and, like many Chinatowns, in the heart of the vice district. The community's growth continued unabated even after the Exclusion Act was passed as more Chinese arrived from the West; by 1883 there were 199 Chinese laundries, and by 1890 the Chinese population would grow to 740.

The Windy City was an obvious destination for any Chinese in America named Moy. The Moy clan has been the dominant Chinese family in Chicago throughout the city's Chinese history. One early immigrant, Moy Dong Chew (*Mei Zongzhou*), technically two generations behind Jin Kee on the family tree but only three years younger, arrived from San Francisco in the 1870s. Known popularly as Hip Lung, which was actually part of the name of his business, he soon sent for many family members, and by 1885 there were already 40 Moys in town. In the 1890s, Chicago would become home to the headquarters of the Moy Family Association (*Mei Shi Gongsuo*), a national organization that established branches in many other Chinatowns. Jin Kee thus had a collection of kinsmen, some more closely related to him than others, on whom he might call for assistance in getting himself established there, and who might feel some obligation to a fellow clan member to do so. And indeed, it was not long before he had set himself up in business – initially in a laundry on State Street – and resumed his quest for citizenship.

The Chinese Exclusion Act had become law while he was back in China, and it was unequivocal on the question of Chinese eligibility for naturalization. Section 14 read: "Hereafter no State court or court of the United States shall admit Chinese to citizenship; and all laws in conflict with this Act are hereby repealed." This seemingly airtight clause, however, did not faze Jin Kee, who had begun to go by the name Moy Ah Kee. Accordingly, on October 18, 1886, he applied to Cook County Court for naturalization as an American citizen.

He must have cut a striking figure when he appeared in court that day. Decked out in flowing silk robes, he wore a Mandarin-style hat with an upturned brim, his braided hair queue dangling down his back. His case was heard by Judge Richard Prendergast, an immigrant himself. The Irish-born Prendergast had arrived in Illinois at age 10 and become a judge at age 28; he had been on the bench only four years. He believed the question of citizenship for Chinese was essentially settled law, but did not shut the door entirely. He declared Jin Kee's first papers to be in order, and while he declined to grant naturalization, he did not reject the claim outright, but directed Jin Kee to engage an attorney to argue his case. His refusal to grant citizenship, however, became national news. The item was picked up by major newspapers in

New York, San Francisco and Washington and even by smaller papers in Vermont, Wisconsin, Nebraska, Georgia and Texas.

Undaunted, Jin Kee went back to court every year to press his case. In the meantime, he and his wife enjoyed a pleasant social life in Chicago, during which his stature in the community – not to mention his wealth – grew steadily. As a fluent English speaker with an expansive personality, he was an obvious source for reporters interested in issues affecting the Chinese community. In 1888, he spoke with a journalist investigating whether a lodge of Chinese Freemasons existed in Chicago. Finding no one at the group's ostensible headquarters who spoke English, the reporter crossed South Clark Street to Jin Kee's cigar shop – he had acquired an additional location and line of business the previous year – to ask some questions about the Masons. Jin Kee confirmed that there was a Chicago lodge, explaining that about half the Chinese in Chicago were Masons, and that he, himself, belonged to the order – called the Chee Kung Tong (*Zhigong Tang*), or "Hall of Universal Justice." The Chee Kung Tong was indeed often referred to as the "Chinese Freemasons," and had some nominal affiliation with the Masons in America, although its origins were entirely distinct from those of its Western counterpart.

In 1891, the subject was cigar makers and labor unions, and in a long essay about the achievements of the unions in this industry, the *Chicago Herald* noted that only two Chinese-owned shops in the city refused to employ non-union labor, and that one of them belonged to Jin Kee. "His desire to become a thorough American has something to do with this," it speculated. Indeed, it probably did. This same desire also manifested itself in the Moys' social relationships, which appeared to extend well beyond the Chinese community into white society. In 1891, at the marriage of Miss Martha Jungblutt and Judge David J. Lyon, whose best man was Mayor Hemstead Washburne, one of the presents displayed on a large table was a magnificent white tea set presented by "Moy Kee, the well-known Chinaman."

During this period, the local media also got a couple of

glimpses of Chin Fung, Jin Kee's wife. The vast majority of Chinese men in Chicago were either single or had left wives behind in China, so there was much curiosity about Chinese women, and in particular about their reputation for having bound feet. More than a dozen Chicago Chinese had wives in America, but most of them were Caucasian, according to the *Chicago Tribune*. Jin Kee was one of the very few who had brought a wife from his native land. The *Tribune* described her as "slightly built, young, and [with] very good features," noting that she "dresses in a long, coat-like garment similar to that worn by the male members of her race" and that "her face was nearly always covered with a veil." A few years later, a reporter for the *Chicago Inter-Ocean* doing a feature on the life of the city's Chinese visited the Moys in their home behind the cigar store. Chin Fung, he wrote:

A sketch of Chin Fung, Jin Kee's wife, that accompanied a September 11, 1892 article about lives of the Chinese in Chicago. Source: Chicago Inter Ocean.

> ... received us – without rising – in delicate heliotrope silk; her hair was constructed in a marvelous fashion and heavily ornamented with gold and flowers. She also wore hoop earrings and her lips and cheeks were rosy red. Several bracelets adorned her wrists and many gold rings glistened on her hands. Curious to see her tiny feet, we were rewarded by a glimpse of green and gold embellished slippers very pointed as she tottered across the room, "pale as rice and graceful as the bamboo."

The article even included a sketch of Chin Fung, although the author got her name wrong, and erred also in identifying her as a "lady of rank," which she most assuredly was not. It went on to describe incense vases and flowers that stood on a small altar in their home, flanked by framed photographs and several scrolls decorated with Chinese calligraphy. And it also gave readers a hint – probably superficial and possibly misunderstood – about the couple's relationship:

> Moy Kee entered in holiday raiment of white silk pongee and greeted us cordially; he is very handsome and intelligent, but Mrs. Moy Kee objected to the information he essayed to give us with such vigorous Chinese chin music that he abruptly left the room, with all the symptoms usually exhibited by an American hen-pecked husband.

Several months later, Jin Kee's desire to become a "thorough American" led him to make another attempt at citizenship. On February 23, 1893, he appeared in Cook County Superior Court before Judge Jonas Hutchinson to press his case for naturalization once again, this time with a lawyer at his side. The attorney – who went by the unfortunate name of C.A. Swine – argued that because Jin Kee's Declaration of Intention had been issued correctly and had been legal when filed in 1880, subsequent passage by Congress of a law prohibiting naturalization of Chinese could not be construed to apply in his case, as to do so would be "of an *ex-post facto* nature." It was a moderately persuasive argument, and the judge took it under advisement, but like his predecessors, declined to grant naturalization.

Jin Kee and Swine were back the following August, this time before Judge Edward F. Dunne of the Cook County Circuit Court, who later became Mayor of Chicago and eventually Governor of Illinois. Dunne also refused to act, then or in October when they appeared before him again. The second time, however, the judge decided to pass the buck. He advised Jin Kee to get all his papers in order and apply for a writ of *mandamus* – an order from a higher court to compel a lower court to perform its duties – and Jin Kee initially promised he would do so. Such a writ - presuming he could get one – might have been sufficient to secure citizenship for him, but it would be based on a technicality and would help no one but himself. Jin Kee was beginning to think bigger, however, and so were Chinese elsewhere in the country.

The Geary Act had infuriated America's Chinese community, and galvanized many into political activism to secure rights for themselves. A Chinese Citizens' Union had met in New York City as early as 1888, and a Chinese Equal Rights League had been formed, also in New York, in 1892, both the creations of Chinese American activist Wong Chin Foo, who believed that Chinese civil rights were winnable, but that his countrymen had to Americanize and eschew their traditional vices if they were to be gained. In the same spirit, on June 20, 1894, to the explosion of giant firecrackers, one hundred and fifty of "the most prominent members of the Chinese colony in Chicago" organized a Chicago Chinese Club.

The festivities were lavish. There were *two* banquets – one at 1:00 p.m. and one at 9:00 p.m. – at the Hing Far Lou restaurant on Clark Street. The first featured bird's nest and shark's fin soup, white and brown chicken tongues, roast duck and several other courses washed down with rice wine and Oolong tea, and four kinds of pudding for dessert. A Chinese orchestra entertained during the meal, and a choir sang Chinese songs. At the second meal, there was mushroom soup, pigeon soup, "pineapple à la Chinese"- whatever that was – vegetable soup, oyster stew, chicken, fruit and rose wine.

The new club's stated object, in addition to the usual functions of Chinese benevolent societies such as caring for the sick and offering language classes, was "to agitate and bring pressure to bear on Congress to the end that the rights and privileges of citizenship may be granted to the Chinese," the *New Haven*

Articles of Incorporation for the Chicago Chinese Club, November 9, 1894. Among the club's objectives were "to establish an association composed [of] Chinamen and others for social, moral and fraternal purposes . . . protect its members in the enjoyment of their property and their personal rights, educate its members in the laws, usages and customs of Americans . . . and work to elevate the social and moral standard and encourage the recognition of honorable Chinamen as entitled to citizenship." Jin Kee was the club's first president. Source: State of Illinois Secretary of State.

Register reported. "In fact, the organization marks the birth of a Chinese political party, although the members have not the power to vote." The group vowed to cooperate with similar clubs to be formed in all American cities with a significant Chinese presence. And indeed, the following year saw the founding in San Francisco of the Native Sons of the Golden State – later the Chinese American Citizens' Alliance – by American-born Chinese dedicated to fighting anti-Chinese activities and advocating civil rights for Chinese Americans. That name was a deliberate take-off on the "Native Sons of the Golden West," an anti-Chinese organization that had been established in San Francisco in the mid-1870s.

Club membership was open only to those willing to give up gambling and alcohol, and who would "declare their intention of making this county their permanent home." These requirements were very significant. The organizers had accepted the argument put forth most eloquently by Wong Chin Foo that in order for Chinese to merit enfranchisement in the United States, they had to change their ways and become more palatable to Americans. On the one hand this meant eschewing the vices that gave Americans a pretext to disparage them, and on the other it meant making an affirmative commitment that they were in America to stay and did not intend to return to China. No other ethnic groups felt the need to make such commitments in order to merit inclusion in America, but then, no other groups were marginalized in quite the same way as the Chinese.

The founders named Jin Kee – whom the *New York Times* dubbed "one of Chicago's richest Chinamen" – as their first president. He was an obvious choice not only because of his leadership skills, but also for his symbolic value. In virtually all of the press coverage, he was touted – inaccurately, in point of fact – as the "first of his race" to apply for, and obtain, his first papers for naturalization.

The organization's first battle came quickly. One of Chicago's evening papers, in reporting about the founding of the club, charged that its members were "highbinders," which the *Chicago Tribune* defined as "a lawless association of murderers sworn to protect each other . . . gamblers and cutthroats." Since protecting Chinese from libel was one of the ostensible goals of the club, Jin Kee had to respond to the malicious attack, and he did so with a lawsuit. He went before Justice of the Peace John C. Everett and swore out a warrant for criminal libel against the newspaper, telling the *Tribune* that the Club was determined to prosecute the suit vigorously.

What became of the lawsuit was not reported, but the libel issue was not the only battle that was being waged. The Chinese community itself was not as united as it might have appeared. The new club's strong stance against gambling and vice was, in fact, highly divisive, as Chicago's gambling houses and drug dens were in Chinese hands – including, and perhaps principally, those of Jin Kee's own kinsmen. Nevertheless, Jin Kee told the *San Francisco Chronicle* that the club intended to hire detectives to hunt down Chinese gambling houses and prosecute the proprietors. And he told the *Tribune* that the establishment of the club had already resulted in siphoning off some customers from the gambling and opium establishments on the city's South Side, and that the proprietors of those establishments had, on several occasions, threatened his life.

This was full-blown war, and Jin Kee's move may not have been its opening salvo. While the effort might be taken at face value as nothing more than a tactic to improve the image of Chinese in America, it was such a gratuitous slap at Jin Kee's own relatives that it smacks of settling some earlier, unspecified score. Its shrewdness resided in the fact that it involved using the levers of law enforcement to do the dirty work.

A second *Tribune* article the following year confirmed that Chicago was experiencing a "Chinese war," evidenced by a conflict over an American flag that hung in the headquarters of the Chicago Chinese Club. According to this account, immediately after the formation of the club, members furnished information to the authorities about local gambling interests, and 38 such establishments controlled by Hip Lung and his brother Sam Moy were raided three times. "All the gambling implements were confiscated and bung-loo and fan-tan stopped with a jerk." Next came the opium dens. The police apparently did such a thorough job of going after them that "not one remains in the Harrison Street district," the *Tribune* crowed.

The bosses suffered such devastating losses that they vowed retribution, and they set out to break up the club. Two could play at the game of co-opting the authorities into doing battle. The gambling proprietors accused several club members of stealing, and once the accused were arrested, hired a law firm to assist in their prosecution. The defendants were convicted and sentenced to two to three years in the penitentiary. Emboldened by their success, the gamblers attempted to raid the Chinese Club's clubhouse at Harrison and Clark Streets and, as a symbolic gesture, steal and burn its American flag, which had been presented by Mayor John P. Hopkins. But they were foiled in this attempt, and Jin Kee took the flag and carried it home. The *Tribune* reported:

> Now, every morning, a Chinaman with a big bundle under his arm and surrounded by his friends, goes to the club. It is Moy Ah Kee with the American flag. Every night the same scene is repeated and Moy Kee carries the flag home. It will take a small Chinese army to capture that flag.

Jin Kee's enemies in this fight – his own kinsmen – then accused him of perjury. They claimed he had inflated the value of the two lots he owned at Seventy-Second and Sangamon Streets that he had posted as bail for one of the convicted men. After a grand jury declined to indict him on this charge, his adversaries attempted to link him to a murder. A Chinese laundryman in Macon, Georgia named Moy Tung Hai had been shot to death at the back door of his laundry on February 13, and Sam Moy made a show of sending a cousin to Georgia to offer a $1,000 reward for information leading to the arrest of the murderer. Members of Jin Kee's club were convinced that the real purpose was to frame Jin Kee by accusing him of personally hiring a hit man to assassinate the laundryman.

Nothing came of these efforts. But taking on the powerful Chicago Moy brothers had been risky and probably unwise, and it is a safe assumption that the animosity engendered in this battle endured for quite some time. It was probably the cause of Jin Kee's sudden departure from Chicago a couple of years later.

Chapter IX
I Created Enmity Among Our Own Countrymen

Jin Fuey was riding high in New York at the close of the 19th century. After he left St. Bartholomew's in 1897, he was appointed official Chinese interpreter for the criminal courts. Louis J. Beck, who interviewed him for his 1898 book, *New York's Chinatown: An Historical Presentation of Its People and Places,* described him as "perhaps the most happy exemplification of the highest attainment of polish and education, made possible for all his race in Free America." Polish and education notwithstanding, Jin Fuey would eventually prove himself something considerably less than an exemplary character, but for the time being he enjoyed the adulation.

He continued to speak out on moral and ethical topics, and on political ones. On February 1, 1898, a member of the New York State Assembly introduced a mean-spirited bill that required all laundry checks in larger cities to be written entirely in English and use Arabic numerals. The measure was an ostensible solution to a problem that really did not exist: Although American customers couldn't read their laundry tickets, the Chinese laundrymen all could. And as the *Brooklyn Daily Eagle* pointed out, "It is not claimed that the work they do is unsatisfactory, or that the check system they use is fruitful of blunders. On the contrary, the system seems to be a remarkably accurate one, for however ignorant the customer is as to the meaning of the hieroglyphics on his ticket, the Chinaman himself finds them a correct index to the identity of his patrons and their wares."

In reality, the measure had nothing to do with improving accuracy in the laundry business, and everything to do with trying to drive the Chinese out of it. When women's rights activist Charlotte Smith, president of the Women's Industrial League of America, addressed the Central Labor Union in support of it about a week after its introduction, she made this abundantly clear. She told them that she wanted to enlist the Union in a "crusade" against Chinese laundries because "these Chinamen are driving white women out of work."

Because it was a life and death issue for them, New York's Chinese laundrymen began to raise funds to fight the bill, and Wu Ting Fang, the Chinese minister in Washington, suggested that they retain counsel to attack the measure in the courts if it passed. The *Times* sought out Jin Fuey for comment, and after he explained the serious consequences that would ensue for the Chinese if the measure were adopted, he offered this view as well:

> Hardly any of them can read or write English. They could not comply with the law. When a Chinaman's laundry slip is lost now nobody who finds it can read it, and it means nothing. But, with the name and address of the laundryman printed on it, anybody who finds it can take it to the laundry and demand the goods it calls for. Then along will come the owner and demand and enforce restitution. To the average Chinaman all Americans and Europeans look alike. He can't tell one from another. His only clue is his own ticket.

Defending his fellow countrymen was something Jin Fuey had been doing for quite a while, but now it would become his turn to go after them. In 1898, he took a job with the Chinese Bureau – the federal government's agency in charge of enforcing Chinese exclusion policies – as an investigator and Chinese interpreter. Following passage of the Geary Act, Chinese could be deported or imprisoned if they were found without proper identity papers, and investigators were charged with seeking out and arresting lawbreakers. For a Chinese, of course, this meant cracking down on his fellow countrymen, but Jin Fuey took his role seriously and stood more than ready to oblige.

"The Chinese population of this city was thrown into a big ferment of fear yesterday," the *North Adams Transcript* declared on December 29, 1898, "through the coming of Dr. Jin Fuey Moy of New York, a United States Treasury official and interpreter" to Springfield, Massachusetts. The visit was the result of complaints lodged in Washington by local labor unions. Many Chinese had been tipped off to the raid and had left the city, but on December 28, Jin Fuey arrived at the laundry of 21 year-old Jue Fun, who was ironing a shirt at the time. Speaking in Chinese, he demanded the latter's papers, and Jue assured him he had entered America in 1894 as a student and had the papers to prove it, though they were not on his person at the time. Together with a police inspector, Jin Fuey promptly arrested him, and he was taken to Boston with four other unlucky Chinese to await trial.

Jue Fun had indeed come to America to study. Under arrangements made by his father, he had attended a Methodist Sunday school in Holyoke, Massachusetts and opened a laundry even as he continued his studies through the beneficence of some Methodist ladies in Amherst. He spoke English rather well. The *Transcript* described him as a "civilized Chinaman," meaning he had adopted Western dress and had cut off his queue. He also had a Caucasian wife. Much the same, of course, could be said of Jin Fuey. The parallels between his own story and that of Jue Fun were, in fact, quite striking.

But duty came first – at least this time – for Jin Fuey, who was the only government witness to testify against Jue when his case was heard the following January. The trial was well-attended, the *Springfield Republican* noting sardonically that there were so many Chinese in the courtroom that the laundries must have shut down for the day. The case ought to have rested solely on the legality of the young man's student papers, which he was ultimately able to produce, but testimony went quite far afield.

At one point, one of Jue's teachers – a Miss Wood of the Second Congregational Church – was asked by the District Attorney if Jue could recite the Lord's Prayer. Her response was that he was better at it than he had been six months earlier, but that there was still room for improvement. His deficient piety notwithstanding, Jue Fun was judged a *bona fide* student and was released, unlike another member of the group who was marked for deportation to China.

Jin Fuey's other well-publicized case involved counterfeiting. In early 1901, working with another Chinese inspector, he arrested 13 year-old Fanny Lenart at the Hung Lee Laundry at 4 Rivington Street in lower Manhattan as she attempted to exchange a roll of 100 bogus pennies for a dollar bill. Agents had been attempting for two years to apprehend a gang of counterfeiters in New York, and in the months before the arrest, as much as $40 worth of the pennies had turned up at the Subtreasury on Wall Street.

The story was picked up by newspapers in Boston, Chicago, Baltimore, Washington, Dallas and New Orleans, with the press almost as impressed with the fact that the arresting officers were Chinese as they were with the girl's age. For her part, Fanny, one of the youngest miscreants ever detained by the Secret Service, claimed she had gotten the coins from a man at the corner of Rivington and Allen Streets. She was committed to the care of the Children's Society. It is not known whether taking her out of circulation succeeded in breaking the back of the counterfeiting ring.

Jin Fuey and his wife had been living in Harlem – at 18 West 134th Street – and then in a two-family house at 43 Kelly Street in the Bronx. But in 1901, they made headlines when they purchased a two-story home about an hour from New York in suburban Woodcliff Lake, New Jersey. It was so unusual for a Chinese to leave the city, let alone have the funds to purchase a country estate, that it merited mention in the *New York Times* in an article headlined "Chinaman Buys a Country Home." Noting that there had been some anxiety on the part of the neighbors at the prospect of a Chinese living among them, the paper reported that "all opposition to his coming disappeared when it was learned that he will live on the place and cultivate it after the Chinese manner with Chinese laborers." Why this was in any way reassuring was not explained.

The bigger question – which no one seems to have asked at the time – was how he could afford it on the salary of a civil servant who had worked for a church in his previous job. A full decade later, his cousin Gop Jung, also an interpreter for the Immigration Bureau, complained that he found it hard to make ends meet on his salary of $100 per month. It is not clear whether

The Colorado Springs Gazette *covered the news of Jin Fuey's purchase of a farmhouse in Woodcliff Lake, New Jersey on December 1, 1901 with images of the home, Jin Fuey and his wife, although it spelled his name incorrectly. Courtesy Colorado College Special Collections. Photo by Mike McEvers.*

Jin Fuey continued to practice medicine during his tenure as a civil servant; what is apparent is that he had developed other sources of income, as subsequent developments would reveal.

In January, 1902, Jin Fuey was suddenly discharged from government service for cause. There do not seem to be any contemporaneous press accounts of the episode, but Jin Fuey himself made reference to it many years later in a deposition given to an Immigration official. He related that he had left the service because he had been accused of smuggling 200 Chinese into the United States from Canada. Presumably, he had also been adjudged guilty, at least internally at the Bureau, of this violation of the law.

The details of his discharge are probably lost to history, because the case file no longer exists at the National Archives. But letters preserved in more general subject files maintained by Immigration do not reflect well on Jin Fuey's rectitude. An April 6, 1901 letter from W. H. Ottis, who appears to have been an undercover employee of the Immigration office deployed to investigate smuggling, was critical of Jin Fuey's involvement in the arrest on March 29 of Goon Dong, a well-known figure in Boston's Chinatown, who had apparently been heavily involved in smuggling.

In the letter, which was written to Assistant Commissioner-General Frank H. Larned, Ottis reported that several Boston Chinese had asserted that Goon's arrest had been "a conspiracy on the part of Dr. Moy and [Inspector] Anderson to injure the Gongs on account of their trap laid for Moy Dew." This was probably a reference to Moy Doon, a cousin of Jin Fuey's, who was occasionally employed by the government as a translator and who had been accused by some Chinese enemies of taking bribes and selling government information. This report sounded plausible to Ottis, who wondered, "if, as Dr. Moy and Anderson claim, Goon Dong and his two assistants have been doing this kind of business right along, how is it that Anderson and Dr. Moy have waited until this late date to expose it?"

The letter did not go so far as to suggest that Jin Fuey was guilty of smuggling, but it did point to his propensity for retribution, intrigue and dishonesty, which would become a repeated theme in his dealings. Whatever the actual circumstances of his expulsion, however, it is clear that Jin Fuey experienced a great deal of difficulty after it occurred. In a letter to his cousin Gop Jung written several years later, he complained, "It has ruined me ... when I was in the service, I created enmity for myself among our own countrymen, for upholding the Chinese Exclusion Laws ... you remember how hard it was for me to make anything after my connection with the U.S. government."

In other words, his reputation had been ruined not because the government had determined that he had broken the law, but rather because he had carried out the government's policies, and in so doing poisoned his relationships in the Chinese community. In his own mind he had, in short, burned his bridges with his compatriots in the service of Uncle Sam. It was not a mistake he would ever make again.

Chapter X
Disaster and Rebuilding

On April 21, 1898, for no apparent reason, Frank Johnson, Malcolm Dunn and Ed Kirby, none more than 14 years of age, attacked Jin Mun in the vicinity of Bush and Kearny Streets in San Francisco. Some adults – it's unclear whether Chinese or white – came to Jin Mun's aid, and he took refuge in a cigar store on the corner. The boys got reinforcements and continued to torment him, and soon there were several hundred onlookers. It took a squad of policemen to break up the incipient riot.

This sort of persecution was, unfortunately, not unusual. Youngsters raised to view the Chinese as a separate class of people with strange customs who did not enjoy, or deserve, the same rights as others – which was, after all, the official view of the country – could hardly be expected to treat them with respect. Jin Mun's brother Jin Fuey had dealt with this same problem in New York as head of the Chinese Guild by attempting to intervene with the police department, but was not able to achieve any noticeable decrease in harassment. Chinese laundrymen and merchants were convenient targets for hoodlums, who attacked them, stole from them and broke their windows, and too often such incidents did not end with the arrest and trial of the offenders. The Johnson, Dunn and Kirby boys were carted off to the California Street police station, but whether they got off with a reprimand or actually went before a judge is unknown.

A year later, Jin Mun found himself in court, but as a defendant rather than a plaintiff, and in a civil, rather than a criminal, case. It concerned a property on the northwest corner of Washington and Dupont Streets that he had leased in 1886 for a twenty-year period. The owner of the property was Erasmus D. Keyes, a Civil War general and businessman who had relocated to California after the war. Keyes had transferred the property to an attorney named Alexander H. Loughborough and asked him to manage it on his behalf, with the proviso that it was to be returned to Keyes' children after the General's death.

The lease had specified rent in the amount of $200 per month, but in 1893, according to Jin Mun, following a precipitous drop in the value of property in Chinatown, the two men had agreed on a lower figure - $140. No amendment was made to the lease agreement, however, and after Keyes' death in 1895 and Loughborough's two years later, there was only Jin Mun's word that an accommodation had ever been reached. Keyes' son, W. S. Keyes, a well-known California winemaker, joined other members of his family in pressing Jin Mun for the full amount due under the original agreement, and the case went to court.

Judge John Hunt ruled in favor of the plaintiffs, though he did not insist on restitution of any sums owed prior to the filing of the suit. He found that $200 had been due the Keyes heirs on April 1, 1899, and that no portion of it had been paid by Jin Mun. The plaintiffs had asked for forfeiture of the lease, restitution of the premises and recovery of $600, three times the rent that was due. The court granted the first two, and in addition, awarded the sum of $400 for "rents" and "damages."

Jin Mun appealed the decision; his attorney asserted the conclusions of law were inconsistent with the allegations of the complaint, and the findings did not support the judgment. The case was ultimately heard by the California Supreme Court, which affirmed the lower court's ruling on March 22, 1902. It found it was proper to assess the defendant for rents accrued after the commencement of the trial, which it believed is what the lower court had done in granting the judgment, and it was a matter of no consequence the sum was described in the decree as "rents" and "damages," because the material question was whether the findings supported a judgment for that sum of money.

Perhaps more important than the legal principles involved in the case is the fact that it was filed at all. It demonstrates how deeply the Chinese had become integrated into the economic life of San Francisco, if not into its political life. Chinese lacked political rights, but they were running successful businesses, paying substantial rents and signing binding contracts. They were also being sued, retaining attorneys and seeking justice through the court system. Most were not citizens, but they nevertheless possessed a certain degree of legal standing, and they appeared before the courts not only as defendants, but also as plaintiffs. The judiciary offered them opportunities for justice unavailable to them through other government agencies.

The day after the original trial that resulted in the appeal, Jin Mun wrote a letter to his Sunday School teacher of many years earlier, a "Mrs. Lick," who was actually a woman named Kate Burton Lake. An Oregon-born schoolteacher widowed before she was 20, Kate had moved to San Francisco in about 1890 and by 1896 was working as a teacher and matron at the Chinese Mission of the Methodist Episcopal Church's Women's Home Missionary Society. She worked in the 22-room mansion at 912 Washington Street until 1902.

Jin Mun wrote to her on behalf of a friend named Boo Hang, his partner in the mining business. Boo was engaged to marry a young Chinese girl, but he had learned that the girl's "master" intended to take her to court to stop the marriage. Perhaps the girl was an indentured servant who wanted to marry before her term of engagement expired; this is unclear, although it is one plausible interpretation. On the other hand, the Missionary Society was deeply involved in rescuing girls from "dens of iniquity" and leading them to "paths of truth and usefulness," which suggests that she was probably working as a prostitute. Jin Mun expressed the wish that Kate take the girl in and give her "good pretection" [sic]. It was a sweet and deferential letter, written in beautiful penmanship, in which Jin Mun proposed to pay a call on Kate together with Boo if she would permit it.

> San Francisco, May 20th 1899
>
> Mrs. Lick.
>
> Dear Teacher,—
>
> The bearer of this is Boo Hang, he has a girl who he engaged for marrige, but now he informed that the girl's Master who want to take the girl before the Court, so he desire you will be kind enough give the girl of good pretection, also the said Boo Hang is one of my partner on the mining business and he wish me come with him to call on to see you, but I do not know that you will permit me to see you or not, if you will permit me to come with him, then I will do so with pleasure, hope that God will bless you forever Your Respectfully
>
> May Jin Mun
> Chinese Interpreter

An 1889 letter from Jin Mun to "Mrs. Lick," actually Kate Burton Lake, whom he had met at the Chinese Mission of the Methodist Episcopal Church. Courtesy of Special Collections and University Archives, University of Oregon Libraries.

In 1900, Jin Mun was enumerated in the census twice – once at his place of business at 735 Washington Street, where he was listed, together with a partner named Leong Hoin, as a merchant selling fancy goods; and a second time at his home at

802 Dupont Street. The double counting was, of course, an error, but census takers frequently made mistakes when it came to the Chinese – reversing or misspelling their names, counting them twice or missing them entirely. Both addresses at which Jin Mun was listed were in the immediate vicinity of Washington and Dupont, the latter of which is known today as Grant Avenue. At his home, he was recorded with his family, and the entry included his *second* wife, Wong Shee. They were listed as having been married for 14 years.

But what had become of his first wife, Gong Shee? Many years later, in depositions before Immigration inspectors, Jin Mun would tell the story. Gong Shee had borne Jin Mun four children: the eldest was a girl named Loy Yee (or Loy Gee), and the second, a son, Dip Tso. Both had been listed in the 1880 census (the latter under the name Sick Hong). Two more sons had followed: Dip Wing, born in 1882, and Dip Jung, born the following year. Then, in 1886, Gong Shee took the children back to China, ostensibly to see to their education. She never returned, although her children eventually did. According to Jin Mun, she died in China, but not until 1906.

Gong Shee made it clear when she left that she did not intend to return, suggesting that their marriage was not all it might have been. Jin Mun recounted that upon her departure, she told him to "pick any woman you want" to replace her. Jin Mun took this advice at face value. Only three or four months after her departure, he wed 16 year-old, American-born Wong Shee, who family members recall was from a well-to-do family. There was "great and lengthy feasting and the roar of millions of firecrackers" when they were married. The account depicts her arriving at the wedding not in a sedan chair, but in a car, "sumptuously draped in vermillion." This, however, was surely not the way it happened, since the marriage took place in 1886, and it would be a full decade before America's first automobile was manufactured.

There is a family story to the effect that the two marriages had overlapped by several years, and that the two wives got along well and cooperated with each other during that period. While that is apparently not the way it happened, the fact that both women were ostensibly married to Jin Mun at the same time most likely accounts for the tale. Wong Shee never knew exactly what had happened to Gong Shee; she thought she was marrying a widower. In back-to-back depositions given in 1913, the couple made this assumption clear. Wong Shee asserted that when she married Jin Mun, his first wife was no longer living. Jin Mun, who was interviewed separately, put it this way: "She don't know anything about that; my first wife was gone to China and she never knew whether my first wife was alive or dead, as she never asked me and I never told her."

Wong Shee related many years later that she had been born at the Kwong Hing Chung store in San Francisco, and that she and Jin Mun had not been married legally, but rather according to Chinese custom only. It is, however, questionable whether a marriage of any sort would have taken place if Wong Shee's family had known that her predecessor was still living; this was not China, after all, and it is questionable whether a wealthy family in San Francisco would have permitted their daughter to become a second wife or a concubine. That being said, Jin Mun, as a successful businessman, would have made a very attractive suitor.

Wong Shee went on to bear Jin Mun as many as nine more children between 1887 and 1905: three daughters and six sons was the count given, but not all of the births are confirmed and the 1900 census record presents a few mysteries in this regard. Living with Jin Mun and Wong Shee at 802 Dupont in that year were two daughters and three sons, all children of Wong Shee. But some of Wong Shee's other children were missing: Dip Young, age 11, Hing Shung (Lydia), age 8 and Dip Yin, age 6, were not listed, and they would have been extraordinarily young to have been separated from their mother. Wong Shee's other two children, Dip Chung (Steven) and Hing Ching (Lillian) had not yet been born.

SCOTT D. SELIGMAN

Although Jin Mun was enumerated in the census as a merchant, he was also pursuing other business interests, principally mining, a lifelong pursuit. An 1895 *San Francisco Chronicle* item noted that he had filed an application to impound tailings in a ravine below the Grizzly Hill Mine near Volcano in Amador County. The *San Francisco Call* reported in the same year that together with some partners, he had purchased a valuable hydraulic mining claim in Placer, California, and had constructed restraining works there to prevent the discharge of debris. Jin Mun had also mentioned mining in the 1899 letter to Kate Lake, and a cryptic announcement in the "Business Changes" column of the *Chronicle* on October 26, 1901 gave notice that, "Moy Jin Mun is no longer manager of the Hong Fat Co. mining property, situated at Howland Flat, Sierra County." There is even a record of him buying placer claims in Oregon as late as 1910. Exactly how he was managing to run a business in San Francisco and manage a mine on the other side of the state – ironically, in the very region of Truckee, California, where he had had such a close call with death a quarter of a century earlier – is not clear; perhaps some of his sons assisted him in the endeavors.

An undated photo of a group of Chinese miners. Jin Mun is standing at far right. Courtesy of Roberta Gee.

THREE TOUGH CHINAMEN

Normal life for Chinatown merchants – indeed, for all San Franciscans – came to a screeching halt just after 5:00 a.m. on April 18, 1906, when the great earthquake struck the city. Felt for about 175,00 square miles – as far north as southern Oregon, as far south as Los Angeles and as far east as central Nevada – the quake was centered quite near to San Francisco, where the few who were awake reported having heard rumbling noises immediately before a sharp jolt. The shock lasted only a minute, but it rattled windows, shook houses and threw many from their beds, even as it damaged and destroyed buildings. But it was not the quake itself that was most devastating. That distinction went to the fires that burned for four days after it was over.

Ruptured gas mains were responsible for the initial blazes, and ruptured water mains prevented them from being extinguished. More fires were set inadvertently through the ham-handed use of explosives to demolish buildings in an effort to create firebreaks. As dozens of fires burned out of control, the wooden buildings and tenements of Chinatown, which by and large had survived the tremors, quickly succumbed. Home to about 15,000 people by this time, the Chinese quarter was completely destroyed. Unlike the other parts of town, however, where little more than heaps of debris were left after the fires finally burned out, the ten square blocks that had been Chinatown appeared as "acres of deep caverns choked by twisted iron and smoking embers . . . [with] black tunnels open on every side." The authorities had long suspected that the Chinese underworld carried out their nefarious activities in subterranean chambers and passageways excavated beneath Chinatown, and here, ostensibly, was the evidence. According to the *Washington Post*, which laid it on particularly thick:

> Deep in the bowels of the earth, the highbinders and gamblers, haunted by fear of the police and of rival tong men, had worked for years, tunneling out underground passages and rooms, one below another. Here the secret meetings of the tongs and the never ending

games of *pi-gow* and *fan-tan* were held. Here also consignments of slave girls from Canton [*Guangzhou*] and Nanking [*Nanjing*] and Shanghai were penned up and sold like cattle, and here amid sweet stifling fumes of opium smoke they lived the lives of troglodytes and died the death of rats.

Soldiers forcibly evacuated the newly homeless Chinese. Some were directed to refugee camps, but most left town, the majority for nearby Oakland, where they hoped to be taken in by friends and relatives in its far smaller Chinatown. Jin Mun and his family, ruined by the disaster, were among them. The *New York Times* estimated that "thousands of Chinese men, women and children, all carrying luggage to the limit of their strength" had headed for the ferries. By one report, all but 400 of the Chinese who survived the quake and the fire went across the bay to Oakland. But there was no guarantee things would be much better there, as food supplies in Oakland were soon exhausted, and real danger of famine and disease loomed.

The family narrative holds that Jin Mun lost three sons in the

Ruins of San Francisco's Chinatown after the 1906 earthquake and fire. This photo was taken at the corner of Dupont and California Streets, looking north. Jin Mun's property was three blocks from this intersection. Source: Bob Bowen Collection, National Park Service.

disaster: Dip Young, age 17; Dip Yin, age 12; and Dip Yook, age 11, all ostensibly children of Wong Shee. Of the three, only Dip Yook had appeared in the 1900 census; there was no record of the others. No death records for the boys exist, but this in and of itself is hardly surprising. The official death count released by the San Francisco Board of Supervisors in 1907 claimed that 478 people had died in the disaster, though later estimates put the figure in the thousands. Only a dozen Asian names appear on any of the lists of the deceased prepared in the immediate aftermath of the tragedy. Given the magnitude of the destruction of Chinatown, it's a safe bet that the Chinese dead were severely undercounted. There is a certain irony in the fact that a government so obsessed with documenting its Chinese residents while they lived was so negligent about recording their deaths.

Whether these three sons actually died in the earthquake is unlikely, and the Immigration Bureau was suspicious of them as early as 1913, when Jin Mun's three youngest sons applied for "pre-investigation of status" in advance of a planned trip to China. Jin Mun testified at the time that the three older boys were in Chicago, and although he was crystal clear about their names and dates of birth, he claimed he did not know exactly where they were, that he had not heard from them in more than a year, and that all the letters he had received from them had recently been destroyed by a gas explosion at his house.

In an internal memorandum, Inspector W. E. Walsh raised questions as to exactly how many children Jin Mun really did have, noting, "he now claims 13 in all." He went on to parse testimony received on two separate occasions from Dip Wing, Jin Mun's second son, in 1907 and in 1911, during which he stated that there were only 10 children in total. "I believe it is quite evident that the alleged father has misstated the number of his children and that later they will apply for native papers."

Whether they ever did apply for native papers is unknown, but it's clear that they were not considered family members in the same way as the other children. As late as 1936, Wong Shee could remember only the name of Dip Young when she testified before the Immigration and Naturalization Service; the names of the other two had escaped her, and she claimed to know only that they were in the eastern United States somewhere.

There was one additional child whose status was also questionable, although there is no doubt of her existence. The girl, Chow Heung, also known as Josephine or Josie, was brought from China by Gong Shee when she arrived in 1875. The orphaned daughter of relatives, she was about two years old when she arrived. Chow Heung did not return to China when Gong Shee went back with all of her children in 1886. She remained in the United States, married in 1891, moved to Denver and bore five children before her marriage failed in 1910.

In 1909, Jin Mun had filed an affidavit certifying that the girl had been born in San Francisco in 1877, but when pressed several years later, after Chow Heung applied for a passport, he changed his story, blaming the notary for having gotten the facts wrong, and blaming himself for having been "sick in my mind" after the earthquake and fire, which had destroyed all of his records. It was not a convincing performance. However, even though Chow Heung was not a biological child, she clearly enjoyed a close personal relationship with Jin Mun's family, and certainly a closer one than the three phantom sons who were supposedly off somewhere in the East.

Mainstream San Francisco did not mourn the destruction of Chinatown. "Chinatown is forever wiped out, and every resident of San Francisco will regard this as a godsend," the *Washington Post* cheered. "In the exasperation following bloody tong wars, the suggestion had been made repeatedly that Chinatown be razed. Providence having performed this task, it may be predicted with assurance that the Chinese will never again be permitted to congregate in the heart of San Francisco."

But congregate they eventually did, Providence notwithstanding, and in the same location. There was, to be sure, a big show of considering alternate sites. Sir Cheng-Tung Liang

Cheng, China's minister in Washington, visited San Francisco and toured several proposed locations together with the mayor. The minister expressed the hope that the new Chinatown would be "free of the squalor which characterized the former locality," but noted pointedly that there were 40 Chinese merchants who owned property in the old Chinatown, that he expected they would be permitted to rebuild there. In the end, Chinatown, a source of not inconsiderable tax revenue to the city and a key to trade with China, was rebuilt precisely where it had stood before.

Jin Mun had to rebuild, too, and the family story holds that he set out in August, 1906 to return to the mines, this time in northern California. He again took up placer mining, this time in the area of Feather River, and used the money he made to purchase additional property. A 1910 item in the *Salt Lake Mining Review* announced the sale of the Brantner group of placer claims, 92 acres located 13 miles above the Applegate Post Office in southern Josephine County, Oregon, to Jin Mun. The *St. John's Review* called the claims "very rich diggings," and revealed that Jin Mun had paid $175,000 for them and stated his intention to equip the property with a modern hydraulic system. Jin Mun was, indeed, back in the mining business.

By 1910, however, he had returned to in San Francisco and he and Wong Shee were living at 886 Washington Street with four sons, two daughters and a granddaughter. He was already 60 years old, but his most important contribution was still ahead of him.

Chapter XI
Meet Me At The Fair

Exactly what caused the peripatetic Jin Kee to pick up and move to Indianapolis in 1897 is not clear, but it probably was related to the animosity that had developed between him and other members of the Chicago Chinese community. It was not the first abrupt transition in his life in the United States. Chicago had been his third home in America, and he had stayed there the longest. Indianapolis would be his last.

There was not much of a Chinese colony in the Hoosier capital in the late 1890s. Like Chicago's Chinatown, it did not get its start until the transcontinental railroad was complete and Chinese began to travel eastward in search of employment. No Chinese at all were enumerated in the town in the 1870 Federal Census, however, and just over a dozen were listed a decade later, all male and nearly all laundrymen. The number continued to increase, but very slowly, and by the turn of the century there were still officially fewer than 30 Chinese men living in the city, mostly along Fort Wayne and Massachusetts Avenues, although the actual number may have been two or three times that. The population was composed principally of Chinese who had lived elsewhere in the United States first and subsequently gravitated to Indiana.

Jin Kee had visited Indianapolis at least once before, in 1894. A curious item in a Logansport, Indiana daily newspaper had announced, "Moy Kee, the Chinese interpreter and adjuster of differences, is down from Chicago." He had come to advise Moy Sing, a kinsman who was suing another laundryman to recover money that had been advanced for the purchase of a laundry.

THREE TOUGH CHINAMEN

Clearly, Jin Kee's reputation had preceded him.

The move to Indiana – after which he became known simply as "Moy Kee" – did nothing to dampen his conviction that he was entitled to citizenship. In 1897, he finally succeeded in his longtime quest. The Circuit Court of Marion County, Indiana accepted his argument that his Declaration of Intention had to be honored because it had been filed prior to passage of the Chinese Exclusion Act. And on October 18, 1897, Moy Jin Kee proudly became a citizen of the United States of America.

At about this time he opened a tea shop – Mee Hing Lung and Company – at 216 N. Delaware, and he and his wife took up residence there. He soon expanded his business to include imported porcelains and other chinoiserie. Two years later, ever the entrepreneur and ever the promoter, he announced a new business venture: a Chinese language school. On August 7, 1899, the *Buffalo Express* reported:

> A Chinaman named Moy Kee, who is a naturalized citizen . . . is making preparations to get some personal advantage out of expansion and the extension of trade to the Far East. He will open an evening school in Indianapolis for teaching Americans the Chinese language – "good Chinese, not pidgin" – and he says they can learn it in six months. He speaks English to perfection and claims to be the only Chinaman in the Middle West who has the accomplishment.

The article went on to say that it was doubtful whether Indianapolis was home to many people likely to take advantage of his proposition, and it appears that few did. The venture – if it ever got off the ground – was as ill-conceived as his hotel in Newark, New Jersey had been 14 years earlier, and seems to have been aborted in the same way.

Chin Fung was the first Chinese woman ever to live in Indianapolis, and still the only one there in 1900. The census record for that year listed her as having given birth to three children, all of whom were still living at the time, though not with their parents. This was a direct contradiction of earlier press reports that the couple was childless. Another reference to children occurred much later, after Jin Kee's death, when the *Los Angeles Times* reported that two sons had been born to Chin Fung and sent back to China "to live as the sons of a man of wealth and caste in that land." If this statement had been true, it would be very puzzling, indeed. A well-heeled Chinese man with U.S. citizenship and no obvious intention to return to live in his native land would normally raise his sons himself, in his adopted country. The ability to do so, for most Chinese in America, would have been one of the most important prerogatives of the citizenship for which Jin Kee had fought so relentlessly. In reality there were no such sons – as would, in time, become clear.

By 1902, Jin Kee had opened a restaurant at 506 E. Washington Street, and he wasted little time in exercising another prerogative of citizenship: in 1901, he sat for – and passed – the civil service examination. Then he announced his intention to lobby Secretary of the Treasury Lyman J. Gage – with whom he professed to be personally acquainted – for a position either as an interpreter or a secret agent. He may indeed have known Gage, who had been a well-known business leader in Chicago before being called to Washington. *The Fort Wayne Evening Sentinel* observed that raising the issue would "renew with the government a disturbing question" as to the effect of the Chinese Exclusion Act. Apparently the question of his potential employment was raised and then dropped, because the Civil Service Commission referred the matter to the Treasury Department and there is no evidence anything further was ever done about it.

A couple of months later, something extremely unusual happened that foreshadowed a larger, more prominent role for Jin Kee in the affairs of his countrymen. It came in the form of a gift of a hundred "100 year eggs" from Viceroy Li Hung Chang (*Li Hongzhang*), a prominent figure in the Manchu court and China's chief diplomat and statesman. The eggs, a traditional Chinese delicacy made by preserving duck (or sometimes chicken or quail) eggs in clay, ash, salt and lime for a period of several months until they take on a strong flavor and a green hue, aroused considerable interest among Americans unfamiliar with them. Taking the translation of the name literally, the press marveled at eggs "that had reached the remarkable age of 100 years [and were] ... still good, [having] ... been cured by some process known only to the cooks of China."

Li Hung Chang had not been in the United States since 1896, and he did not visit Chicago on that trip; if he had ever met Jin Kee it is not recorded. But he did enjoy preserved eggs, and as a matter of fact didn't travel without them. In addition to the clothing and daily necessities that he and his retinue of 18 staff members and 22 servants carried with them during their visit to America, there were also liquor, water for his tea (melted from snow collected in China's far West), two English-speaking parrots and "cassia flower century eggs." Whether the Viceroy had jettisoned 100 of them before returning to China and arranged several years later for them to be forwarded to Jin Kee (they would, presumably, not have gone bad) or simply sent a fresh batch from Beijing is unclear. It's also entirely possible, and quite a bit more likely, that while the gift was sent in Li's name, it was really masterminded by Chinese diplomats in the United States. The Chinese government was concerned about the status of Chinese in America, and it was clearly romancing Jin Kee in the belief that he could prove useful in improving it. The gift and the revelation of the giver's identity was well-publicized in newspapers all across the United States – and it certainly helped raise Jin Kee's stature in the eyes of both Chinese and Americans.

America's ill-treatment of its Chinese was understood to be the reason the Qing government had declined to exhibit at in the 1893 Columbian Exposition in Chicago, but in 1904, in an effort to improve relations, it decided to participate in the St. Louis World's Fair, a commemoration of the 100th anniversary of the Louisiana Purchase. China's pavilion was a partial replica of the summer home of Manchu Prince Pu Lun, a cousin of the Guangxu Emperor, and the monarch tapped up the Prince himself to head up China's delegation to the Fair. Pu Lun was on hand to review the parade on opening day, and he stayed in St. Louis for two months after visits to Honolulu, San Francisco and Washington.

China spent 750,000 taels of silver, the equivalent of about half a million dollars in gold, on its pavilion and on arrangements for the Pu Lun delegation visit. The goods exhibited were valued at an additional $650,000. Chinese artifacts and manufactures on display included jade, cloisonné, crystal, lacquer ware and porcelain objects; tools and weapons; cotton, wool and silk goods; furs and animal pelts; carpets and paper goods; as well as 1,300 photos illustrating Chinese dress, manners, customs and pursuits that filled 20 albums.

An 1897 photo of Viceroy Li Hung Chang, China's chief diplomat and statesman, who presented Jin Kee with 100 "century eggs." Reports that the two were blood relatives were surely untrue. Source: Edward Bangs Drew Collection, Harvard-Yenching Library, Harvard University. Copyright President & Fellows of Harvard College. Used with permission.

Jin Kee was one of the local Chinese exhibitors at the Fair, so it is all but certain that Pu Lun met him for the first time in St. Louis. If he did not, however, he definitely did so in Indianapolis, which was also on the Prince's itinerary. After leaving the Fair and spending some time in Chicago, the Prince arrived in the Hoosier capital for a ten-day visit on May 18, 1904. The trip had been arranged by Wong Kai Kah, Chinese Imperial Vice Commissioner-General to the World's Fair, an American-educated Cantonese who had studied at Yale in the 1870s and was fluent in English. Indianapolis had been selected because of

Wong's friendship with William Fortune, one of the city's civic leaders.

Pu Lun, believed by many likely to become China's next emperor, arrived at Union Station in Indianapolis, alighting to a 21-gun salute. "It was not known how many guns a Chinese Prince should receive according to Chinese etiquette," explained the *Indianapolis News*, "but it was believed that a salute that was suitable for the President of the United States would be equally suitable for his highness from the Orient." An official welcoming party was at hand, led by Mayor John W. Holtzman, and after speeches and formalities, the Prince greeted some of the attendees. Jin Kee and Pang Wah Jung, leaders of the local Chinese community, welcomed him with deep bows – "almost touching the floor with their heads" – and presented him with flowers. Jin Kee's bouquet was wrapped in red paper, his business card attached.

Then it was off to a reception at the State House. Jin Kee and Pang rode with the Prince in the parade, a spectacle that would have been absolutely inconceivable in their home country, where Manchu princes did not, as a rule, condescend to consort with the sons of Cantonese peasants. But these were unusual times, and the Prince's trip in itself was more or less unprecedented. The Chinese community of Indianapolis amounted to at most 100 men plus, of course, Chin Fung, but respect had to be paid to its presumed leader while the Prince was in town.

Prince Pu Lun, cousin of the Emperor of China, represented China at the 1904 St. Louis World's Fair, visited Indianapolis and was instrumental in elevating Jin Kee to the titled elite.

Chinese Exhibitors at the St. Louis World's Fair. Jin Kee is standing in the front row, second from the right. Pang Wah Jung, also a leader of the Indianapolis Chinese community, is shown third from left. The figure in the center appears to be Wong Kai Kah, Chinese Imperial Vice Commissioner-General to the World's Fair. The image is from the 1905 History of the Louisiana Purchase Exposition by Mark Bennitt, editor-in-chief, and Frank Parker Stockbridge, managing editor, Universal Exposition Publishing Company. Courtesy St. Louis Public Library.

Accordingly, Jin Kee and Pang were later granted a private meeting with the Prince at the Claypool Hotel.

Jin Kee worked hard behind the scenes to negotiate hosting the Prince at his restaurant for a luncheon with the Chinese community, or at very least a short courtesy call. Pu Lun eventually accepted his invitation, and a banquet was arranged for May 27. In preparation, Jin Kee closed his establishment to his usual patrons for a day. A large lantern was hung outside the restaurant's door, and the façade was festooned with colorful tissue ribbons. The *News* described the scene this way:

> Oriental rugs were spread from the street to a teakwood table, where were placed two beautiful inlaid chairs covered with crimson satin draperies. The carved table stood on beautiful rugs, and upon it were placed burning incense, chop suey and Chinese wine. These refreshments were partaken of by the Prince, Mayor Holtzman, James Whitcomb

Riley [the well-known poet], Mr. and Mrs. Cass Conaway, Charles Jones and William Fortune.

Exactly what delicacies were served at the luncheon are not recorded, but it's a safe bet that Jin Kee's honored guest was offered a good deal more than mere chop suey. At a banquet Jin Kee had thrown for American friends the previous month, the fare had included shark's fin, bird's nest soup, water chestnuts, fruits, candies and rosebud wine as well as preserved eggs, and surely a Manchu Prince would have rated nothing less. The repast reportedly pleased the Prince, who presented Jin Kee with a silk scarf. Then came a surprise announcement that "lifted Moy Kee into the seventh heaven of delight and set Mrs. Moy Kee bowing in devotion to the Prince":
Pu Lun declared that upon his return to China, he intended to recommend to the Emperor that Jin Kee be granted a title.

The *News*, in a pitiful attempt to offer some background for this unusual action, explained that Jin Kee was already a person of status in China, since before his departure from his native land, "rank was given him by the mayor of his city, and the brass

PU LUN CALLS ON HIS NEW FRIENDS

Meets Members of Commercial Bodies and Auto Club, and Wives To-Night.

WILL LUNCH WITH MOY KEE

Chinese Household is Thrown Into Raptures by Unexpected Honor— Preparations for Event.

Tired out by the succession of affairs at Lafayette, and the long run to Indianapolis in an automobile, Prince Pu Lun retired at 8 o'clock last night, and did not arise until nearly noon to-day. Servants and secretaries paced in front of the prince's room, but none disturbed him. He declared himself this noon fit to do it all over again.

Prince Pu Lun is regarded as a mascot by the automobile club, for considering the number of machines, accidents in the run were few. The prince landed from William Fortune's car at the Claypool just in time, for after he alighted and the car had gone fifty feet farther, it "went dead." Not a drop of gasoline was left.

Prince Pu Lun's acceptance of Jin Kee's luncheon invitation was big news in the city, as this May 26, 1904 headline from the Indianapolis News suggests.

button of dignity was presented him." This statement was pure drivel; mayors did not confer titles in China, and Jin Kee had come from a tiny village, not a city. Nor did the "brass button of dignity" exist anywhere but in the reporter's imagination. But the Prince proved as good as his word. Two months later came the news that Jin Kee had received official certificates bearing the seal of the Emperor of China, elevating him to the rank of Mandarin of the Fifth Degree.

Ohio's *Piqua Leader-Dispatch* decided to have some fun with the announcement, speculating about Jin Kee's political aspirations:

> The one thing to be feared is that Mr. Moy Kee, pardonably proud of his new acquirements, may look over the list of senatorial aspirants and conclude that he is fit to succeed Mr. [Charles W.] Fairbanks in the Senate. Mr. Moy is a naturalized American, a stalwart Republican and speaks the English language fluently – much better, indeed, than some of the gentlemen who aspire to the prospective vacancy in the upper house of Congress.

The *Leader-Dispatch* needn't have worried; Jin Kee had not set his sights on the Senate. But he would soon find himself in Washington anyway. Not to assume office, but to lobby for the rights of his countrymen.

Chapter XII
Leading the Fight

The title of Mandarin of the Fifth Degree had not been conferred on Jin Kee simply because Prince Pu Lun had enjoyed his company. That honor was certainly part and parcel of a business transaction of some sort. The declining Manchu government was aggressively courting overseas Chinese merchants because it needed capital, and it is quite conceivable that Jin Kee paid for his title, as many others did. But it is also clear that the Chinese government saw in Jin Kee a possible standard bearer for its drive to persuade the United States to ease restrictions on America's Chinese population. It might well have granted him the title to encourage him in this effort and to signal others that China's government was behind him.

In the spring of 1905, an obsequious article about Jin Kee and his wife appeared in several newspapers around the country. The gist of it was that Chin Fung was "received in the most exclusive social circles" in Indianapolis, that she was a Mandarin's daughter and that her husband was a distant relative of Viceroy Li Hung Chang, who by this time was dead. In one version he was also said to be a cousin of Prince Pu Lun. While the Moys had indisputably achieved a measure of social acceptance in the Hoosier capital, the other assertions were patently untrue. Mandarins' daughters did not, as a rule, marry poor young provincial men, still less émigrés, and Jin Kee shared neither a surname, nor a dialect, nor a home province, nor a social class with the venerable Li Hung Chang, let alone with the Prince, who was of Manchu rather than Chinese descent. While it's doubtful that this article was orchestrated by Chinese sources, these particular pieces of misinformation surely had the effect of raising the stature of the couple in the eyes of naïve and credulous Americans.

That the Chinese government had plans for Jin Kee, however, is undeniable. The year 1905 saw several manifestations of homegrown Chinese outrage at the mistreatment of their compatriots in America, stories of which had been circulated widely back in China. Reports of a Supreme Court decision that denied due process to a Chinese *habeas corpus* petitioner, of the incarceration in Boston of a Chinese student suspected of being a laborer and of the failure of a new treaty negotiated by the two governments to curb the abuses of the exclusion policy all played a part in a May announcement by Shanghai merchants of an unprecedented boycott of American goods to begin in July. Also in May, about a month after the articles about Chin Fung appeared, Sir Cheng-Tung Liang Cheng, China's minister in Washington, issued instructions to Chinese subjects in America to band together to protect their rights in a new organization that would take instructions from him. The group, whose establishment was linked explicitly to Pu Lun's visit the previous year, was to be headed by none other than Moy Kee of Indianapolis.

Jin Kee's credentials for the assignment were summed up in a syndicated follow-up article that appeared in several publications:

> He is very, very wealthy, being a merchant, and he is beside a well-educated man. He is broad and liberal, and with his wife is received in exclusive society here. He exerts not a little influence in state affairs, as he is a citizen. Besides, he is supreme grand master of the Chinese Free Masons, and when Prince Pu Lun visited Indianapolis last July he made Moy Kee a mandarin. He is known locally as the mayor of Chinatown. He is famous for his generosity and entertains lavishly. He contributed a large sum to the Japanese Red Cross fund and was decorated by the Mikado.

THREE TOUGH CHINAMEN

TO LEAD THE FIGHT TO LET CHINESE IN

MOY KEE, WEALTHY AND INFLUENTIAL CHINAMAN AT INDIANAPOLIS, WILL DIRECT THE BATTLE FOR THE SIX COMPANIES

MOY KEE,
Who is leading the fight of the Six Companies against the deportation of the Chinese.

Illustration from "To Lead the Fight to Let Chinese In," a Newspaper Enterprise Association dispatch that appeared in several newspapers, including the Fort Worth Star-Telegram *on May 26, 1905.*

The author might also have added Jin Kee's excellent communication skills, the fact that he already had experience running an organization committed to securing rights for Chinese – the Chicago Chinese Club – and that his connections included some powerful Washington figures, including Vice President

Charles W. Fairbanks, the former senator from Indiana.

Jin Kee did not admit to the reporter who interviewed him for the article that he had been selected to lead the charge, but he did acknowledge that he intended to devote his energies to arguing for the repeal of the Exclusion Act. And he was more than willing to speak – eloquently, as usual – about the injustices visited on the Chinese as a result of it:

> My people are honest. They come to help build up the farms and cities. In the far west they follow agricultural pursuits. There are millions of acres of untilled land in this country. The Chinese can make these deserts bloom . . . It is manifestly unjust to the Chinese to say that they are inferior to others who come here. In the arts and sciences, the Chinese acknowledge no superiors . . . I claim for my race high-mindedness, honesty and industriousness. In our fight to secure the repeal of the Exclusion Act, you will find us honorable – straightforward. We will use only such arguments as all the people may understand.

On May 21, the *Cleveland Plain Dealer* reported that Jin Kee, together with one of the leaders of St. Louis' Chinatown, would soon make a visit to its home town to investigate recent arrests of men accused of violating the Exclusion Act. The article quoted Ben Lee of the local Chinese community, who had recently paid a call on Moy in Indianapolis, as saying that "we are hoping to establish a national organization soon so that by united movement we may be able to exert some influence in the direction of our rights."

Cleveland was, in fact, a very appropriate city for Jin Kee to choose for his first visit in his new capacity, because it had been quite active in the enforcement of exclusion policies. The previous year, Judge Francis J. Wing, a McKinley appointee, had issued a startling decision in the case of Hong Chang and six other Chinese men arrested after entering the United States illegally from Canada. Wing ruled that the defendants could not be compelled to admit that they were Chinese, since to do so would be tantamount to incriminating themselves. He put the onus on the government to prove nationality, which of course was all but impossible in most cases. The maverick decision effectively nullified the Chinese exclusion laws, at least temporarily, and was immediately appealed by U.S. District Attorney John J. Sullivan.

Because of the constitutional questions raised, Sullivan was able to get the question put directly before the Supreme Court, bypassing the circuit court in Cincinnati, although only after overcoming legal obstacles artfully placed in his way by Judge Wing. On March 14, 1904, Attorney General Philander C. Knox appealed to the Supreme Court to issue a writ of *mandamus* to compel Wing to enforce the Exclusion Act – the first time in the history of the Supreme Court that the government had ever sought such a writ against a Federal judge. The Court obliged, issuing the document on May 2.

Sullivan believed that Wing's initial ruling, which had stayed the arresting power of Federal officials in exclusion cases, had made northern Ohio a haven for undocumented Chinese immigrants. So after the decision, he decided to send a strong signal that his turf was no longer a safety zone. In early 1905, he ordered the imposition of a "dragnet" to pursue Chinese residents who did not have proper identification papers, maintaining that all such men "must be apprehended, brought to trial and deported." The tactic chosen was a census of all the Chinese in the district, and midnight raids were launched in Cleveland's Chinese quarter for this purpose.

By mid-May, nine Chinese men had been arrested and six had been ordered deported and had appealed. The *Plain Dealer* reported that the "ablest legal talent in the city" had been retained to defend them. The legal team was led by none other than Judge Wing, who had stepped down from the bench the previous December and returned to private practice. According to the *Plain Dealer*, the defense was to be part of a broader, nationwide effort whereby legal talent would be retained and pooled to defend Chinese such as those arrested in Cleveland, with the goal of a constitutional victory in the Supreme Court. Cleveland was to be the epicenter of the effort, and Jin Kee's new organization was to coordinate it. It was probably his group that underwrote the legal defense.

The legal "dream team" developed a novel argument. It asserted that the Exclusion Act had effectively expired because it had not been renewed by mutual agreement between the United States and China, as the original Act required. When the cases were lost in Federal Court in Cleveland and the Court of Appeals in Cincinnati, Judge Wing filed an appeal with the Supreme Court. But the Court, which had opined previously on the constitutionality of the Exclusion Act, refused to hear the case, effectively upholding the decisions of the lower courts and ending the matter.

Jin Kee's planned journey to Cleveland might have been timed to permit him to attend the court proceedings against the Chinese defendants, which took place in late May, but there is no record that he actually took such a trip. What is known is that in early 1906, Jin Kee and Pang Wah Jung, the so-called "Vice Mayor" of Indianapolis' Chinese residents, visited Washington, DC, no doubt to further the goals of the new organization. One purpose of the trip was to discuss strategy with the Chinese Legation. Their stay overlapped with the tail end of a visit to Washington by a 62-person delegation from China, led by two imperial commissioners, Tuan Fang (*Duan Fang*) and Tai Hung Chi (*Dai Hongci*), who had been charged with studying the political and social institutions of the United States and Europe. These officials may also have taken part in the discussions.

Jin Kee and Pan went to the Capitol in full national dress to pay their respects to Vice President Fairbanks. While they were there, they were intercepted by Senate Chaplain Edward Everett Hale, who mistook them for foreign dignitaries and immediately spirited them in the direction of the diplomatic gallery, only to realize his mistake when they were halfway there. As the *New York Times* snickered, they were redirected when "it was discovered that their diplomatic experience was confined to the adjudication of differences between rival tongs of Indianapolis."

The most important audience the two Chinese men secured in Washington was one with President Theodore Roosevelt on February 1. According to the *Washington Post* and several other newspapers, Representative Jesse Overstreet, a Republican congressman from Indiana, took them to the White House and made the introduction, and the two were seen having a conversation with a member of Congress in the anteroom to the President's office, suggesting strongly that the presidential audience took place there. Roosevelt's appointment book records no such meeting, but it does show that he hosted a congressional reception on that date to which Overstreet and his wife had been invited, so it's more than likely the meeting took place in conjunction with that event.

No record of their conversation survives, but it is known that Roosevelt had taken the Shanghai boycott of American goods quite seriously, and that while he had pressured the Chinese government to suppress it, he had also ordered more courteous treatment of Chinese in the United States as a result of it. The month before meeting with Jin Kee, in fact, the President had devoted three full paragraphs to Chinese exclusion policies in his State of the Union message to the Congress. Although he defended the exclusion of Chinese laborers as a settled and even a non-controversial issue, he allowed that in the course of excluding workers, many abuses had occurred and much injustice had been done to other Chinese. He said, in part:

> We must treat the Chinese student, traveler, and business man in a spirit of the broadest justice and courtesy if we expect similar treatment to be accorded to our own people of similar rank who go to China. Much trouble has come during the past summer from the organized boycott against American goods which has been started

in China. The main factor in producing this boycott has been the resentment felt by the students and business people of China, by all the Chinese leaders, against the harshness of our law toward educated Chinamen of the professional and business classes. This Government has the friendliest feeling for China and desires China's well-being ... Such an attitude tends to the peace of the world.

Whether this topic, or modification or repeal of Chinese exclusion legislation came up in Roosevelt's meeting with Jin Kee and his colleague is not recorded, but the President's conviction that Chinese should be afforded courteous treatment by his government was probably the reason for the audience in the first place. Whatever was discussed, meeting in the White House with the President of the United States was surely the apotheosis of Jin Kee's career. Before long, his fortunes would begin to decline, and they would do so precipitously.

Chapter XIII
I Deem It To Be A Lesson

Within a few months of Jin Fuey's unceremonious discharge from the Immigration Bureau on charges of smuggling, his cousin Gop Jung joined the same Bureau's Brooklyn, New York office. Jin Fuey had probably been instrumental in the younger man's hiring. Gop Jung was very close to him, and called him "uncle" throughout his life, even though he was born only two years after him and was not actually his nephew, but rather a first cousin once removed. The "uncle" title was an honorific reserved for a kinsman belonging to the previous generation on the family tree. Throughout his tenure in the Immigration Bureau, Gop Jung would frequently seek advice from his "uncle" on matters related to his employment there.

Like Jin Kee, Jin Mun and Jin Fuey, the portly Gop Jung was born in Hai Yang village and emigrated to America as a young man. He arrived in the mid-1870s and moved around quite a bit, generally perching in cities in which Moy relatives preceded him, including San Francisco, Peoria and Washington. In 1890, he returned to China for a year and married 19 year-old Hu Shee, whose hometown was not far from Hai Yang, but he left her in China and went back to the United States alone. A decade later he proceeded to marry again – this time to an American woman – although Hu Shee was still very much alive.

Gop Jung met Lillian Patton while working in a laundry in Gouverneur, New York. He returned to Washington in 1898, where he had a relative who was also a laundryman. The next year she followed him there, and in early 1900 they were wed. Because District of Columbia authorities were unwilling to perform a mixed-race ceremony, they married across the Potomac River in Alexandria, Virginia, Gop Jung apparently having made no mention to her or to the authorities of the existence of a first wife. The union did not last more than a couple of months, however. By June 4, when the census taker visited, Lillian had disappeared, although there was never a formal divorce.

Gop Jung made one more trip back to China in 1900, this time staying just under a year, but when he returned to America it was, again, without Hu Shee. A year later, he joined the Immigration Bureau, and in 1907 was transferred to Baltimore, where his kinsman in nearby Washington persuaded him to invest in a corporation in the capital. The District of Columbia was home to about 500 Chinese men at that time, nearly all of whom occupied a three-block stretch of Pennsylvania Avenue just a stone's throw from the Capitol Building. The firm, Yuen Chong & Company, was headquartered at 318 Pennsylvania Avenue, N.W., the heart of the Chinese quarter.

The business was established by 32 investors, 20 of them named Moy and nine named Lee. Most contributed $1,000 to capitalize the company, which seems to have earned its revenue primarily through illegal gambling, although there were probably some legitimate lines of business as well. There were very occasional distributions of dividends – "$50 one year and $200 another year" per share, according to one source - but earning money was of decidedly secondary importance to the investors. The company's principal purpose was to provide a fig leaf for Chinese laborers who wished to enjoy the privileges reserved for merchants under the Exclusion Act. Travel back and forth between China and the United States was easier for businessmen, and most importantly, as members of an "exempt" class under the Act, they were permitted to bring their wives and children into the United States. For Chinese who preferred to remain in America, this was a significant consideration, and Gop Jung was one of those Chinese. He had no intention of moving back to his native land.

THREE TOUGH CHINAMEN

In 1910, Gop Jung was transferred to the Bureau's Pittsburgh office, and two years after his arrival, he applied for entry for Hu Shee and for a son, Moy Sher Park. The son, he explained, had been conceived during his 1900 trip and born shortly after his departure for the United States; Gop Jung had never seen him. Since there was no exemption in the law for government employees, Gop Jung applied as a merchant, citing his association with Yuen Chong to justify the status. He acknowledged that he did not actually work in the business – his government service made this impossible – but asserted that his standing as an investor in the firm entitled him to be considered a merchant. He certainly did not qualify as a laborer, he argued, because he had not worked as one since his entry into government service a decade earlier.

To spare himself the expense of ocean passage for his wife and son if they were only to be turned away when they reached San Francisco, he applied to the Bureau for predetermination of his own status as an indication of whether his family would be eligible for entry. Initial signals were not encouraging. Since government interpreters were not an "exempt" class, the Service was inclined to base its decision on the position of an applicant during the year before he entered government service. In Gop Jung's case, that job had been in a laundry, and laundrymen were considered laborers. His investment in Yuen Chong, which did not take place until 1909, was not, it was argued, germane.

Gop Jung fought back, naming several other cases in which interpreters who had run restaurants or laundries before their government service had been permitted to bring in families. He lobbied friends in the Immigration Bureau and consulted an attorney. He even tried to enlist his old Sunday School teacher, Abby Gunn Baker, in the effort. Mrs. Baker knew First Lady Ellen Axson Wilson personally, and Gop Jung hoped she would ask her to intervene on his behalf with her husband, President Woodrow Wilson. Not surprisingly, Baker rebuffed him, unwilling to use her high-level connections on such a matter. Eventually,

The first page of Gop Jung's February 15, 1913 application for pre-investigation of his immigration status, the initial step in bringing his wife and son to the United States. Source: National Archives and Records Administration, Philadelphia, PA.

however, perhaps because Gop Jung had ingratiated himself with several of its officials, the Immigration Bureau relented, and on May 28, 1913, the decision was made to concede Gop Jung's "exempt" status and permit the entry of Hu Shee and Sher Park. They would be allowed in provided their identity and their relationship to him could be established to the satisfaction of the Immigration officer who examined them.

Once his wife and son had set sail for San Francisco, Gop Jung had to make arrangements for their landing and safe transfer to a train for Pittsburgh. He decided to ask a Chinese colleague – Young Kay, an interpreter in the San Francisco office – to look after them. All was arranged until Young was suddenly sent to Los Angeles on assignment. Hu Shee and Sher Park were due to arrive aboard the S.S. *Siberia* on March 29, 1914, and the interpreter would not be back in time. So Gop Jung decided to write to his "uncle" Jin Mun and ask for assistance. He probably did not know Jin Mun well; the latter had already left China by the time he was born, and had returned only briefly to marry and to retrieve his wife. They might have spent some time together in San Francisco in the late 1870s, but the relationship was not a close one, or Jin Mun would surely have been his first choice to care for Hu Shee and Sher Park.

Jin Mun agreed to help, and the woman and the boy arrived on schedule, but they were held for a medical examination at Angel Island, the station in San Francisco Bay where, beginning in 1910, most immigrants from China were processed. When they were released on April 2, they were taken to 886 Washington Street in San Francisco, Jin Mun's business address. Two days later, Gop Jung received a long telegram in English written in their names (even though neither spoke any English) requesting $150 for attorneys' fees associated with their immigration formalities and for the purchase of clothing.

Hu Shee and Sher Park's case was straightforward and ought not to have required the intervention of a lawyer, and Gop Jung, experienced in immigration matters, suspected he was being swindled. He imagined Jin Mun's fingerprints all over this undertaking, and complained about it in a letter to two of his brothers, of which an English translation survives:

> I have received telegrams and letters from uncle Yiu Mon [Jin Mun], of San Francisco, requesting me to send him $150, which, he alleges he expended in the interest of my family's admission. One of the items included in this account was the sending of a motor boat to receive my family. He threatens with the detention of my wife and son in San Francisco unless I pay him this money, as per bill rendered. He thinks he can extort this money from me, but I am not to be fooled by him. His action certainly has rendered the relations between him and me as nephew and uncle very unpleasant.

For guidance on how to handle the situation, he immediately wrote to Jin Fuey, his consigliere, who counseled him to ask for assistance from Samuel Backus, the Immigration Commissioner at Angel Island, which he did. This was curious advice, because seeking government adjudication of an internal family squabble ran decidedly counter to normal Chinese practice. Jin Fuey was in an excellent position to have mediated this petty argument, so one can only speculate as to why he declined to do so, and instead advocated going to the authorities, which could serve only to get his brother into trouble. Perhaps, for some unknown reason, his own relationship with Jin Mun was strained and he wished to cause him problems. If so, it would not be the only time Jin Fuey had used such a tactic on an adversary.

Backus' first act was to remove Gop Jung's wife and child

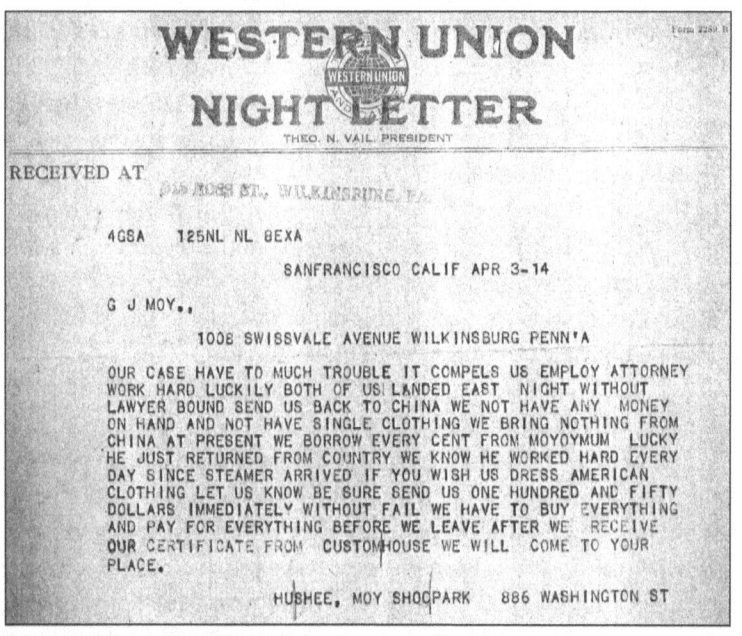

Telegram written in the names of Hu Shee and Moy Shoo [Sher] Park, probably by Jin Mun, asking Gop Jung to send $150 to see to their ostensible needs. Gop Jung saw it as an extortion attempt and asked Immigration Bureau officials to intervene. Source: National Archives and Records Administration, Philadelphia, PA.

from Jin Mun's custody and spirit them off to Pittsburgh. In the interim, Gop Jung received – presumably from Jin Mun – a letter containing a detailed list of expenses: $15 each for two steam launches from San Francisco to Angel Island; $50 for lawyer's fees and a "certain sum" for bribing the doctor who conducted eye examinations on Hu Shee and Sher Park. Backus requested a copy of this itemized list, and declared his intention to conduct an investigation of Jin Mun's connection with the case.

Jin Mun got wind of this plan and tried to pre-empt what assuredly spelled trouble. He wrote Backus on April 10 disclaiming any responsibility. "Moy Gap [sic] Jung is my nephew and is laboring under some mistaken hallucination," he declared, "as no one ever demanded money for him or his wife to assist in their landing, or in payment for services rendered in the matter of their landing." He explained that the attorneys, who were friends of his, had worked free of charge, and that he was treating the two new arrivals as "honored guests" and would accept no money for their care. He added that he intended "to read Moy Gap Jung 'the riot act' for daring to insinuate such untruth against myself or my family."

By May 18, however, when Jin Mun gave a lengthy statement to Inspector Phillips B. Jones on Angel Island concerning his role in the matter, his story had changed. He was shown a copy of the letter written to Gop Jung with the list of expenses, signed with his own name and stamped with his own "chop" – his official seal – and asked if he had written it. He denied doing so, but allowed that he had told his nephew, Moy Quong Poy, to write it, and that they had similar handwriting. He was then asked to provide handwriting samples, which he did. He was also questioned in detail about why and when he had hired the attorney, whether instructions had ever been given to bribe the doctor and whether he himself had visited Hu Shee – or the doctor – on Angel Island. Jin Mun's answers were evasive, and from Inspector Jones' report it is clear he did not believe much of what the old man said. Jones also suspected, as did the interpreter, that Jin Mun had deliberately disguised his handwriting.

What remained was for the handwriting sample to be compared with a specimen of Jin Mun's known script, and on May 18 Backus wrote to Gop Jung asking for one. It was not to come. Gop Jung, whose only objective had been to see to his family's safe transit without being swindled in the process, had sent Jin Mun $15 for what he deemed were legitimate expenses,

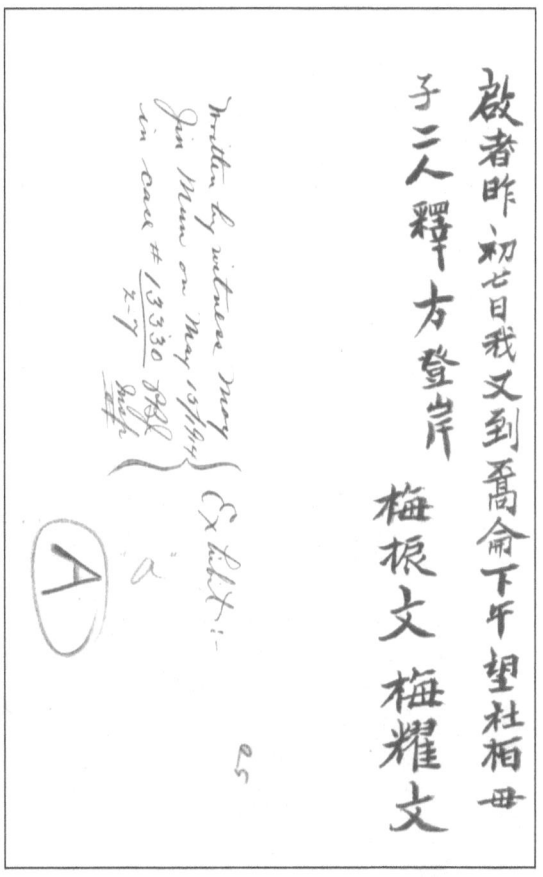

Handwriting sample with two signatures by Jin Mun submitted to the Immigration Bureau on Angel Island on May 18, 1914. He provided these in connection with an investigation into alleged extortion related to the arrival in the United States of Gop Jung's wife and son. Source: National Archives and Records Administration, Philadelphia, PA.

though the latter returned the money to him. And on May 21, Gop Jung wrote to Backus and officially requested that the entire matter be dropped.

As he put it, "he is a distant relative, and if anything should befall him, I only not inflict punishment on him alone, but upon his whole family who depending [sic] on him for their support. Since you have frightened him, I deem it to be a lesson for him," he wrote, and the distasteful matter ended there.

Chapter XIV
Less Than Savory Characters

On May 2, 1911, while taking his wife Hattie and his 23 year-old daughter Josephine out for a ride near their country home in Woodcliff Lake, New Jersey, Jin Fuey was arrested by a United States Marshal. The charge was smuggling Chinese immigrants into the United States.

The warrant for his arrest had been issued by U.S. Commissioner James D. Carpenter of Jersey City after notification came from Boston that Jin Fuey had been indicted on April 23, together with three white men, for plotting to smuggle 100 Chinese from Jamaica. He was accused of having colluded with Goodman Phillips, Harvey C. Daly and George A. Gardinier, all of Massachusetts, to charter a vessel and bring the laborers to the United States, charging each $400 to $500.

At the arraignment, Jin Fuey contended that the indictment was the result of a conspiracy to do him harm, exclaiming, "President McKinley was my friend. I was an inspector of immigration at Boston during his administration and if he were alive the arrest would not have happened. Since he died, I have been persecuted." He did not specify by whom, or for what, nor did he explain how he had come to know McKinley personally through his previous employment. Hattie Moy was equally vocal, protesting the arrest angrily. "I'm ashamed of my own country," she cried. "I'm ashamed to live in a country where so much cruelty is visited upon my husband's countrymen. It makes me sorry to think that my daughter was born in the United States," she added oddly, as if she anticipated that her daughter's birthplace might one day become a point of contention.

> # THE UNITED STATES OF AMERICA.
>
> At a District Court of the United States of America, for the District of Massachusetts, begun and holden at Boston, within and for said District, on the third Tuesday of March in the year of our Lord one thousand nine hundred and eleven.
>
> The JURORS for the United States of America, within and for the District of Massachusetts, upon their oath, present that
>
> GOODMAN PHILLIPS and HARVEY C. DALY, both of Boston, and GEORGE M. D. GARDINIER otherwise called CHIC GARDINIER of Wellfleet, all in said District of Massachusetts, and JIN FUEY MOY otherwise called DOCTOR MOY of New York in the southern district of New York, heretofore, to wit, on the first day of November in the year nineteen hundred and ten, unlawfully did conspire together and with other persons to the grand jurors unknown, to commit an offence against the United States of America, that is to say, the offence of unlawfully bringing into and landing in the United States from a foreign country, to wit, Jamaica, by some vessel, the name and a more particular description whereof is to the grand jurors unknown, divers, to wit, one hundred Chinese persons, the names and a more particular description of said Chinese persons being to the grand jurors unknown, which said Chinese persons were not then nor thereafter entitled to enter the United States under the Acts of Congress in such cases made and provided; that

U.S. District Court for Massachusetts indictment against Jin Fuey and his co-defendants on the charge of conspiracy to import Chinese illegally into the United States. Source: National Archives and Records Administration, Waltham, MA.

Bail was set at $5,000 and Jin Fuey offered a bag allegedly containing $6,000 worth of jewelry as collateral, but it was refused. A Miss Anna M. Dodd of Newark, however, came forward and posted bond, permitting Jin Fuey to be released for several days. It is not clear who she was or the nature of her relationship with Jin Fuey; she was listed in the Newark city directory merely as a "copyist" – that is, a transcriber. Perhaps she was a patient of his, or someone he knew through the church. Miss Dodd, however, soon thought better of her decision, and on May 12 sent her sister to Jersey City to report that she would not renew the bond. Jin Fuey was then taken to Hudson County Jail, and on May 13 was transferred to Boston to stand trial.

In the decade since his discharge from the Immigration Bureau, Jin Fuey may have practiced medicine, but if he did so, it is not clear how robust his practice was, for he appears constantly to have been on the lookout for ways to add to his income. In 1906, he had applied for a patent on a new and improved kind of nutcracker. His invention involved the addition of a simple attachment to the traditional implement that enabled it to hull chestnuts even as it was cracking them. His application was approved in 1908 and assigned patent number 883,558. He also applied for protection for the same invention in Canada. Whether the item was ever manufactured, or ever resulted in any income for him, is not known, but Jin Fuey may well have been the first Chinese in America ever to apply to the U.S. government for patent protection, although he was not the first to have a patent granted.

In addition, he earned money from his work as a court interpreter, charging $5 a day for his services, plus incidental expenses. He was not picky about his clients. He translated at the 1905 Baltimore trial of an alleged triad member accused of swindling and forgery, for example. The following year, he was obliged to bring suit for non-payment of $1,088.10 against the Baltimore-based Wah Gee Tong, or Chinese Harmony Society, which had retained him in the case. Perhaps most ironically, he served as a government interpreter in Buffalo in a 1908 smuggling case in which a motorboat filled with "contraband Chinamen" had been wrecked on a breakwater in Lake Erie, causing three deaths.

Now it was Jin Fuey's turn to be charged with smuggling. Or, more precisely, it was his turn once again, since his discharge from government service in 1902 had occurred because of alleged

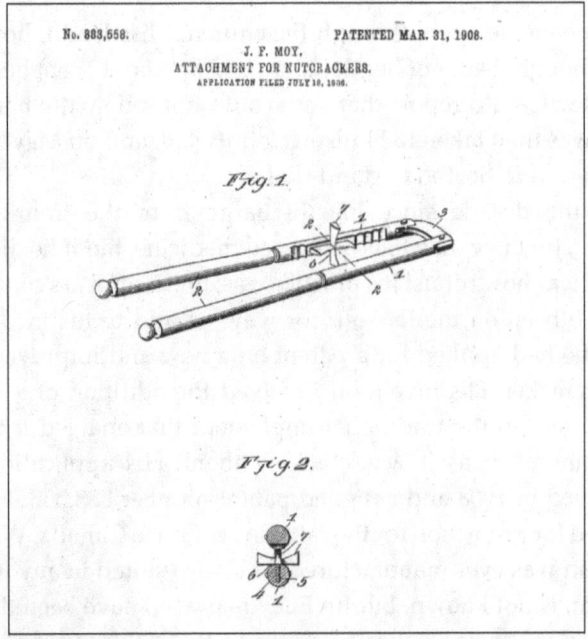

U.S. Patent number 883,558 for an attachment for nutcrackers was issued to Jin Fuey on March 31, 1908. Source: United States Patent and Trademark Office, Alexandria, VA.

trafficking in Chinese laborers. After he arrived in Boston, he was given over to the custody of U.S. Marshall Thomas J. Alcott and held for trial, which began on May 16. The *Boston Journal* reported, without foundation, that he was "reputed to be the wealthiest Chinaman in America, and a merchant in Mott Street." The former assertion may have been a popular impression, but it surely was as untrue as the latter. In a letter to Gop Jung written just nine months before the indictment, Jin Fuey had bemoaned his lack of funds:

> Now, my dear Gop Jung, I have long been thinking of going back to China, but where is the money or any prospect for me to raise enough money for my expenses for going over there. I mean enough expenses just for my own self, without anyone else. I know that there

is a better opportunity for me, but I am crippled just on account of the traveling expenses for going. I have heard of this same advice nearly from everyone I know, but everyone thinks that I am a millionaire, and have had some money hidden somewhere, and afraid to reveal it. If I have five hundred dollars, you will not see me here long.

This was apparently the second time in his life that Jin Fuey flirted with returning to China. He had inquired with the government in 1889 about procedures for readmission in the event of a trip back. His reference to the prospect of a "better opportunity" for him in China is curious, especially so late in his career. He did not elaborate on it, but perhaps he believed that he could make a better living there as a Western-trained physician. However, the fact that he was not envisioning taking his wife with him, coupled with the reality that his re-entry into the United States would be anything but guaranteed, calls into question how seriously he was really considering a trip, or a permanent return, to his native land.

The common belief that Jin Fuey was well-heeled may have had something to do with his comportment. A press account of his appearance before Commissioner Carpenter in Jersey City prior to his transfer to Boston noted that "a quiet looking citizen enough is Dr. Jin Fuey Moy, who appeared with his American wife, his American frock coat, his almost American daughter and $4,000 worth of American made family jewels before the Federal commissioner in Jersey City the other day," going on to describe his "slick, short hair, his smile and his pearl stickpin."

Jin Fuey's lament to his cousin belies the fact that he and Hattie lived in a lovely home and were able to come up with $6,000 worth of jewelry on short notice to offer up for bail. But appearances to the contrary notwithstanding, it does suggest that money remained a problem for him. He was either unable or unwilling to produce bail in the amount of $3,000 in Boston, and consequently remained in jail throughout the trial.

Jin Fuey's co-defendants in the case, all of whom pleaded not guilty, were less than savory characters. Gardinier, known as "Chick," was well-known to Federal authorities, having recently served a sentence for mail fraud. He had sold hen and duck eggs for $2.80 each, claiming they were the eggs of rare fowl. He had met Phillips, a former tailor, in jail; the latter was serving a term for the attempted smuggling of Chinese from Mexico. Both had been released the previous summer. Daley, too, had spent time in prison for conspiracy to smuggle Chinese; he had been freed the preceding June. Federal agents had been watching all three of them, confident they would be up to something again before long.

First to testify in the trial was U.S. Special Agent Clyde Ambrose, a former constable and private dick. Posing as a wealthy man seeking profitable investments, he had met

Jin Fuey was unable, or unwilling, to produce bail in the amount of $3,000 in Boston. He remained in jail throughout the trial. Source: National Archives and Records Administration, Waltham, MA.

Gardinier in Jamaica, he attested, and it was Gardinier who had proposed the smuggling scheme, promising Ambrose a quick return of thousands of dollars for each $150 invested. The plan was to use Daley's $25,000 steam yacht to travel from Boston to Port Antonio, Jamaica, pick up the Chinese laborers and discharge them in several locations near Boston, on Long Island and on the Potomac River. There was apparently an arrangement to import and sell opium as well.

When Gardinier and Ambrose returned to the United States, Ambrose recalled, they met with Jin Fuey, whom they expected to furnish letters of introduction to Chinese in Jamaica. Later, at the Adams House Hotel in Boston, there was a final meeting on the eve of the planned departure in which Ambrose handed Gardinier a check for $700. He and Phillips were immediately taken into custody by U.S. marshals for accepting the money; Daley was arrested later.

The principal witness for the prosecution was a Miss May Graham of Philadelphia, who had met Gardinier aboard ship on his way to Jamaica and been his companion there. He had disclosed his plans to her and she had lent him $1,000, ostensibly to buy fruit – he claimed to be a produce dealer – but actually to hire a boat. A letter Gardinier had written her after his arrest that had been spirited out of prison was read aloud in court; apart from revealing his plans to divorce his wife for her, it also contained damning instructions not to mention to anyone that the money was to be used to procure a boat, or that the boat was to be used to smuggle Chinese into the United States.

On May 18, after the letter was read, the government rested its case, and it was the defense's turn. Jin Fuey was the only defendant to take the stand. He admitted meeting Ambrose at the Broadway Central Hotel in New York and at 11 Mott Street in Chinatown, but disavowed any conversation about smuggling. He denied any complicity in the plot and testified that he knew at once that Ambrose was a government agent from a letter marked "Department of Justice" visible in his pocket, and that he told him to leave the shop. Hattie Moy testified as well, as did Mrs. Daly, but what they said is not recorded. No transcript of Jin Fuey's statement survives, but his testimony was covered in the *Boston Globe* and a detailed account of his story, which reveals that the plan was as much about smuggling opium as laborers, exists in a letter he wrote the following month to his cousin Gop Jung:

THREE TOUGH CHINAMEN

Ambrose insisted I should go up to Gardinier's room . . . After entering said room, Ambrose stated that he had smuggled 400 cans of Lai Yuen opium, and paid $8 per can in Jamaica. In the forenoon of that day, Ambrose caused the sale of 14 cans at $24 per can, realized $336, and were [sic] desirous for me to sell same for him. I told Ambrose that I knew nothing about opium, nor know any way that I was able to dispose of it for him; but I asked him in what way was he able to land the 400 cans of opium weighing 200 pounds, without detection by the custom inspectors on the dock or wharf. Ambrose replied that he could do it again.

He continued:

At 12:10 at noon on April 3, 1911, Ambrose called at No. 11 Mott Street . . . He greeted me and wished to see me privately . . . He stated he had sold all the opium and made over $6,000, and wished to go down to Jamaica, with Phillips and Gardinier, and Captain Daly, to smuggle Chinamen into the United States. I told him then and there, I did not know Phillips nor Captain Daly, and told him to get the hell out of there, or else I would kick him out.

He went on to say that Ambrose had received a letter from Gardinier stating that Jin Fuey could demand $450 per Chinaman, and that he was personally indicted by the letter. But apparently he had known Phillips, because the latter had been found with a check signed by him. Jin Fuey acknowledged that he had sent the check, and said it was for tickets to bring over two of his nephews from Liverpool to Canada, and that he had post-dated it so he could stop payment if the ticket orders turned out to be fraudulent. The orders were also produced as exhibits in the trial.

The principal evidence against Jin Fuey was the check, and while it was suggestive of complicity, it was not conclusive. The jury retired at 4:30 p.m. the following day, May 19, and reached a verdict after only four hours: Phillips and Gardinier were found guilty, but Daly and Jin Fuey were acquitted. Hattie Moy embraced her husband tearfully and ran to congratulate his attorney. Jin Fuey crowed to a reporter, "They arrested the wrong man when they arrested me."

The verdict, however, belies the larger picture of the company Jin Fuey kept, his detailed knowledge of the economics of smuggling, his "street smarts" in such matters and his expressed need for money. If he truly "knew nothing about opium," as he asserted, he soon would know all there was to know about it. And if he was not, in fact, already corrupt, he soon would be.

Chapter XV
Reversal of Fortune I

In early 1906, Jin Kee had traveled to Washington as the "mayor" of Indianapolis' Chinatown, a fifth-degree Mandarin and the titular head of a national effort to secure rights for Chinese-Americans. He had collaborated with the Chinese Legation and met with President Theodore Roosevelt. By late 1907, however, all of that had changed. On October 19, he received a letter from the Chinese minister in Washington informing him that he had been ousted from his Chinatown position and stripped of his rank as a Mandarin.

The "mayors" of America's Chinatowns during this period were apparently appointed, not elected. Such titles may have seemed informal, but the selection of incumbents was serious business, and was almost certainly a process undertaken in consultation with the Manchu government, acting through the Chinese missions in Washington and elsewhere in the country. After all, very few Chinese in the United States were American citizens; they all remained subjects of the Emperor, and, as such, ostensibly continued to live under his authority. Jin Kee's elevation in 1904 had been choreographed by China's U.S.-based diplomats, and so, in 1907, was his demotion.

The reason for this reversal of fortune is not entirely apparent. There were several versions of the story. The dubious report that circulated at the time of the announcement was that Jin Kee and Pang Wah Jung, the "vice mayor," had accepted a contract to settle a longstanding land dispute between their two clans in China for $1,000, which was not paid to them as it should have been. Their enemies, so the story went, obtained an audience with the Empress Dowager and accused them of fraud. The result was an official order depriving them of their rank. At the time, Jin Kee dismissed the allegations as trumped up charges and complained that neither he nor Pang had been given an opportunity to be heard before the decision was handed down.

It is not at all likely that a private land dispute among Cantonese clans would have been adjudicated in far-off America or would have come to the attention of the Empress in Beijing. What is more probable is that Jin Kee had enemies who were determined to depose him, and that these adversaries were closer to home than China. After all, except for two brief interludes, Jin Kee had by this time lived in America for about half a century. He had certainly left behind some seriously frayed relationships in Chicago, but one did not need to look any further than Indianapolis to find detractors. One irritant was his interpretation in the trial of the accused murderers of "Doc" Lung, an Indianapolis laundryman who had been bludgeoned to death with a meat cleaver and nearly decapitated in 1902. Three black men had been tried for his murder, which was allegedly committed in the process of robbing him, but which may also have been commissioned, along with several others, by two local physicians seeking cadavers for dissection. Jin Kee told a reporter that he had earned the enmity of some local Chinese who had felt he was working against their interests in providing interpretation. He suspected it was they who were behind the action of the Chinese minister.

A year and a half later, Jin Kee related yet another, more plausible, version of his fall from grace to a U.S. Immigration officer while he and his wife, on their way back from China, were detained in Smith Cove, Washington. According to this story, his ouster had nothing to do with land in China or court interpreting and everything to do with the alleged mishandling of funds in the United States:

> After the earthquake at San Francisco we subscribed some money

for the relief of the sufferers at San Francisco and I had charge of taking the subscriptions and then during the flood in Quong Si [*Guangxi*] China I went and took up another subscription to send for their relief and I gave receipts for all money collected and had it published in the papers, and some members of the Pong [sic] family owed me some money and I went and collected the debts they owed me and this Pong Que Fong went and told the Acting Minister at Washington that I was going around swindling money from the Chinese and that way the Acting Minister said he would reduce my rank.

Yet a fourth account was published years later in Jin Kee's *Indianapolis Star* obituary. According to the *Star*, it was "through some unfortunate circumstances in which he was accused of illegally assisting two Chinese youths into this country, and of defrauding some of the local Chinese."

The decision to strip him of his rank was far more likely made in Washington than Beijing, but it is absurd to believe that the Chinese government would have retaliated against Jin Kee for fraudulently importing Chinese youths into the United States. Doing so would have been a violation of an American law, not a Chinese law, and in any case it was a widespread practice during this era. Mishandling of relief funds, however, could well have provided sufficient reason, or at least sufficient pretext, for the demotion. Friends of Jin Kee appealed in vain to Minister Wu Ting Fang, who once again was heading the Chinese mission, to reverse the order.

Whatever the proximate cause of Jin Kee's demotion, it was a deeply humbling experience for someone who had been so prominent and had commanded so much respect. The disgrace may have led directly to the decision by Jin Kee and Chin Fung the following year to pull up stakes and go back to China. Whether they intended ever to return to the United States is open to question. On the one hand, they sold their restaurant at 506 E. Washington Street for $1,000 to their three business partners,

Dong Gum Hong, Moy Hee and Moy Hun – all Jin Kee's cousins – although the finality of this sale would later be denied. And Jin Kee was reported to have announced, before his departure, his intention to live out his remaining years in China.

On the other hand, Jin Kee and his wife each filed a "Statement of Registered Chinese Laborer About to Depart from the United States with the Intention of Returning Thereto" with the Immigration Bureau on October 15, 1907. Laborers who owned more than $1,000 worth of property or had uncollected debts in the United States of at least that amount – or some combination of the two – were permitted to return as long as they reported their financial details on the form and received return certificates before they left the country. Both Jin Kee and Chin Fung listed the following assets: "Half interest in restaurant No. 506 E. Washington St., Indianapolis worth $2,500. Also half interest in lots 142 & 143 Vajins [Vajens] So. Brookside addition of Indianapolis on Oxford St. worth $1,300." Thus, each of them claimed $1,900 in assets, which was more than enough to ensure re-entry.

Although the couple did own the restaurant when they filled out the form, they actually sold it two days later, after they and their three partners had all been deposed in connection with the applications for return certificates. No one technically supplied any false information. The partners readily admitted they were going to run the business in Jin Kee's absence and affirmed that no assets had been transferred. The transaction does muddy the waters, however, as to whether the couple really intended to come back. Probably they did not know themselves; after all, neither had set foot in China for nearly 25 years, and it's likely that they wanted to see what living there would be like for them after so much time in America. In disposing of assets but pretending they had not done so, they were simply hedging their bets.

The Immigration Bureau was satisfied that Jin Kee's restaurant was worth at least what he claimed, and also examined the deeds

THREE TOUGH CHINAMEN

STATEMENT OF REGISTERED CHINESE LABORER ABOUT TO DEPART FROM THE UNITED STATES WITH THE INTENTION OF RETURNING THERETO.

Made in compliance with the act of Congress "An Act to prohibit the coming into and to regulate the residence within the United States, its Territories, and all territory under its jurisdiction, and the District of Columbia, of Chinese persons and persons of Chinese descent", approved April 29, 1902; and the Rules and Regulations of the Secretary of Commerce and Labor in conformity therewith.

I HEREBY DECLARE that I am Chinese laborer, duly registered as such, under the act of May 5, 1892, as amended by the act of November 3, 1893. My certificate of residence which is attached to this statement was issued by the Collector of Internal Revenue for the _First_ district of _Illinois_, at _Chicago_ dated _April 13 1893_, and numbered _53274_.

Name _Mrs Chin Fung Kee_
Present age, _51_ years
Local residence, _Indianapolis Ind_
Occupation _Restaurateur wife of Moy Kee_
Height: _5_ feet, _X_ inches.
_____ lbs.
Color of eyes, _brown_
Complexion _dark_
Physical marks or peculiarities for identification _bound feet_

I CLAIM TO POSSESS THE FAMILY, or property, or debts described below:
PROPERTY: Full description, _Half interest in restaurant at No 58 & E Washington Indianapolis Ind worth $2500. also half interest in lots 142 & 143 Vajens & Brookside addition of Indianapolis on Oxford St worth $1300.00_ Value, $_1900.00_

I HEREBY AGREE that none of such property or debts shall be diverted, transferred, or collected during my absence, and that the above described claims shall remain as they now exist until my return.
I RESPECTFULLY REQUEST a certificate of my right to return to the United States.

Subscribed & sworn to before me Oct 15" 1907
L. R. Plummer
Chinese & Immigrant Inspector

Chin Fung Kee
mark

Pre-Departure statement with photo filed by Chin Fung, known as Chin Fung Kee, on October 15, 1907. Source: National Archives and Records Administration, Chicago, IL.

for the lots, which had been purchased on the installment plan, and found that the couple had recently acquired full title to them. It therefore authorized the issuance of return certificates for them on October 19, and within a day or two they left Indianapolis for Seattle, where they would actually receive the certificates. They set sail for China on October 26.

What happened to them in China is not known, except that after a year there they had clearly decided that living in America was preferable. On February 14, 1909, they boarded the U.S.-bound S.S. *Suveric* in Hong Kong, and on March 11 landed at the Port of Tacoma, Washington, intending to resume their lives in Indianapolis. Doing so, however, turned out to be far more difficult than they expected. The two were detained by Immigration officers, who must have found some reason to question their eligibility. On March 13, the Seattle office wired the Chicago office, which held Jin Kee and Chin Fung's files, inquiring as to whether there had been any change in their status since their departure in 1907. Within a week came the response, in the form of a cryptic telegram: "Adverse report Moy Kee and wife forwarded today. Find property transferred," it read.

This initial report did not constitute sufficient evidence to deport the couple immediately, but nor was it a green light for re-entry. What it did was to trigger a full-scale investigation to determine whether they were entitled to readmission. In the meantime, they were lodged in a two-story building at Smith Cove that had been constructed for the Immigration Service two years earlier by the Great Northern Railway in order to entice shipping lines to dock there, so that disembarking passengers might board its trains for points east. Great Northern had promised the Immigration Service a first-class station, "modern in all respects," with hot water baths on each floor. What it delivered, however, was a drab firetrap that included a small hospital, office and a canteen, but lacked indoor plumbing and was poorly ventilated. Women were assigned to the first floor and men to the second. It was already overcrowded by 1909

THREE TOUGH CHINAMEN

First page of the Chinese passenger manifest from the S.S. Suveric, which docked at the Port of Tacoma, Washington on March 11, 1909. Jin Kee, a.k.a. Moy Kee, and his wife Chin Fung are listed on the last two lines. Source: National Archives and Records Administration, Washington, DC.

when Seattle's Chief Sanitary Officer proclaimed it one of the most unsanitary structures in the city.

Upon receipt of the inquiry from Seattle, the Chicago office dispatched an inspector to Indianapolis to determine whether there had been any material change in the couple's financial situation there. He discovered that the restaurant, its fixtures and its inventory had all been sold prior to their departure and acquired a copy of the bill of sale. And with only the two Oxford Street lots as assets – even at the declared value of $1,300, which was a stretch – the couple fell short by $700 of the $2,000 minimum – $1,000 per person – that would permit their re-entry.

Word of the Moys' predicament got out, whether from Jin Kee himself, who was allowed to write letters while detained, or because of the investigation itself. The result was that pressure to admit the couple was brought to bear from several quarters on Lorenzo T. Plummer, the Chinese Inspector in Charge at the Bureau's Chicago office. On March 23, Plummer received a letter from Charles W. Moores, a well-known Indianapolis attorney and civic leader. Moores wrote on the letterhead of his law firm, but made it clear that he was inquiring not as Jin Kee's lawyer, but rather in his capacity as a Federal commissioner "interested in having Moy protected, if he is entitled to protection." He noted that Jin Kee had been granted U.S. citizenship, and sent proof of it along as an enclosure. Why the fact of Jin Kee's citizenship alone did not obviate the need for an investigation and ensure immediate re-admission for the couple is certainly a valid question, and the inescapable conclusion to which it points is that the Exclusion Act and its successor legislation had, in the eyes of the government, cast serious doubt on the validity of that citizenship, even though it had never officially been revoked.

In his response, Plummer noted that Chinese workers seeking readmission could base their claims on familial relationships with others already in the United States. He mentioned an event that had taken place in Port Huron, Michigan five years earlier, when two young men were granted entry after Jin Kee testified, and Chin Fung confirmed, that they were their sons. Oddly, Jin Kee had made no reference to the two men in any of his arguments for admission.

On March 26, Plummer was visited in Chicago by Dr. E. C. Bachfield, an Indianapolis dentist who had known Jin Kee for eight years. Bachfield came to share information about additional American assets he believed Jin Kee might not have reported, specifically 40 shares of stock in the Indiana Broom Company, a manufacturer of brooms and cleaning supplies that Bachfield had helped establish in 1907. He was the corporation's Secretary, and he produced a certificate for 40 shares of stock that had been issued to him on November 18, 1907 and that he, in turn, had endorsed and transferred to Jin Kee on November 28. And he informed Plummer that while the stock's par value was $25 per share, its actual value could be calculated at 75 cents on the dollar.

Because this alleged transfer of assets had occurred a little more than a month after Jin Kee had departed for China,

Plummer pursued the topic with follow-up questions. Jin Kee, it turned out, had paid for the stock not with cash, but with two diamond rings, one valued by a diamond expert at $260 and the other at $300. Since the stock Plummer owned was denominated in lots of 40 shares, he had transferred one entire lot to Jin Kee, at a price of $18.75 per share. Thus Jin Kee owned the stock, but by that calculation he also owed Backfield $190.

Backfield also produced a sworn statement from George F. Young, Treasurer of the Mutual Ice Company of Indianapolis, to the effect that Jin Kee held $50 worth of that corporation's bonds and an unspecified number of shares of stock. And he provided further information on the disposition of the restaurant. He said he had learned from Moy Hee and Dong Gum Hong that the $1,000 Jin Kee had received from his partners was, in fact, borrowed money; that the bill of sale for the restaurant was merely collateral for the loan; and that their intention was to transfer the property back to Jin Kee upon his return from China and repayment of the loan.

At this point, Plummer decided to broaden the investigation, and over the next several weeks he cast a wide net in order to gather all relevant information about the Moys. The first step was another visit to Indianapolis. He dispatched Inspector Harry E. Tippett to interview Jin Kee's business partners and the attorney who had drawn up the papers for the sale of the restaurant. In light of the information provided by Bachfield, the questioning of the Chinese partners centered on the precise terms under which title to the restaurant had been conferred upon them.

Moy Hee asserted he had lent Jin Kee $333.33 before his departure, that the restaurant had been offered as collateral for the debt, and that he expected the property to revert to Jin Kee when the latter returned and repaid the loan. Dong Gum Hong's story was quite different. He maintained that the property *had* been sold and that he had paid his share of the $1,000 directly to Jin Kee. He also acknowledged receiving the bill of sale from Cass Conaway, the attorney who had handled the transaction.

And in his own deposition, Conaway made it clear that all four men had fully understood the terms of the transaction at the time it took place, and that it had been a *bona fide* sale.

Moy Hun denied he had purchased the restaurant, and, in fact, denied paying Jin Kee anything at all before his departure. He characterized his arrangement with Jin Kee as a promise to maintain and pay taxes on the property during the latter's absence, but nonetheless referred frequently in his deposition to his "interest" in the restaurant, which he said would revert to Jin Kee upon his return and upon his making a payment to

Moy Hee, Jin Kee's first cousin, who took over the Indianapolis restaurant together with two others when Jin Kee returned to China in 1907. Source: Indiana Historical Society.

him. He also allowed that he had been born in the same village as Jin Kee and had known him since they were boys, prompting Inspector Tippett to probe into the matter of Jin Kee's alleged sons. Moy Hun affirmed that Chin Fung was Jin Kee's one and only wife, but was vague – surely deliberately so – on the subject of whether she had ever borne children.

The questions Tippett asked in Indianapolis gave a fairly clear idea as to what Immigration likely now believed about those children. In 1904, Jin Kee had gone to Port Huron to testify that two 21 year-old men who had been detained there were his sons Ning Tong and Ning Yip, and were entitled to enter because they were American-born. They were in reality members of a family named Ning and surely foreign-born. Once Jin Kee had vouched for them and Chin Fung had submitted an affidavit, however, they were admitted. But then he allegedly brought them to Indianapolis and confined them in his basement for five or six weeks until the Ning family secured their release with a $750 payment.

It was common practice for Chinese to make representations to the government claiming parentage of non-existent children in order to create a paper trail that could be employed later to arrange the fraudulent admission of the children of relatives, or even those entirely unrelated, in exchange for payment. Hence the term "paper sons," which was often used to describe them. In all likelihood, the need to create such a paper trail in anticipation of the arrival of the young men is why Chin Fung had told a census taker in 1900 that she had given birth to three children.

Since Jin Kee and Chin Fung would potentially have had a

Record of the case of Ning Yip, a.k.a. Hai Gim, who, together with Ning Tong, a.k.a. Say Fong, was suspected of entering the United States illegally and arrested on July 15, 1904. The two were released and admitted when Jin Kee testified falsely that he was their father and that they had been born in San Francisco. Source: National Archives and Records Administration, Chicago, IL.

valid claim for readmission if their sons had been American-born and were living in the United States – even though they had not advanced any such claim – Plummer wrote for the files relating to the cases of the two young men. He also made an effort to find others who might confirm whether Jin Kee and Chin Fung had actually had any children. For this, he didn't need to look beyond Chinatown in Chicago, where he worked. Jin Kee, after all, had lived there for 11 years between 1886 and 1897. He was also, of course, reviled by some in Chicago's Chinese community, and his list of enemies, which extended to several members of his own clan, included Moy You Bong (Moy Sing), Moy Dung Hoy and Hip Lung.

Plummer had Tippett depose the three of them as well as two other Chicago Chinese on April 5. Among the five were men who had known Jin Kee in China (one was from his home village), in San Francisco in the 1870s and later in Chicago. The men were unanimous in affirming several key facts: that Jin Kee had only one wife, Chin Fung; that she had not been with him while he lived in San Francisco; and that the couple was childless. ("She never give birth to anything," Moy Dung Hoy sneered). And while some of these witnesses were probably still hostile to Jin Kee and would have relished causing him trouble, it's unlikely all of them were lying.

Tippett summarized his findings in a formal report to Plummer on April 7. Among them:

- The bill of sale for Jin Kee's restaurant represented an absolute sale, rather than a loan;
- Shares of Indiana Broom Company, even if Jin Kee had claimed them, were worthless;
- The two lots on Oxford Street in Indianapolis were worth only about $375 each;
- A claim made by Jin Kee that Dong Gum Hong owed him $500 for interpreting services provided several years earlier was bogus;
- Shares of the Mutual Ice Company were valueless; and

- The court at Port Huron that had permitted the two ostensible "sons" to enter the United States had "been imposed upon," and Jin Kee could not possibly have been their father.

His conclusion was that "Moy Kee and his wife have not established property rights sufficient to comply with the law or to warrant their admission into the United States. So far as to their claim of children here, I think there has been enough testimony obtained to show that he never had any children, and that the two boys that were landed by the U.S. Commissioner at Port Huron were admitted upon the perjured testimony of Moy Kee and his wife, the applicants."

Plummer accepted Tippett's conclusions and forwarded the report to Seattle with a comment of his own: "While it is true that the Commissioner at Port Huron is *res adjudicata* [a matter already judged] as to the fact that the two boys who were discharged September 15, 1904 were born in the United States, I do not believe the decision is binding upon the Government to the extent that they are the children of Moy Kee and his wife." In other words, Jin Kee and Chin Fung would not necessarily derive any benefit from the earlier decision about the birth of these two young men if Immigration now doubted the veracity of their story.

After receiving the Tippett report, the Seattle office ordered Acting Inspector in Charge Harry A. Monroe to re-examine Jin Kee and Chin Fung and permit them an opportunity to refute the findings. The couple was questioned separately, Jin Kee on April 14 and Chin Fung on April 17. Much of what they said simply contradicted what others had said about them without offering any new evidence that might be persuasive. But on the subject of children they made matters worse, for more conflicting information came out.

Chin Fung testified that she had borne two children in China before coming to the United States, but that both had died. Jin Kee had initially maintained that they had had no children in China, but eventually allowed that they had had a daughter there. Jin Kee said Chin Fung had given birth to their eldest child in San Francisco in 1883, their second child 18 months later and a third two years after that. Chin Fung named the three children – Mong Bin, Moy Ming Gen and Ning Fong – but gave their ages as 28, 25 and 24, which did not comport with Jin Kee's recollections. Jin Kee said the children had been sent back to China in the care of an uncle because Chin Fung had been too ill to care for them; Chin Fung said it was a sister-in-law who had taken them back because she and Jin Kee had been moving around too much. And none of the three names or ages she gave squared with those of the two young men who had been admitted at Port Huron in 1904 as their sons.

"In view of the fact that you are not able to give the date of the birth of your children and the further fact that you do not seem to have cared for them and especially as Chinese do for their male children," Inspector Monroe asked Jin Kee, "are we not justified in believing and placing some credence in the statements made by Moy Sing, Moy Sung You, Lee Park, Hip Lung and Moy Dung Hoy, all of Chicago; all of your family some of whom claim to have known your family in China yet all say that they never heard of your ever having any children born to your wife in this country or in China?" It was essentially a rhetorical – if an appallingly ungrammatical – question.

In a surprising turn of events, however, Inspector Monroe wrote Plummer on April 22 giving his reasons for concluding that the two applicants should be admitted after all. He based his recommendation solely on the value of their American-based assets, tipping in Jin Kee's favor on the more controversial claims, such as the finality of the sale of the restaurant. Between the two lots, some valid claims Jin Kee possessed against Dr. Bachfield, the Mutual Ice Company and Moy Hun and the value of the restaurant – two thirds ownership of which had just been deeded back to Jin Kee by Moy Hun and Moy Hee – Monroe calculated that Jin Kee and Chin Fung's assets exceeded $2,000 and concluded they were therefore eligible for re-entry.

Behind-the-scenes politics was very likely responsible for this decision, because the facts as recounted by Plummer certainly did not support a positive recommendation. But whether Monroe had made a good faith re-assessment of the situation or had been leaned on by some unseen force, on April 21, 1909, after more than five weeks in detention, Jin Kee and Chin Fung were once again admitted into the United States. After spending a few days with friends in Seattle, they proceeded to Indianapolis to resume their lives in America.

Despite this latest humiliation at the hands of the U.S. government, and despite his demotion from the position of "mayor" of Indianapolis' Chinatown by the Chinese government two years earlier, Jin Kee's reputation seems to have remained relatively untarnished. In July, he took a short trip to Kalamazoo, Michigan as the guest of Charlie Lamb, the Chinese owner of a local chop suey restaurant and of Doc Waddell, general agent for the Lambrigger Wild Animal Show, a circus that was, at the time, performing at the city's Haymarket. Both were old friends, and Jin Kee was doing

A prominent international visitor is due in Kalamazoo today. He will be the guest of Charles Lamb, owner of the Chop Suey parlor on South Burdick and of the Lambrigger Wild Animal show exhibiting on the Haymarket. The Celestial is Moy Kee, the Chinese mayor of America. He is the only Chinaman who ever hunted wild animals and has been over the territory now being covered by Roosevelt. He has also hunted in India and helped capture the big snake of the Lambrigger show. It is given out Moy Kee will be present when the big monster Python is fed.

On July 23, 1909, the Kalamazoo Gazette hailed Jin Kee as the "Chinese Mayor of America." Article used with permission. Copyright 1909, Kalamazoo Gazette. All rights reserved.

business with Waddell, because he was listed as the manager of the show's commissary department.

Jin Kee's trip was covered in the *Kalamazoo Gazette*, which celebrated him as "the Chinese Mayor of America." It described his appearance in vivid detail, noting his "stunning gowns" in one article, his "loose silk toga" and his "coal-black silken queue" in another. It also printed some bogus "facts" about him: that he was "the only Chinaman who ever hunted wild animals," that he had hunted them in India, and that he had helped capture the monster python then on display in the Lambrigger show.

The *Gazette* followed Jin Kee for three days, describing his activities in some detail. On his third day in Kalamazoo, Jin Kee visited the circus. "Austere in mien, stern of countenance and with the bland eye characteristic of his race, Mr. Moy carefully scrutinized each animal and bird in the show, expressing keen interest," The *Gazette* reported. He also was the subject of a verbal attack from Prince, a large parrot, who, at the sight of him, "flapped his wings and screeched a horse laugh that brought the bird and animal kingdom to attention."

Jin Kee did not apparently take umbrage at this embarrassment, and instead accepted it as good fun. And it certainly was, compared to another indignity he would soon face at the hands of the U.S. government, which unbeknownst to him had already begun a formal inquiry into the legality of his citizenship.

Chapter XVI
Reversal of Fortune II

In 1910, His Imperial Highness Prince Tsai Tao (*Zaitao*), brother of the Prince Regent of China and uncle of the young Emperor Pu Yi, set out on a month-long visit to the United States to study the American military system. The Prince was chief of the general staff of the Imperial Army, which he was determined to modernize. He stopped in Japan for a week and Honolulu for a few days on the way to the U.S. mainland. "To the astonishment of his countrymen," the *New York Times* reported after he landed in Hawaii, "the Prince was dressed in the conventional civilian dress of Europeans and Americans, wearing a frock coat and high hat. For a Chinese official to wear such a garb on a ceremonious occasion was declared to be unprecedented, and caused much comment."

By 1910, the Qing Dynasty was on the verge of collapse, and much of what was happening was unprecedented. The Prince arrived in Washington on April 28 and called on President William Howard Taft, and later that evening attended a cavalry drill at nearby Fort Myer, together with 10 officers from China's army and navy. The following day, he inspected the gun foundry, ordnance shops and storehouses at the Washington Navy Yard. He then went on to West Point, and while there delivered a startling announcement: The queues of all the soldiers in the Chinese army would soon be cut off, and he expected to remove his own upon his return to China, provided the Prince Regent approved. The officers traveling with him had already been shorn of their pigtails.

The Chinese had first adopted queues when the Manchus,

who had established the Qing Dynasty in 1644, ordered them to wear their hair in this fashion as a symbol of submission. The penalty for non-compliance was death, as was made clear in the popular slogan, "Keep your hair and lose your head, or keep your head and cut your hair." Many Chinese who had resisted the humiliating order had lost their lives as a result. After a few hundred years, however, queues gradually came to be accepted, paradoxically, as a symbol of national culture and pride, and even many Chinese living abroad refused to part with them, especially those who expected to return to China at some point.

But things were changing. During some anti-Manchu demonstrations in China, people had begun to cut their hair as a political statement against the weakening dynasty. Many overseas Chinese, including some in America, had already parted with their pigtails and adopted a totally Western appearance, and the younger they were and the more Americanized they became, the more willing they were to do so. Now, some of the ruling Manchus themselves were beginning to talk seriously about getting rid of the queues.

When Prince Tsai Tao returned to Beijing, he reported that the wearing of queues was making the Chinese look ridiculous in the eyes of Westerners, and though there was some opposition, the Prince Regent, who had also traveled abroad, apparently agreed with him. In the fall of 1910, an Imperial edict was sent by telegraph to Chinese missions around the world ordering all Chinese diplomats to remove

Prince Tsai Tao, uncle of the Emperor of China, in military regalia. The Prince, who was Chief of the General Staff of the Imperial Army, favored the removal of queues by all Chinese soldiers.

their queues. China's consul in San Francisco appeared without his for the first time on November 4. And the *San Francisco Chronicle* reported on November 7 that "there was a steady procession of well-known residents of the local Oriental colony to the barbershops of Chinatown yesterday, and many queues which had for years been a source of pride to their owners fell victims to the operators' shears."

Jin Kee – initially, at least – was appalled by the rush to chop off queues. "Moy Kee has revolted; he is defiant," the *Indianapolis Star* reported on November 14, 1910. "By all his ancestors he vows . . . he will not forswear his queue." Though no longer officially the "mayor of Chinatown," Jin Kee was still occasionally referred to as such, and in any event remained prominent; with his excellent English skills, he continued to serve as a source for reporters writing stories about China. "Not if every other Chinese in the world cuts off his cue will Moy part with his," the report went on to say.

Early the following year, his Excellency Wu Ting Fang, by now the former Chinese Minister to the United States, announced that on January 30, 1911 he would cut off his own queue. This was taken as a signal by Chinese in the United States, and there was an understanding among them that on that same day, Chinese across America would do the same. "Great preparations for the 'cutting day' are being made among the 2,000 inhabitants of Chicago's Chinatown," the *Star* reported on January 16, "likewise at San Francisco and other large cities." But Indianapolis' Chinese would not participate, at least not as a group. "There will be no action among members of our colony," Jin Kee told the newspaper. "There are about fifty Chinamen in Indianapolis and all but a few have long ago parted with long braids of hair."

Astonishingly, though, he seems to have had a complete change of heart in just a month's time. "It is a sensible idea," Jin Kee was quoted as saying in January. "I had my queue cut off several years ago and I don't know that I ever felt the loss of it." This, of course, in no way squared with the comments attributed to him by the same newspaper the previous month, or the 1909 description of him with his queue intact that had appeared in the *Kalamazoo Gazette*, but no one apparently pursued the point. "Chinamen the world over will welcome the decree to cut off their queues," he opined. Whether he had truly changed his mind, or whether pressure had been brought to bear on him from some quarter, is unclear.

A Chinese man in San Francisco with a queue, photographed before 1910 by Laura Adams Armer. Courtesy of California Historical Society, FN-08023. Used with permission.

Queue-cutting was the least of the changes in store for Chinese in 1911 when revolutionary forces ended more than 2,000 years of dynastic rule in China, overthrew the Manchus and established the Republic of China. For Jin Kee, however, change of a different and most unwelcome sort was imminent, and much closer to home. His native land had visited an indignity on him when it summarily stripped him of his rank in 1907. In 1911, it was the turn of his adopted country to disgrace him. It set out to deprive him of his hard-won citizenship.

The impetus for the effort to rescind his citizenship came from the State Department before he and his wife returned from China, and was not a result of the Immigration Bureau's investigation of them upon their return. On February 17, 1909, the Department had sent Jin Kee's naturalization certificate to the Commerce and Labor Department, to which the Bureau of

Naturalization belonged, "for appropriate action." Although the cover letter from the State Department was silent on the matter, the Naturalization Bureau understood that the reason for the dispatch was that the Department considered that, as a Chinese, Jin Kee had been rendered ineligible for citizenship.

"Appropriate action" meant forwarding Jin Kee's file to the Justice Department, which the Bureau did on February 24, noting that Chinese were ineligible under section 14 of the Chinese Exclusion Act. The matter was then referred to the U.S. Attorney in Indianapolis for investigation, with the proviso that if legal warrant were found, "proceedings be instituted at the earliest practicable date for the vacation of the order of the court admitting the said Kee [sic] to citizenship, and for the revocation and cancellation of the order to naturalization." There was little question, of course, that legal warrant would be found.

The matter was therefore pending when Jin Kee returned to Indianapolis after emerging from detention in Smith Cove on April 18, but little attention seems to have been paid to the exhortation to address it at the "earliest practicable date." In fact, very little happened until the middle of 1911, which was the first time Jin Kee found out about the proceedings. On August 4, as he waited on a customer in his restaurant on E. Washington Street, he received word that a petition had been filed in federal court to strip him of his citizenship, and he dropped a dish and stared silently for several moments, according to the *Indianapolis Star*. "A look of anguish clouded his customarily smiling countenance. It was one of the saddest moments of his life," the paper added.

"It's no use to buck Uncle Sam, I guess," Jin Kee said, even though few Chinese had a record of bucking Uncle Sam as long as Jin Kee's own. "I'll not fight it. If they don't want me to be an American, I'll still be a Chinese citizen. No, it's no use to fight them – I haven't enough money to do that, even if I wanted to. It's too bad."

The petition alleged that Jin Kee had obtained his certificate of citizenship wrongfully and asked that it be cancelled. But the

Star was sympathetic. "Moy always has been regarded as a loyal citizen," it declared in a caption under a portrait of him that occupied two columns, "and his many friends are expressing regret that he may have to forgo the privileges of citizenship. When delayed by Customs officials recently in Spokane, Washington, Moy declared that he was a citizen of Indianapolis, 'the best city in the country.'" The love, it would seem, was mutual.

One of his many supporters in the town was the mayor, Samuel L. Shank, who wrote President William Howard Taft at Jin Kee's request. He explained that he had known Jin Kee personally for 16 years, and that the Chinese man was regarded as one of Indianapolis' best citizens. Taft received the letter, according to his secretary, Charles D. Hilles, and referred it to Secretary of Commerce and Labor Charles Nagel. Whether the matter was ever seriously considered is doubtful.

Served with notice of the court proceedings, Jin Kee chose not to attend. There would have been no point in appearing in person to suffer what was sure to be a humiliating loss of face. He was, however, represented by counsel. On October 9, the court issued a decree revoking his citizenship. But the official date of the order was October 18 – 14 years to the day since the same court had naturalized him. Whether this was a deliberate attempt at symbolism or simply an unfortunate irony is a matter of conjecture. Perhaps significantly, on the very same day, the court also annulled the citizenship of Syrian-born Mohammed Amon of Michigan City, Indiana, suggesting that the action against Jin Kee was neither directed at him personally nor solely at Chinese. The deputy court clerk did, however, also notify the Federal authorities after Jin Kee's citizenship had been cancelled that another Chinese named Yick Tong had been naturalized in Indiana on the same day as Jin Kee in 1897, and that if he could be found, he would probably be subject to the same ruling.

The day after the court handed down its decree – October 10, 1911 – was the day of the Wuchang Uprising, the coup that began

THREE TOUGH CHINAMEN

The U.S. citizenship of Moy Jin Kee, a.k.a. Moy Ah Kee, was revoked by the Circuit Court of Marion County, Indiana on October 18, 1911, exactly 14 years to the day after the same court had naturalized him. Source: National Archives and Records Administration, Washington, DC.

the revolution that was to topple China's Qing Dynasty. Within a month, the establishment of the Republic of China had been proclaimed, and most Chinese Americans were jubilant. The event was seen as signaling emancipation for China and Chinese everywhere, and there was a heady sense that the country would now be open to new ideas and new influences.

In Indianapolis, the Chinese New Year, which occurred in February, 1912, was celebrated in the usual way. Jin Kee and his friends gathered in his restaurant, smoked Chinese tobacco in pipes and American cigars, drank tea, ate Chinese food and enjoyed American candy. Firecrackers had been shot off the night before, and candles and incense burned at a miniature shrine in the restaurant. It was the last time the small colony of Chinese planned to mark the new year according to the lunar calendar, Jin Kee explained to a reporter from the *Star*. In a departure from the past to mirror the changes occurring in China, New Year's Day – for them as well as the rest of America – would henceforth be celebrated on January 1. And it would be a celebration that would "surpass all others in the past."

The following year, Jin Kee marked his 64th birthday with another elaborate celebration. He invited 50 friends to his restaurant, which he decorated with Chinese and American flags. The summary revocation of his citizenship notwithstanding, Jin Kee still felt himself to be American. Chin Fung, attired in a blue and black silk suit imported from China, greeted the guests, and the dinner menu consisted of bird's nest soup and entrées of duck and turkey, accompanied by Chinese apricot wine and imported preserves. Toasts were drunk not only to Jin Kee and his success, but also to the new Chinese Republic.

It was probably the last such gathering he enjoyed with his many friends. On January 6 of the following year, while seated at a table in his restaurant, he suddenly fell to the floor and was dead of a heart attack by the time the doctor arrived. He had been in failing health for several weeks. Chin Fung made futile efforts to revive him, but after the coroner declared him deceased, his body was given over to a funeral home.

According to his obituary, he was the wealthiest Chinese in Indianapolis, his "fortune" estimated at $25,000. The article described many of the events of his life, focusing on his time in Indianapolis and conveniently omitting mention of his sojourns in New York and Chicago, both of which had ended unfortunately. It recounted that he had raised funds in Indianapolis to relieve famine in China, that he had been elevated to the Chinese titled elite, that he had met with difficulty at the hands of Immigration officials in Seattle when he returned from China, and that he had served as "the prominent local source of information on questions relating to Chinese affairs." The *Tipton Daily Tribune* from nearby Tipton, Indiana, in a front-page obituary of its own, commented on his intelligence, on the fact that he had come from "the higher class of his race" and on "his powerful influence among the people of his race and his wide acquaintance among all classes of people."

There was a good deal of curiosity in Indiana about Chinese customs relating to death. The newspapers couldn't seem to say enough about them, and they followed the story of Jin Kee's funeral arrangements voyeuristically over several days. The *Star* reported that Chin Fung had knelt at the side of his body and chanted a death song. The *Tipton Daily Tribune* related how she sprinkled rice over his face in hopes it might "rekindle the fire of life." On January 15, the *Star* described his attire in great detail:

> Moy Kee's body, dressed in the costume that he wore when he was elevated to the fourth rank of Chinese caste, lies on a couch, the features preserved almost as naturally as though he were asleep. On his head is the cap that he wore as a part of the uniform. The cap is surmounted by the flowing peacock feather that is a part of the insignia of his rank. In one hand a fan, outspread, has been placed. In the other is held a folded paper, which, though blank, carries out the custom of providing the deceased with fare on his journey into the hereafter.

American friends were permitted to call at the undertaker's on the morning of January 15; Jin Kee had a lot of them, for he was a beloved figure in Indianapolis. Then a brief funeral service, open only to Chinese, was conducted in the afternoon by what was termed "the Chinese order of the Masons" - the Chee Kung Tong - of which Jin Kee had been an officer. A grief-stricken Chin Fung, who had almost never been apart from her husband since her arrival in America more than 30 years earlier and who had sat vigil at his side every day since his death, announced plans to depart a week and a half later to accompany his body back to China, making it clear that she did not expect to return to the United States. A Chinese woman with no real identity independent of that of her husband, she surely would have found it difficult to remain in America as a widow. In China, with the savings the couple had accumulated in their many years in the United States, she could live very comfortably.

"Before an altar from which arose the pungent odor of burning incense, their hands bathed in wines considered sacred in China, a dozen prominent Chinese yesterday paid tribute to the memory of Moy Ah Kee," the *Star* recounted on January 16, its sixth day of coverage of Jin Kee's death, Indianapolis' morbid curiosity apparently not yet satisfied. "The copper-lined casket of richest walnut was covered in floral offerings from American friends of the deceased," it reported. "At one end of the casket stood a huge Masonic square and compass wrought of blossoms. Before this was the altar of burning incense, before which each of the Chinese knelt in turn . . . making the obeisances and going through the forms peculiar to a Chinese funeral service." The Americans who attended the funeral were moved to tears by the widow's grief, the *Star* reported, suggesting, however, that "little sympathy was reflected in the stern faces of the [Chinese] men, for it is the custom of the Chinese to express no sorrow for the widow."

Before she departed, Chin Fung made sure her affairs were

in order. Through her husband's attorney, Cass Conaway, she sold her home and the Moy Kee Chop Suey House on E. Washington to Chin Gum Shing, also known as E. Lung, owner of a chain of Chinese laundries who had succeeded Jin Kee as "mayor" of Chinatown and who announced plans to keep the business open. And she posted a notice in the *Star* informing Jin Kee's creditors that any outstanding claims had to be presented to her on or before January 22. Prior to her departure, Indiana Governor Samuel M. Ralston presented Chin Fung with a letter of introduction asking for all courtesies to be extended to her on her journey home, a facsimile of which was printed in the January 22 edition of the *Star*.

Stopping over in Los Angeles, Chin Fung gave an interview to a *Los Angeles Times* reporter that, in print, appeared as cloying and self-serving as it was misleading. "The love of a Juliet or a Virginie are no greater nor more touching than that love which is taking little Mrs. Moy Ah Kee, a dainty bit of faded Chinese femininity, all the way from Indianapolis to Canton with the body of her dead husband," it gushed. Chin Fung, it reported, blamed American doctors for her husband's death, maintaining that in China, seemingly dead people were often only comatose and were routinely revived after three or four days. "To carry out her plan she has sacrificed all her old friends, the respect perhaps of her two sons and the little fortune that remained to Moy Kee at his death," the *Times* intoned. "She has sold her slender stock of jewels, disposed of the properties belonging to her dead husband and is spending her all, a little more than $1,000, in order that his spirit may join that of his ancestors and that she may find a high place in the heaven of the Celestials." And in taking her husband's body back to China, she was "beggaring herself . . . and promising to die, self-slain, on his grave."

Chin Fung was surely still grieving, and she was not an educated woman, nor one accustomed to the limelight. But none of that changed the fact that the sons were almost undoubtedly fictitious, that in any case no Chinese son would lose respect for his mother for returning his father's body to his homeland, that her husband had left her an estate in excess of $25,000 which would be a king's ransom back in China, that she was "beggaring herself" in a comfortable room at Los Angeles' tony Hollenbeck Hotel and that the suggestion that there is a Chinese custom that requires widows to commit suicide on their husbands' graves is ludicrous. Whether the exaggerations were the product of Chin Fung's flair for the dramatic, poor translation or the wild imagination of the reporter is impossible to say.

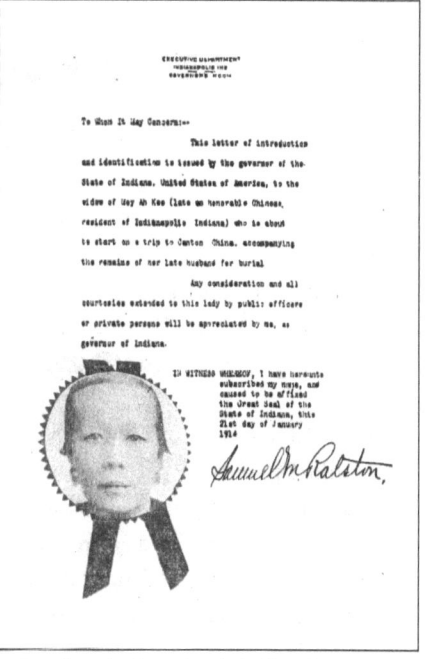

Letter of introduction written by Indiana Governor Samuel M. Ralston on behalf of Chin Fung, asking that courtesies be extended to her on her journey back to China with the remains of her husband. Source: Indianapolis Star, January 22, 1914.

From Los Angeles it was a short journey to San Francisco, where, on January 26, Chin Fung set sail for China, bringing Moy Jin Kee back for his final journey, to rest with his ancestors in Taishan.

Chapter XVII
Many Impeachable Practices

On January 21, 1916, a letter was delivered to the headquarters of the U.S. Immigration Bureau in Washington that changed the life of Gop Jung, the Moy brothers' cousin. It read as follows:

> Moy Op Jing [sic] your interpreter at Pittsburgh now has committed criminal perjury to get a son of his brother into the United States with his wife and claimed as his own. I live in same town with him in China. He never had a son born to him. I know his family as well as mine. You will find my information absolutely true if you will investigate this matter scrupulously.
>
> He is a member of On Long [Leong] Tong and rely on its power for his protection. His conduct such as gambling in Chinatown evry [sic] night, accept money from Chinese for official information, associate with a few bad Chinamen to smuggle Chinese from Canada by way of Buffalo. Uses his cousin Dr. Moy Jin Fey [sic] translating official letters and many other impeachable practice.
>
> Your [sic] very truly,
Moy Ling

The letter, although in English, appeared to have been written with a writing brush, and local Bureau officials soon determined that Moy Ling was not a real person, but a pseudonym. The letter was forwarded to the Philadelphia Bureau, which had oversight over all Pittsburgh-based employees, including Gop Jung. Philadelphia was ordered to take the lead in investigating the charges, which were too serious to ignore. Washington also forwarded Gop Jung's personnel file, which contained references to previous allegations of malfeasance: a 1907 letter mentioning an investigation that "tends to show that this interpreter has been practicing blackmail," and a 1912 allegation that Gop Jung had leaked official information about a particular case to his brother.

In response, Elmer Ellsworth Greenawalt, Commissioner of Immigration for the Port of Philadelphia, vowed to "settle once and for all time the question of the integrity in office of Moy Gop Jung." He charged Charles V. Mallet, a Philadelphia-based Immigration Inspector, with conducting the investigation. Mallet's work plan included deposing Gop Jung's colleagues and known associates in Pittsburgh, in the New York and Baltimore bureaus where he had previously served, and in Washington and Gouverneur, New York, where he had once lived. It also involved auditing his bank accounts and asking him, as a token of his "good faith," to surrender all of his personal papers for detailed examination.

The investigation of Gop Jung went on for months. Inspectors spoke with his Chinese wife and son, who had joined him in Pittsburgh in 1914; his brother; several officers of Yuen Chong & Company, the Washington, DC corporation in which he had invested; an ex-girlfriend and several colleagues. They also located and visited his Caucasian wife, with whom he had not had contact for more than a decade. He himself was deposed 13 times. And the inspectors interrogated his cousin, Dr. Jin Fuey Moy.

Among Gop Jung's personal papers that were examined were several letters from Jin Fuey written between 1909 and 1911. They attest to a rapport between the two men, who had known each other since childhood. The letters dealt chiefly with Gop Jung's employment at the Immigration Bureau; Jin Fuey knew its ways from his own four-year term as an interpreter before he was discharged. He offered advice on how to avoid a transfer, how to get a raise in pay and why Gop Jung ought to husband his money carefully in case he were someday dismissed, as Jin Fuey himself

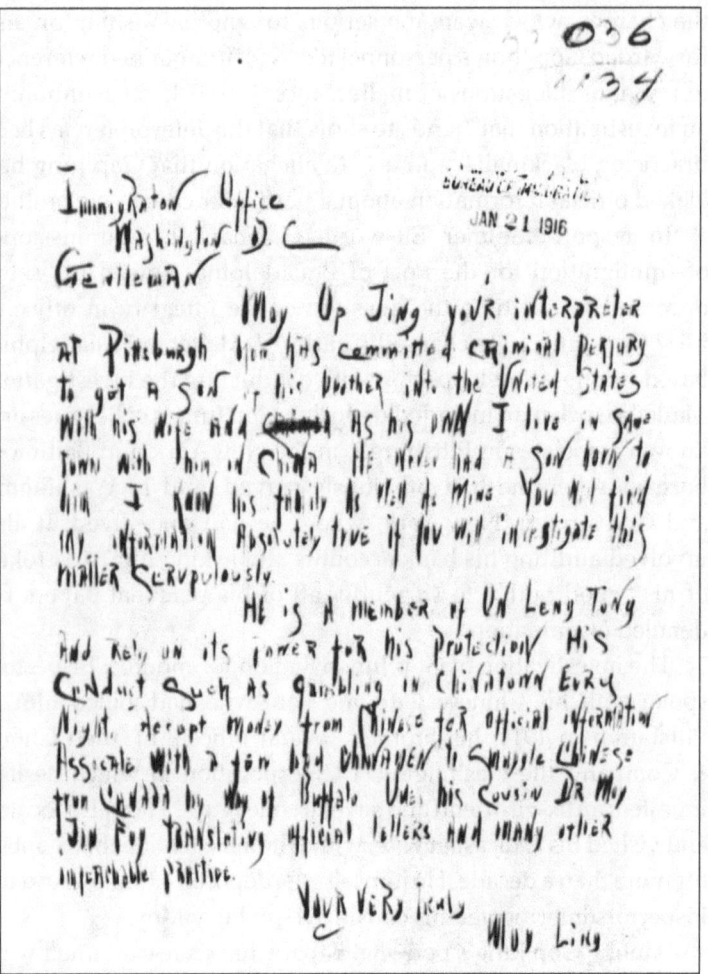

This letter, signed with the pseudonym Moy Ling, was received on January 21, 1916 at the headquarters of the U.S. Immigration Bureau in Washington, DC. It proved to be Moy Gop Jung's undoing. Source: National Archives and Records Administration, Philadelphia, PA.

had been. He also complained about his own financial situation and gave Gop Jung his account of the smuggling case that had brought him to Boston for trial in 1911. Gop Jung's letters to Jin Fuey do not survive, but the latter's missives bespeak a warm, personal relationship between the two cousins, deferential on the part of Gop Jung, who sought and valued the counsel of the more canny and worldly wise Jin Fuey.

Jin Fuey was deposed not only because he knew Gop Jung well, but because one of the accusations in the anonymous letter concerned him. His wife Hattie was also present at the interrogation. After Jin Fuey testified that he had been born in China and had known Gop Jung since he was a little boy, Mallet asked about Gop Jung's family and his activities, and Jin Fuey steadfastly defended his cousin's probity. He acknowledged that he had occasionally helped Gop Jung with difficult translations, but maintained that the names of the individuals had always been removed from the documents before he saw them.

Then the questioning got more personal, as this surviving verbatim transcript of the interview testifies:

> Q: Do you write your Chinese letters with a brush?
> A: No, sir, with a pen.
> Q: Have you a Chinese brush and pad here?
> A: No sir. I have not used any here for about 30 years. When I go into the Chinese store sometimes I use it for signing a bill or something like that, but that is all. I got out of the way of using them 30 years ago.
> Q: There is a matter of this investigation which connects you with it, Doctor. The Immigration Service in Washington has received a complaint against Moy Gop Jung and it is said that you write the letter.
> A: I never write a letter with a Chinese brush or Chinese ink for the past 30 years.
> Q: I did not say it was written with a Chinese brush or ink. Why did you think it was?
> A: It was just a supposition.
> Q: Does it get down to the heart of the matter do you think that the letter was written with a Chinese brush or ink?
> A: I think so. I do not write Chinese letters any more.

THREE TOUGH CHINAMEN

Hu Shee and Moy Sher Park, pictured with Gop Jung soon after their arrival in Pittsburgh. Source: National Archives and Records Administration, Philadelphia, PA.

Q: I would like to say that there is very strong evidence that the letter came from you?
A: There is?
Q: Yes sir.
A: I would like to see it. Because I do not write Chinese letters except to one party in New York.

Next, Mallet asked Jin Fuey to provide a handwriting specimen that could be compared with the writing in the letter, but Jin Fuey categorically refused to cooperate:

Q: I would like to have you demonstrate for me please for the satisfaction of the record that so that anybody cannot charge you with duplicity in this matter.
A: I do not think it would be justice to me to demonstrate to you, and somebody might forge my handwriting, and I prefer not to do it.
Q: I do not believe in letting anybody rest under a cloud. I should

like if you are innocent of having written this letter of charges to make it so that your worst enemy cannot say that you wrote it.
A: That would not induce me to put anything in black and white.

The interview ended with a strong vote of confidence in Gop Jung's integrity on the part of Jin Fuey. "Nothing would make me believe that he would accept a bribe or do anything wrong or do anything crooked," he declared.

Mallet was lying when he told Jin Fuey that there was "very strong evidence" that he had written the letter, but he was not alone in suspecting Jin Fuey of complicity in it. Gop Jung himself believed that either the doctor or his wife had been behind it, and he had told this to Mallet during an interrogation the previous day: "My idea is that it was written by the wife of Dr. Jin Fuey Moy or she had somebody do the writing for her," he had said. What Jin Fuey and Hattie Moy might have had against Gop Jung to cause them to undertake such a vicious effort to destroy him is not clear. But some of the evidence did point to them, and not only for the reasons outlined by Mallet. If Jin Fuey had written the letter, it would not have been the first time he had used this tactic. In 1905, he had accused immigration inspectors in the Philadelphia office and a Chinese interpreter in the St. Louis office of blackmail and other improper practices. The Bureau had investigated the complaint at the time and concluded it was "actuated by spite," because the interpreter in question had testified against Jin Fuey in the incident that had resulted in the latter's own dismissal from the Bureau.

It is also possible Jin Fuey did not actually pen the missive himself but was behind the effort. The letter is poorly written, with many errors in spelling and grammar uncharacteristic of Jin Fuey, who wrote English quite well. And it is hard to fathom why Jin Fuey, if he were truly out to harm his cousin, would have mentioned himself in the letter or spoken so glowingly about Gop Jung during the deposition, except perhaps to throw the inspectors off of his scent. On the other hand, words like "impeachable" and "scrupulously" and expressions like "by way of Buffalo" that appear in the letter do not suggest authorship by a Chinese with a limited command of the language. And Jin Fuey did seem to slip when he "supposed" that the letter had been written with a Chinese writing brush.

As the investigation progressed, more evidence was teased out of the interviewees and the documents. Investigators reviewed the circumstances surrounding Gop Jung's campaign to bring Hu Shee and Moy Sher Park to the United States. Despite the discovery among the confiscated papers of a "coaching letter" – detailed instructions to the child as to how – and how *not* – to answer certain questions that Immigration officials might pose to him upon his landing in San Francisco, they more or less concluded – rightly or wrongly – that the child was probably his son. They examined the books of Yuen Chong & Company and found them wanting, and strongly suspected that its business was "not conducted in good faith in its relation to the Chinese and Immigration laws."

Mallet and his colleagues ruled out gang membership – there was no evidence for it – and did not find Gop Jung to be a high-stakes gambler. They strongly suspected, however, that he had had an affair with his ex-girlfriend, a white woman who lived in Baltimore and who had since married someone else. They delved into how he had afforded a "head-shaving" banquet – a Chinese "first haircut" celebration for a newborn child to which his wife had given birth after she arrived in America – to which he had invited a large number of people, some of them colleagues, who were of course government officials. And they concluded that he had been guilty of bigamy, even though that particular accusation had not appeared in the letter.

Although Mallet and his colleagues had clearly reached certain conclusions about the accusations against Gop Jung – guilty on some counts, innocent on others – no final report was ever written, nor was any remedial action ever taken. The file is silent on why the investigation stalled, but the whole affair was put to rest in April 1918, when Moy Gop Jung died suddenly, still in the employ of the government for which he had worked for 16 years. He was only 54.

While Jin Fuey and Hattie were being deposed by Inspector Mallet, one of them had alluded to the fact that certain lawyers who enjoyed the official confidence of Immigration inspectors in the Pittsburgh office had "accorded courtesies or considerations" to the inspectors, implying that they had done so to secure favorable outcomes for their clients. When pressed about it, Jin Fuey declined to identify any specific individuals. A few months later, however, Commissioner Greenawalt decided to give it another try. He wrote Jin Fuey on July 11 inviting him "to advise me just what may have been implied" by the remark about "courtesies or considerations" to Inspector Mallet during the deposition. He asked Jin Fuey to be "perfectly free" to report just how he knew, or why he believed, that the law, or any of its inspectors, were being "imposed upon," and offered the possibility of making an oral statement if the doctor preferred not to commit anything to paper.

The brief but carefully worded response from Jin Fuey just over a month later spoke volumes about his own attitude toward the Service that had, he believed, ruined his life by discharging him improperly so many years earlier. He said simply:

> While I have the greatest respect for the integrity of those persons employed in the service of the government of the United States of America, my experience in the past with your superior officers has taught me that silence is the best policy, for the information I withhold will not improve the service, nor benefit me personally in the least. It will only create animosity.

Chapter XVIII
The Chinese Nightingale

Shortly after his 1911 acquittal in Boston on charges of smuggling Chinese immigrants, Jin Fuey and his wife Hattie relocated to Pittsburgh, where he set up a medical practice. Their adopted daughter Josephine was already 24, and although she lived with them there for a short time and considered Pittsburgh her permanent home, she was actually busy pursuing a career in show business that kept her in New York, Philadelphia and on the road.

Josephine stood five feet two inches tall and had an oval face, dark brown eyes, a sharp chin, a small nose, small eyes and black hair. She had inherited her tan complexion from her mulatto mother. Known as Josie within the family, she was a talented singer and performer who created an exotic identity for herself on the stage and, later, on screen, as the "Lady Tsen Mei," which is how she was always billed when performing.

Unlike Josie, however, the Lady Tsen Mei was ostensibly Guangzhou-born, a fiction that continues to be perpetrated to this day in most of her film biographies. She bore the title "Lady," she told reporters, because an ancestor was "a Mandarin way back in 1500 B.C." She had been schooled in China, she said, where she read American history and then induced her father to take her to America. He purportedly sent her to Columbia University, where she claimed to have received her A.B. degree after finishing the classical course. (In another version she also became a member of the New York bar). After graduation, she asserted, she had studied music at New York's Metropolitan College of Music (by one account with Mme. Katharine Evans Von Klenner and Sergei Klivansky, both well-known artists) and entered concert work. Soon an offer came from Vaudeville, and she eventually played "on all the large circuits in the East," and made her way into films. She vowed pompously to one reporter, "I am going to show the world through the medium of the screen that the Chinese women have come out of their lethargy and are ready to take part in the world's affairs."

Most of this biography was pure invention, but the part about being a performer was true. Josephine was, indeed, a vaudevillian, and by most accounts a rather talented one. Billed as the "Chinese Nightingale," she traversed the country in the 1910s and 1920s offering a "full-blooded Chinese girl's conception of American vaudeville versatilities." She appeared with the likes of The Four Readings, Jugglers of Human Beings; Samayoa, the Spanish Aerialist; and Don Stanly and Al Barnes, performing in "Julius Sneezer." While she did not always ring true as a full-blooded or native-born Chinese – the *New York Clipper* sniffed that she "does not look the part" and that her style and vocal finish "strongly suggested American teaching," – she did earn consistently good reviews. She had quite a broad vocal range: Her voice extended from male baritone to lyric soprano, and she was a pianist, a comedienne and an accomplished mimic, delighting audiences with her imitations of birds and animals.

Josephine also appeared in three motion pictures. She was called "the first Chinese screen actress to rise to stellar fame" and was associated with the Betzwood Film Company, a 340-acre studio on the Schuylkill River in suburban Philadelphia that produced more than 110 films and shorts between 1912 and 1921. "Quite apart from the novelty of Tsen Mei's nationality, her ability to portray many types other than Celestial ones make her a real 'find,'" the *New York Sunday Tribune* declared.

Josephine – or, rather, the Lady Tsen Mei – acted in *For the Freedom of the East* (1918), a love story played out against a backdrop of American, Japanese and allied troops driving the Germans out of the Orient. She also appeared in *Lotus Blossom* (1921), said to be "the first Chinese-made motion picture in the history of the cinema industry." It featured an all-Asian cast save Tully Marshall and Noah Beery, Caucasian actors made up to look Chinese. And her third film was "The Letter" (1929), adapted from the Somerset Maugham stage play of the same name.

Of the three, only *The Letter* apparently survives today. Set on a rubber plantation on the Malay Peninsula and in nearby Singapore, it is a dark tale of infidelity, deception and blackmail. It starred

Josephine Augusta Moy, a.k.a. the Lady Tsen Mei, as she appeared in the 1929 film, The Letter.

stage and film actress Jeanne Eagles, who was nominated posthumously for an Academy Award for her performance. The screenplay is more or less faithful to the Maugham drama, but among the liberties the screenwriter took with it was the building up of the Lady Tsen Mei's part. Known only as "the Chinese woman" in the play and without lines because she ostensibly spoke no English, the character got a name in the film – Li Ti – and became a "half-caste" Chinese woman, no doubt because Josephine was part black and did not look entirely like a full-blooded Asian. The character was portrayed as "painted and powdered," was made to run a brothel, and appeared in spots throughout the movie but was the focus of only one campy scene in which she humiliated the leading lady. Overly melodramatic for today's tastes, it was a creditable performance by the standards of the day, and it showcased Josephine's ability to portray exotic characters.

In 1916, Josephine was invited to perform in Australia and

China, and she made plans to sail across the Pacific with Hattie. On October 13, 1916, at the U.S. District Court in Pittsburgh, the two filed forms as native citizens desiring passports. Josephine, who had publicly professed Chinese birth as the Lady Tsen Mei, did not attempt to make the same claim before the Immigration Bureau, and she listed her date and place of birth as March 29, 1888 and Philadelphia. She and Hattie stated that they intended to leave the United States from San Francisco aboard the S.S. *Ventura* on November 7. But the process would prove more complex than either of them expected. Their applications triggered an investigation by the U.S. Immigration Bureau in Philadelphia as to their birth and citizenship. And that, in turn, meant looking into the circumstances of Jin Fuey's birth.

A week later, after receiving the forms from Pittsburgh, the Bureau of Immigration in Washington directed its Philadelphia office to undertake a prompt investigation of Hattie's claim to be the wife of Jin Fuey Moy, and, at the same time, to probe Josephine's assertion that she was American-born. Accordingly, on October 24, Jin Fuey was deposed in Pittsburgh by William W. Sibray, chief inspector of the Pittsburgh Bureau. He claimed, under oath, that:

> I was born on a sailing vessel in San Francisco Bay in 1862, the said sailing vessel being of the Tien Tsung Line plying between Hong Kong and San Francisco; my father, Moy Yuen Bong being one of the owners of the Line and was at that time employed on the ship. I remained in San Francisco with my parents, as I was subsequently told by my father, for about three months when I was taken to China. I resided in Wing Ning village, Sun Ning District with my parents until I was 13 years old when I came to the United States accompanied by my older brother, Moy Kee, who died some years ago, and I have never gone back to China but have resided in the United States continuously since my arrival 41 years ago.

He supplied the date and place of his marriage to Hattie and

THREE TOUGH CHINAMEN

Josephine Augusta Moy's Application for a U.S. Passport, October 13, 1916. Source: National Archives and Records Administration, Washington, DC.

described the circumstances under which Josephine had come to live with them. He did not assert that the couple had formally adopted her; only that they had raised her as their daughter after she was given to them by her father. He also named others who could attest to the circumstances of her birth.

After Jin Fuey had described the situation surrounding his own birth, Sibray was quick to point out that he had given an entirely different account to Inspector Mallett only eight days earlier in his testimony in connection with the investigation of his cousin Gop Jung. At that time he had said he was born in China. Cornered, Jin Fuey immediately, if not convincingly, explained the discrepancy by saying that he always gave his birthplace as China because he lacked sufficient evidence to prove that he was actually born in San Francisco Bay.

The next step was to depose others who could shed light on the birth and citizenship of Josephine and Hattie. For Josephine, these included Moy Chong, the Philadelphia laundryman who was her biological father; Moy Hand Fun, her blood brother; and George W. Cliffe, the banker who many years earlier had attempted to get her and her siblings admitted to a Methodist orphanage. They all confirmed that Josephine was, indeed, the daughter of Moy Chong and the late Jessie Whitehurst, and that she had been born in Philadelphia, as she claimed. While interviewing Moy Chong, however, the inspector casually questioned him about Jin Fuey. He volunteered that Jin Fuey had been born in China in a village very close to Moy Chong's own. But after a bit more probing, Moy Chong realized that he had blundered and refused to say any more.

As for Hattie, the legality of her union with Jin Fuey was established by a copy of their marriage license, but her birthplace still needed to be investigated. Because birth records at the Wilmington, Delaware Court House and at Wilmington City Hall went back only to 1881, there was no official record of Hattie's birth in 1869. Immigration officials therefore sought out individuals knowledgeable about her origins. They questioned former U.S. Senator Willard Saulsbury, who had been connected with litigation concerning the estate of King Dolbow, Hattie's grandfather, many years earlier; Charles M. Curtis, Chancellor of the Orphan's Court in Wilmington, who had been opposing counsel in the same case; George E. Lyon, one of Hattie's cousins; and Mary Dolbow, Hattie's sister. All confirmed that Hattie had, indeed, been born in Wilmington.

For Josephine's part, she had never been adopted legally by Jin Fuey and Hattie Moy, and her father, Moy Chong, was clearly not a citizen. Her claim to citizenship, therefore, rested solely on the location of her birth. That having been established to the satisfaction of the Immigration Bureau, she was judged to be an American citizen and a passport was issued to her. Hattie, however, was a different story. Although Immigration was satisfied that she had been born in Delaware, she had also married a Chinese, and it was the custom during this era that wives adopted the citizenship of their husbands. Thus, her own status as an American citizen hung on the question of whether Jin Fuey had, indeed, been born in San Francisco Bay.

An unsigned note in Hattie's Immigration file provides an interesting window on the Bureau's reasoning:

> There is not one iota of evidence in proof of the claim of the citizenship of Dr. Moy except his own bare claim ... this leaves the *woman* without evidence of her citizenship – while it is shown she was born here, she is married to a Chinese who is not a citizen.

Appended to this note was a handwritten paragraph, dated November 1, 1916 and signed simply "A.W.P.," which stood for A. Warner Parker, an attorney at the U.S. Bureau of Immigration in Washington. It read:

> The girl's application should be favorably reported upon. The woman, presumably, is not a U.S. citizen. Her application cannot be reported favorably, but she is not a Chinese *racially* and of course can re-enter.

That is, permission to re-enter the United States, in Hattie's case, would be a function not of citizenship, but purely of race. Hattie never got her passport, however, and she did not accompany Josephine on the trip.

Some time in late 1916 or early 1917, Parker had an informal conversation with Charles F. Baker, Jin Fuey's attorney, and the two discussed the question of the doctor's nativity. Parker mentioned the different accounts Jin Fuey had given of the circumstances of his birth, and particularly the admission during the investigation of Gop Jung that he had been born in China. Baker, in turn, related the essence of the discussion to Jin Fuey, who maintained that "in this investigation I made no statement as to the place of my birth, except Charles Mallet raddled [sic] off but he wished to have the record shown until I objected."

Jin Fuey asked Baker to inquire further as to the Bureau's official opinion on the matter, which the attorney did in a January 10, 1917 letter to Parker. The response, which came two weeks later from Assistant Commissioner-General Alfred Hampton, confirmed that as far as the Bureau was concerned, Jin Fuey had, indeed, told Inspector Mallet that he had been born in China, and had known Gop Jung there as a little boy.

More than a month later, Baker forwarded to the Bureau a response written by Jin Fuey in which he maintained that the Bureau's records were unreliable, and that he had never testified as the transcript indicated. "Before I learned the object of their mission," he recalled, "Mr. Mallet... began firing off his questions like a Gatling-gun. He was persistent in his declarations that I was the author of a letter making a complaint against Moy Gop Jung, and demanded that I should acknowledge as the authorship of that instrument... I denied all the allegations there was any such letter ever in existence, and demanded for further proof." And he went on to repeat his assertion that he had not been asked about his birthplace at the time.

Then, incredibly, he offered a third version of the story of his birth:

THREE TOUGH CHINAMEN

Since my childhood, I have been told by my grandmother on my father's side that my father, Moy Yuen Bong, my three uncles, Moy Yuen Kwok, Moy Yuen Tsok and Moy Yuen Tung, were born in the State of California. My father and mother told me I was born in San Francisco, Cal., February 20, 1862. They died in China in the years 1879 and 1884, respectively. Upon my return to the United States in the year 1875, my elder uncle, Moy Yuen Kwok, pointed out to me the second floor in the frame house on the northeast corner of Jackson and Dupont Streets, San Francisco, Cal. in the year 1875.

In other words, not only was he now saying he had not been born in China, but that he hadn't been born aboard ship, either. He was maintaining he had been born in San Francisco's Chinatown, and to bolster his claim, he named his two living elder brothers, whom he said had been present at his birth, as witnesses that he could produce: Moy Jin Mun of San Francisco, and Moy Kye Hin of Philadelphia.

He never did so, however. The last word on the matter was delivered by the Immigration Bureau in a March 21, 1917 letter to Baker's law firm:

> The Bureau can only repeat what was said in its letter of January 25 to the effect that the statement made by Dr. Moy regarding his birth in China was both positive and circumstantial, and there would seem to be no reason why the doctor should not have testified to the true facts on that occasion. In view of this previous statement of Dr. Moy it would seem to the Bureau that proof of his claim of birth in the United States will now be very difficult.

Jin Fuey and Hattie never pursued the matter further. Had they done so, the Bureau would certainly have allowed her to return – indeed, as noted above, there was an internal memo to this effect. But it is highly doubtful that Jin Fuey, neither a merchant, a diplomat, nor a scholar, and with three conflicting stories of his birth and not a shred of proof for any of them, would have been permitted to re-enter. This is surely why, in the 42 years he had lived in the United States, despite occasional musings about going back to China, he never actually did so.

Chapter XIX
The Man Who Took the Teeth Out of the Drug Act

Jin Fuey's medical practice in Pittsburgh turned out to be the most lucrative venture of his questionable career. Like other physicians, he was permitted to prescribe opiates and patent medicines that contained them, a freedom obviously open to misuse. Nationwide, the abuse of opiates was difficult to quantify, but one estimate put the number of addicts in the United States at a quarter of a million in 1900. Growing concern about the problem had prompted the government to create the U.S. Opium Commission in 1903 to study ways to regulate the substance.

In 1911, the organization's Commissioner, Hamilton Wright, who had been appointed by Theodore Roosevelt, observed that the United States consumed more habit-forming drugs per capita than any other nation. He pointed out that there were far fewer safeguards against the distribution of opium in the United States than in any other country, China included, and that some American doctors were unfortunately part of the problem. Physicians in the United States "use it recklessly in remedies and thus become responsible for making numberless 'dope fiends,'" he declared.

The federal government had relatively few tools at its disposal to fight drug distribution, however, since under the Constitution the matter was basically under the purview of the individual states. But this was the Progressive Era, and the urge to attack the problem at the national level was strong, especially after Wright estimated that, in 1907 alone, 160,000 pounds of opium had been imported into the United States for smoking and consumption. Various strategies were discussed, among them the use of international treaties as a means of compelling federal action, and the use of the government's taxation powers to monitor and control domestic drug distribution. Both would eventually be employed.

In 1909, Congress passed the Opium Exclusion Act, which outlawed the importing of opium processed for smoking, but not for medical use. This may have been as much a foreign policy gambit as a serious effort to control drug use, however, as the United States was interested in developing the Chinese market and hence in ingratiating itself with China, and this effort placed America in stark contrast to Britain, whose history of forcing opium on the Chinese was a continual source of resentment. At the urging of the Roosevelt Administration, thirteen countries participated in an International Opium Commission meeting in Shanghai which led to a 1912 follow-up meeting in The Hague. The result was a convention signed by the participating

This 1913 view of 308 Grant Street during street repair shows the office of Dr. Jin Fuey Moy. His sign, not easily legible, announces the hours of his practice, which were 9 a.m. to 9 p.m. He and his wife Hattie also lived in the building. Source: Pittsburgh City Photographer Collection, 1901-2002, AIS.1971.05, Archives Service Center, University of Pittsburgh. Used with permission.

nations that bound them to restrict the manufacture, trade and international distribution of opium. In the United States, this treaty would lead to the passage of the Harrison Narcotics Tax Act in 1914.

Congress had actually begun debating an early version of what eventually became the Harrison Act in its 1910-11 session. But even in advance of its passage, the federal government did have ways of cracking down on physicians, druggists and others engaged in drug distribution, and Jin Fuey became ensnared in one such effort. On November 21, 1912, federal officials arrested 173 people in a 72-city raid, charging them with soliciting illegal medical practice and distributing unlawful medicines, all by means of the Post Office. Because misuse of the mails was alleged, it was within the purview of the federal government to police these practices, and, indeed, the operation was carried out under the personal direction of Postmaster-General Frank Harris Hitchcock.

The "most extensive and far-reaching raid ever made by any department of the government," followed seven months of diligent work on the part of 390 inspectors to work up all the individual cases. Five of those arrested were from Pittsburgh, and one of them was Jin Fuey; of all those detained, he was the only Chinese. He was able to produce the $2,000 bail, and so he was released. It is not clear whether he was ever convicted, however; the case file does not survive, nor are there contemporary press accounts of anything but his arrest.

On December 17, 1914, President Woodrow Wilson signed the Harrison Narcotics Tax Act into law; it would go into effect on March 1, 1915. Congress adopted it at the urging of Secretary of State William Jennings Bryan, who argued that passage was vital for the United States to fulfill its obligations under the Hague Convention. The legislature had circumvented the thorny question of constitutional federalism – the right of the states to govern their own affairs in all areas except those explicitly delegated to the federal government – by relying on its powers of taxation, and the result was essentially a criminal and regulatory measure that masqueraded as a tax law.

The Act imposed a registration requirement and a nominal tax on everyone who "produces, imports, manufactures, compounds, deals in, dispenses, distributes or gives away opium or coca leaves or any compound, manufacture, salt, derivative or preparation thereof." It also required that records of sales be kept for two years on forms provided by the Bureau of Internal Revenue and subject to inspection by Bureau officials, who were charged with enforcing the law because it was tax-related. The legislation criminalized possession of the drugs by unregistered individuals, but carved out an exception for doctors, specifically exempting "the dispensing or distribution of any of the aforesaid drugs to a patient by a physician, dentist, or veterinary surgeon registered under this Act in the course of his professional practice only."

What the Act did not make clear was whether physicians were permitted to supply opiates to addicts for no reason other than to support their addictions. Was doing so within the scope of "professional practice"? Reasonable people differed on the issue. Some felt no good could come of feeding the habits of "dope fiends." But others, including some doctors, truly believed that sustaining addicts until such time as a cure for their addictions became available was a perfectly legitimate medical practice.

Detailed regulations for enforcing the Act promulgated by the Treasury Department in early 1915 made it clear that the only legal means for individual consumers to obtain these drugs was from a registered doctor, dentist or veterinarian. Arrests of rogue physicians began soon after, but usually a stern warning was given before one was made. Whether Jin Fuey ever received such a warning is unclear. What is known is that on April 16, 1915, he became one of the first physicians arrested under the new regulations.

If Treasury officials had been looking for a test case involving a physician who was prescribing opiates in large quantities and under questionable circumstances, they needed look no further than Dr. Jin Fuey Moy. The government had surely been keeping an eye on him, at least since his 1911 arrest, and he was highly visible in any event as one of only a handful of Chinese doctors then practicing in America. When he was arrested, U.S. Attorney E. Lowry Humes announced that almost 1,000 people had received opium through Jin Fuey and an accomplice, and the Bureau of Internal Revenue reported that he had, during one 23-day period, written prescriptions for 10,000 heroin tablets and additional ones for morphine. Jin Fuey was clearing an estimated $100 per day from this enterprise. As the *Macon Weekly Telegraph* put it in a distasteful headline, "Chink Doctor Gets Rich But His $100 a Day Drug Profit Causes His Arrest."

At his arraignment, Jin Fuey was charged with conspiring with an addict named Willie Martin to place opium and its compounds "unlawfully and feloniously" in the latter's possession. He had done this, the government contended, by issuing Martin a prescription not for medicinal purposes, but merely to support his habit. Oddly, the charge was made under Section 8 of the Act, which made possession of such drugs by anyone not registered to have them unlawful. That is, Jin Fuey's ostensible crime was to cause the drug to be in the possession of Martin, who, as an addict, was by definition an unregistered person, since the Treasury Department had refused registration to addicts. Charging Jin Fuey under this provision proved to be a serious mistake on the government's part.

The U.S. District Court for Western Pennsylvania heard arguments in the case of *United States* v. *Jin Fuey Moy*, and on May 12 rendered a verdict with which the Wilson Administration was wholly dissatisfied. The court ruled that the statute was binding only on individuals who imported, produced and dealt in opiates – the ostensible targets of the tax that was the fig leaf that lent the law its legitimacy. Addicts like Martin, who were not importers, producers or dealers, were thus not covered by it. And if it was not illegal for Martin to possess the drug, then it was not illegal

394	OCTOBER TERM, 1915.	
	Syllabus.	241 U. S.

UNITED STATES v. JIN FUEY MOY.

ERROR TO THE DISTRICT COURT OF THE UNITED STATES FOR THE WESTERN DISTRICT OF PENNSYLVANIA.

No. 525. Argued December 7, 1915.—Decided June 5, 1916.

A statute must be so construed, if fairly possible, as to avoid not only the conclusion that it is unconstitutional, but also grave doubts upon that score. *United States* v. *Delaware & Hudson Co.*, 213 U. S. 366.

This court cannot assume to know judicially that no opium is produced in this country; nor is it warranted in so assuming when construing a statute itself purporting to deal with producers of that article.

When Congress contemplates the production of an article within the United States, this court must construe the act on the hypothesis that such production takes place.

An attempt of Congress to make possession of an article—in this case opium—produced in any of the States a crime, would raise the gravest question of power. *United States* v. *De Witt*, 9 Wall. 41.

United States v. Jin Fuey Moy *was argued before the U.S. Supreme Court on December 7, 1915.*
Source: United States Reports, Vol. 241.

for Jin Fuey to have prescribed it for him. The court found, in essence, that the Harrison Act, or at least the section of it under which Jin Fuey had been charged, did not apply to the case.

The government appealed the decision, and in what appears to be a procedural rarity, the case bypassed the circuit court entirely and went directly to the Supreme Court. Assistant Attorney General William Wallace, Jr. argued the government's case on December 7. He contended that the Harrison Act had been passed to carry out obligations under the International Opium Convention to which the United States was a signatory, and that under the Constitution, such treaties constituted the supreme law of the land. He also asserted that, its status as a tax measure notwithstanding, the Act was really a police measure and thus applied to everyone, not just to those subject to the tax. Jin Fuey's attorneys, for their part, averred, as the lower court had ruled, that the scope of the law was limited to those specifically named in it, and did not extend more broadly.

Associate Justice Oliver Wendell Holmes, Jr., delivered a 7-2 majority opinion on June 5, 1916, and in so doing made it clear that the Supreme Court had little use for the government's arguments. Like the lower court, the Court believed the pivotal issue in the case was whether possession of the drug by Martin was illegal under the Harrison Act. Holmes concluded that the wording of the section under which Jin Fuey had been charged did not support the contention that it had been passed to fulfill commitments under the Opium Convention, and that "only words from which there is no escape could warrant the conclusion that Congress meant to strain its powers almost if not quite to the breaking point to make the probably very large proportion of citizens who have some preparation of opium in their possession" subject to criminal punishment. Accordingly, it upheld the lower court's decision to quash the indictment against Jin Fuey Moy, and, in a stroke, largely gutted the Harrison Act.

The press was quick to latch on to the significance of the decision, and covered it broadly. "Government officials declared that this interpretation will ruin the effectiveness of the measure to a large extent," wrote Maryland's *Hagerstown Daily Mail*. "The Supreme Court's interpretation takes away from the law about half of its force," opined Indiana's *Ft. Wayne News*, noting that the measure still provided for rigid supervision of drug dealers, but also that "experience has shown that victims of narcotics do not always obtain the drugs from public dealers."

Indeed, they did not, if Jin Fuey was any example. The case earned him the sobriquet, "the man who took the teeth out of the Harrison Drug Act." But while the Supreme Court's decision established that addicts were not covered by the Act, it gave no cut-and-dried answer to the question of whether it was legitimate for physicians to distribute drugs merely to sustain them. The Bureau of Internal Revenue's opinion on the matter was apparent enough, but the issue remained to be clarified in the courts. In the meantime, the government kept Jin Fuey, who apparently saw no reason to change his practices after his acquittal, squarely in its crosshairs.

Sure enough, on May 12, 1917, just short of a year after Jin Fuey's exoneration, a federal grand jury in Pittsburgh returned an indictment against him, another physician and three officers of the Joseph Fleming & Son Drug Company for alleged conspiracy to violate the Harrison Act. The *Washington Post* reported that unnamed officials at the Bureau of Internal Revenue called it "the most extensive known conspiracy for illicit traffic in narcotics in the country." According to the indictment, the *Post* wrote, 3,500 ounces – more than seven million doses – of morphine had been distributed by the alleged conspirators in just over two years, with nearly 12,000 narcotics prescriptions having been written by Jin Fuey himself.

This time, however, the government charged Jin Fuey under Section 2 of the Act, the portion that made it unlawful to sell, barter, exchange or give away any of the drugs covered, but exempted physicians, dentists and veterinarians who prescribed the drug in the course of their professional practice. The indictment contained 20 counts, all in the same basic form; only the names of the people who received the drug and the amounts differed. The government's contention was that Jin Fuey's actions, some of which involved dispensing drugs to people who were not even his patients and without adequate direction, could not be considered to be part of his professional practice.

When the case came to the trial court, Jin Fuey's attorneys moved on several grounds that the indictment be dismissed. They contended:

- That the Harrison Act was unconstitutional;
- That the defendant was not charged with actions prohibited under

the Act or other federal law;
- That to dispense drugs by prescription was different from selling, bartering, exchanging or giving them away, which were the acts specifically prohibited by Section 2; and
- That no competent evidence was submitted by the government to sustain the jury's verdict.

In its opinion, the trial court dispensed with each of these arguments in turn. First, it found the Act constitutional, arguing that in light of earlier legislation restricting the import of opium into the United States, it could be read merely as the regulation of the use that may be made of opium that is imported. Second, the court concluded that there was no question that the indictment charged an offense under Section 2. On the third point, the court held that Congress, concerned with unlawful distribution of drugs and not ownership *per se*, did not intend the words "sell, barter, exchange or give away" to be read narrowly: "Whether the victim procured the drug from the hand of the physician, or through the druggist on an order or prescription of the physician, can matter nothing," wrote Federal District Court Judge W. H. "Seward" Thomson, a nephew of the late William H. Seward, Secretary of State under Abraham Lincoln - "unless we look blindly at the letter of the Act, wholly forgetting its spirit and purpose."

And finally, the court rejected the claim that no competent evidence had been submitted, damning Jin Fuey in a blistering paragraph that sought to quantify the extent of his perfidy:

> On the contrary, there was a superabundance of such evidence. Unless this section of the act is a dead letter, it would be hard to conceive a more flagrant case of its violation. The defendant seems to have obtained an extended and unenviable reputation as a dispenser of morphine sulphate. From Brooklyn to Chicago, from all the Lake cities, the victims of the drug habit came to Dr. Moy and procured the drugs. When we remember that the testimony

showed that morphine sulphate is at least eight times as powerful and deadly as opium; that one-half grain is a large dose, and a grain a fatal dose to the nonuser; that there are 60 grains in one dram, and that the defendant time and again issued prescriptions for as much as 16 drams to one person, or 960 grains, enough to kill an entire regiment; that he issued, in the two years preceding the indictment, 11,687 prescriptions, calling for 15,796 drams, and in addition 43,200 one-half grain morphine tablets and 30,600 one-quarter grain tablets, we can have some conception of the magnitude of the defendant's unlawful business in the distribution of narcotics; and when we consider that for every dram prescribed he received $1, the commercial feature of the unlawful business becomes painfully and alarmingly apparent.

On February 6, 1918, Jin Fuey was convicted on eight of the 20 counts. The maximum fine prescribed by the Harrison Act for violations of Section 2 was two years' imprisonment and a $5,000 fine. He was given the full prison term, but fined only $1,000.

This time it was he who appealed the case, and once again, the appeal went directly to the Supreme Court. It was not argued there for more than two years, however, and the delay proved highly significant. In the interim between the verdict and the Supreme Court's consideration of the case, the Court ruled on two other important cases involving the Harrison Act – *Webb* v. *United States* (1919) and *United States* v. *Doremus* (1919), and it was apparent it had begun to change its mind somewhat about the Act. In both cases, the Court ruled against physicians who were merely "maintaining" drug addicts by writing prescriptions for them. In the *Webb* case, it went so far as to declare, "to call such an order for the use of morphine a physician's prescription would be so plain a perversion of meaning that no discussion of the subject is required."

Jin Fuey Moy v. *United States* was argued before the Supreme Court on October 11, 1920. The appeal had been based on several assertions, the first of which was his attorneys' continued insistence that the Harrison Act was unconstitutional. In the eyes of the Court, however, that question had already been put to rest in the earlier *Doremus* case, so the Justices considered the others: the sufficiency of the indictment, the adequacy of evidence, the instructions given to the jury and the admissibility of certain evidence rejected by the trial court.

The "sufficiency of indictment" argument was more or less a replay of the assertion made at trial that writing a prescription was not tantamount to selling or giving the drug away in the manner envisioned by the statute. The Court rejected this reasoning in its ruling of December 6, 1920, concluding that there was "no necessary repugnance" between prescribing and selling. As for the adequacy of evidence, the Court recounted some of the salient accusations in the case: that Jin Fuey had issued prescriptions without an official, written order; that he had issued them to persons not his patients and not previously known to him; that he had sometimes dispensed entirely with a physical examination of the person receiving the prescription; that his prescriptions had called for large quantities of drugs and his directions as to how to use them had been vague; that he had charged according to the amount of drug prescribed ($1 per

---

JIN FUEY MOY *v.* UNITED STATES.

ERROR TO THE DISTRICT COURT OF THE UNITED STATES FOR THE WESTERN DISTRICT OF PENNSYLVANIA.

No. 44. Argued October 11, 1920.—Decided December 6, 1920.

1. In a case properly here on a constitutional question under Jud. Code, § 238, the court retains its jurisdiction to decide other questions presented, after the constitutional question has been settled in another case. P. 191.
2. In an indictment charging defendant with unlawfully selling mor-

Jin Fuey Moy v. United States *was argued before the Supreme Court on October 11, 1920. Source:* United States Reports, *Vol. 254.*

dram); and that all the prescriptions had been filled by a single drugstore under circumstances highly suggestive of collusion. The Court concluded that in each instance in which Jin Fuey had been found guilty, the evidence fully warranted finding him so, and at the same time it rejected the objection to the instructions that were given, and not given, to the jury.

The sole remaining argument – the admissibility of certain evidence – referred to the refusal by the lower court to permit Hattie Moy to testify on her husband's behalf. Jin Fuey's attorneys had argued that she should have been allowed to testify because she had not been offered as a witness "in behalf of her husband," but rather to contradict another witness as to an event that had allegedly occurred in her presence. The Supreme Court failed to see the distinction, however, concluding, "the rule that excludes a wife from testifying for her husband is based upon her interest in the event, and applies irrespective of the kind of testimony she might give."

Why did the Court appear to change its mind between the first and second case involving Jin Fuey? Some observers have suggested that the Court became increasingly tolerant of an encroachment of federal power on the states because of a growing consensus of the evils of opiates and the absolute necessity of cracking down on them. Dr. Kurt Hohenstein, however, has argued that in fact, the crucial change was that the Court began to make distinctions among doctors, and to look at the "bad" ones as essentially little more than drug dealers themselves. If a distinction could, in fact, be drawn between "good doctors," and "bad doctors," then it is abundantly clear to which group Dr. Jin Fuey Moy belonged.

The decision, which upheld the verdict of the trial court, did not attract much attention in the press, but it sealed Jin Fuey's fate. There could be no more appeals. He was bound for the United States Penitentiary in Atlanta.

Chapter XX
Prisoner #11990

When it opened its doors in 1909, the Federal Penitentiary in Atlanta, Georgia, was hailed as "Uncle Sam's model prison." The federal government had only three penal institutions of its own at the time – the others being Leavenworth in Kansas and McNeil Island in Washington State – and Atlanta was the destination of choice for those sent from New England, the Mid-Atlantic states and the South. Located about four miles from the city center on a 321-acre site, the complex was made up of brick and granite buildings built largely by prison labor and 100 acres of farmland on which prisoners raised some of the food they ate. A concrete wall four feet thick at the base and two at the top surrounded the complex. It was rounded at the apex so no hook could be used in an escape.

Every modern convenience was provided, including running water, steam heat, electric lighting, glazed tile walls and concrete floors and ceilings. Prisoners who did not work on the farm could work in the tailor shop, shoe shop, pharmacy, laundry, infirmary or barber shop. Religious services were held regularly – an inmate choir performed at compulsory Sunday services, accompanied by an inmate orchestra – and prisoners had access to a 6,000-volume library under the direction of the chaplain, who also served as librarian.

When Jin Fuey arrived on January 27, 1921 to serve his two-year term, he followed the normal prison routine. He was given a bath, outfitted in prison clothing (a dark blue uniform, not prison stripes), weighed and measured, given a medical examination, issued a book of rules and escorted to a holding cell. After an interview with a prison official, he was initially assigned to kitchen duty and then sent to a cell. Like all the others, it was eight and a half feet long, nearly six feet wide and just under eight feet high, and contained two bunk beds. It is not clear whether he had a cell mate. Friendly relations between cell mates was encouraged, but apart from communicating in the course of their work, inmates were not permitted to talk with others, nor were guards permitted to communicate with them except as necessary to perform their duties.

Life was highly regimented and the schedule provided for eight hours of work per day. Prisoners rose at 6 a.m. and lights went out promptly at 9 p.m. All inmates were assigned a grade, which determined the privileges permitted them. Like all new prisoners, Jin Fuey was designated "first grade," a classification he would lose if he were found guilty of a willful violation of the rules. This designation enabled him to receive letters, to write friends and receive visits once every two weeks (always in the presence of prison officials), to use the library and to smoke or chew tobacco – but only if he had done so before entering prison. He was also permitted to receive newspapers and magazines, save "sensational or sporting publications," which presumably meant pornography.

Had he broken any rules and been reassigned to the second grade, he would have had to exchange his blue uniform for stripes, submit to a close haircut and forfeit a portion of his "good time allowance," which was essentially a reduction in the maximum sentence offered in exchange for good behavior.

Federal Penitentiary, Atlanta, Georgia, ca. 1910. Source: Library of Congress.

THREE TOUGH CHINAMEN

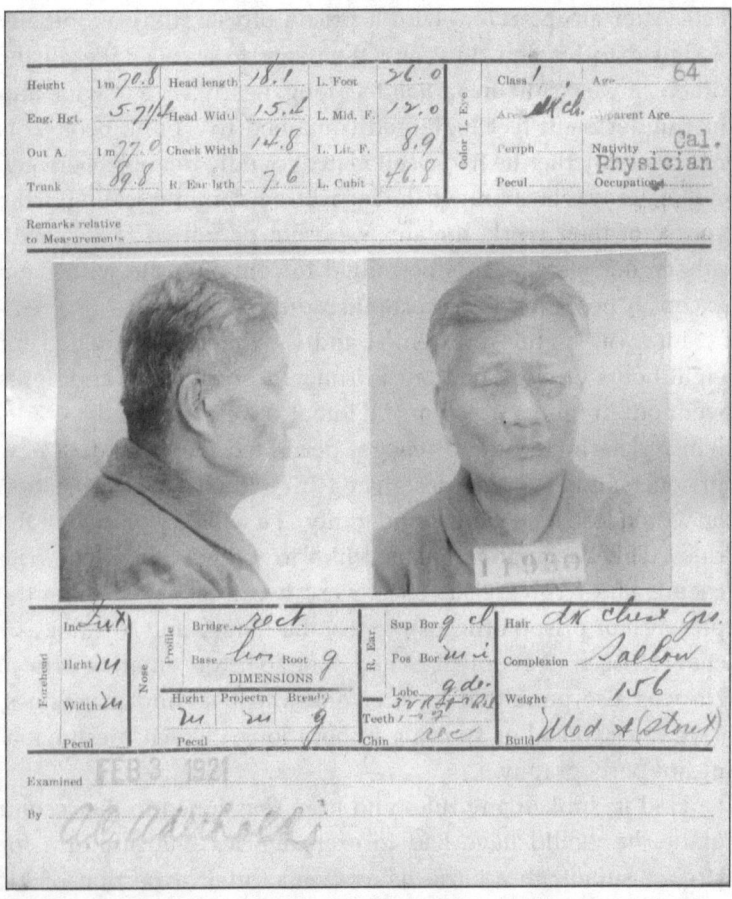

United States Penitentiary, Atlanta, GA record of the physical examination of Dr. Jin Fuey Moy, 3 Feb 1921. Source: National Archives and Records Administration, Atlanta, GA.

And for more serious violations, such as attacking an officer or a fellow prisoner, demotion to the third grade meant red and black striped clothing, loss of all special privileges and a ball and chain. Ninety days without a serious breach of conduct was required to restore a prisoner to the next higher grade. Below grade three, for those who committed heinous acts, there were concrete isolation cells, where in some cases the prisoner's diet – subject to veto by the prison physician –was limited to bread and water in order to provide "ample opportunity for meditation."

Atlanta Penitentiary had just about 2,000 inmates when Jin Fuey entered in 1921. They were serving time for crimes like counterfeiting, tax evasion, mail fraud, forgery, perjury and murder. American labor leader Eugene V. Debs was there; he had been sentenced to a 10-year term for urging resistance to the military draft. He was actually nominated for president by the Socialist Party and received 2.2 percent of the national vote, all while incarcerated. Another of Jin Fuey's fellow inmates was Charles Ponzi, who gave the world the "Ponzi scheme." He had been charged with 86 counts of mail fraud, had pleaded guilty to a single count, and had been sentenced to five years.

Jin Fuey entered the prison with an overcoat, a cap, a coat, a collar, two pairs of drawers, a pair of gloves, three handkerchiefs, a hat, a cap, three sweaters, a shirt, two undershirts, a pair of shoes, two pairs of socks, a pair of trousers, a pair of suspenders, a tie and a vest. He also had $78.04 in his pocket, one watch and chain and a pocketbook. These were confiscated and not returned to him until his discharge.

Shortly after his arrival, prisoner number 11990, as he was designated, petitioned the warden to permit him the freedom of the prison yard enjoyed by his fellow prisoners between 1:00 and 3:30 p.m. on Sundays. This privilege required pledging that he would make no attempt to escape, would be especially observant of the rules and would conduct himself in "a gentlemanly and orderly manner."

Records in the penitentiary were kept in excruciating detail, and included documentation of all the letters Jin Fuey sent and received and all the visitors who came to see him. He had correspondents in a wide variety of locations, including Washington, Indianapolis, Jacksonville, Philadelphia, Chicago, Seattle, Buffalo, Atlanta and Cleveland in addition to Pittsburgh. The majority were Caucasian Americans, not Chinese.

He had to request writing paper if he wanted to send a

THREE TOUGH CHINAMEN

> Department of Justice
> United States Penitentiary
> Atlanta, Georgia
>
> No. 11990
>
> I certify that Jin Fuey Moy was received at this penitentiary February 2, 1921 75 with a commitment showing a sentence of two years imprisonment and ($ 1,000.00) fine and costs, the sentence to begin January 27, 1921
> Short term expires September 4, 1922
> Crime Vio. Drug Act
>
> September 26, 1922
>
> Warden

Jin Fuey's term in Atlanta began on January 27, 1921 and was set to run until September 4, 1922, contingent on good behavior. Source: National Archives and Records Administration, Atlanta, GA.

letter, a process that necessitated filling out a form specifying the intended recipient, the person's address, the subject of the correspondence and the number of sheets of paper being requested. He exchanged letters with his wife every week; Hattie numbered hers so that he could acknowledge receiving them and so that they would both know if any had been intercepted. There was never any evidence of tampering.

From the beginning, it was clear Jin Fuey had no intention of accepting his incarceration passively. Although he was a model inmate, he was determined to use every legitimate means at his disposal to press for early release or, failing that, to secure better treatment for himself. Shortly after he arrived in Atlanta, Hattie, prompted by one of his letters, complained to his attorney that her husband was being "compelled to do work too heavy for a man of his years." The attorney, in turn, contacted the Justice Department, and the warden received the complaint in the form of a letter from the Assistant Attorney General.

The warden responded that the only work required of Jin Fuey was peeling potatoes for an hour or two a day. He had since been reassigned to work in the hospital. Apparently this job did not suit him either, however, for he soon determined that he didn't have much respect for the physician in charge. He wrote Hattie that the doctor "might be a fair surgeon, but not proficient in medicine from my experience with him."

In another gambit to make his life easier, Jin Fuey got one of his relatives, through an attorney the latter knew in Washington, to arrange for Scott Ferris, a personal friend of Warden J. E. Dyche, to write Dyche on his behalf. In his letter, Ferris allowed that while dispensing opium was a crime "detestable to the American to the last word, to the Chinese it is about as common as dispensing cigarettes or tobacco is among our people." He asked Dyche to "let one of your clerks give a little attention to Dr. Moy, get a report on him and see if there is not some way in which you can make his sentence as comfortable as [possible] for him."

By June, Jin Fuey had begun a campaign to seek executive clemency due to declining health. On June 30, 1921, no doubt in response to Hattie's protests, the Justice Department's pardon attorney wrote the warden that "strong overtures are being made that the application [for clemency] be granted on the ground of illness." He asked that the prison physician examine Jin Fuey and report as to whether further confinement would jeopardize his life. The physician reported that a physical examination revealed that Jin Fuey's urine showed signs of albumen and a slight trace of sugar, but that he could not see how further confinement would in any way be life-threatening.

Jin Fuey, a physician himself, conducted a self-diagnosis based on those symptoms, however, and pronounced himself ill with both diabetes and Bright's Disease, that is, chronic nephritis, an inflammation of the kidneys. He saw in those complaints a way to energize his friends to work for his release. As he wrote to Hattie in July:

> Now here is a good and solid cause about which Judges Cohen and Kleine and others can write to various persons for their helping hands

in my behalf, owing to my illness with diabetes and Bright's Disease, with which I am suffering . . . I asked for the particular drug for the treatment in my case, but none can be had here, so you can readily see the supply of drugs for the hospital is incomplete . . . Please advise Burton of these facts at once . . . for his immediate prompt and active attention for my freedom, and secure affidavits if necessary, from two reputable physicians as to the peril of the life of a person that has sugar and albumen in his urine, to rebut any statements made to the contrary.

Hattie wrote immediately to the Justice Department about Jin Fuey's illnesses, and the Department once again demanded a medical report. The doctor reported on August 8 that there had been no change in his condition, adding: "I still fail to see why further confinement would jeopardize his life." Jin Fuey, of course, was orchestrating all of Hattie's moves from his prison cell. But all of the pressure for clemency he was able to muster in Washington proved insufficient to secure his release, especially with no corroboration of any serious health issues from the prison doctor. And in another setback, at a hearing on October 21, he was denied parole.

Convinced that the Supreme Court had erred, Jin Fuey also attempted to advance a legal strategy for early release. In late 1921, he sought to retain M. Hoke Smith to persuade the Court to vacate its judgment. Smith, an attorney who had served as Secretary of the Interior under President Grover Cleveland, as Governor of Georgia and, most recently, as a U.S. Senator, was an odd choice. He was a white supremacist who had advocated disenfranchisement of blacks during his gubernatorial campaign earlier in the century. Nor was he any friend of Chinese immigrants; he had once proclaimed before a joint session of the Georgia legislature his sympathy with "the determined purpose of the white people of the Pacific coast to protect themselves against Asiatic immigration." But he was indisputably influential in Washington, and influence was what Jin Fuey needed.

Smith was practicing law in Washington after his 1920 defeat for re-election, and in response to an inquiry from Jin Fuey, asked a friend in Atlanta, an attorney named Ronald Ransom, to call on the latter at the penitentiary. That meeting occurred in late December. Then, in early January 1922, Jin Fuey had Hattie send the former senator a letter to which she attached a 12-page legal brief. In her note, Hattie made reference to a rumor she had heard in Pittsburgh that "personal bias and prejudice" on the part of the trial judge and the U.S. attorney had been behind the failure to grant Jin Fuey parole the previous October. Surely Smith had been approached not so much for his legal acumen as for his perceived sway in the corridors of power. If influential people were set on keeping Jin Fuey in jail, then perhaps others with even more clout could be recruited to help secure his release.

When no word had been received from Smith by late February, Jin Fuey followed up in a letter to Ransom in which he reiterated the main points of his case. Although not trained as an attorney, Jin Fuey was highly intelligent and strategic, and he evinced, in his hand-written summary, a remarkably detailed and nuanced grasp of the legal issues surrounding his case. Ransom immediately forwarded the letter to Smith, noting that Jin Fuey "seems to be a man of very considerable means who is quite anxious to pay some fees if he can find some attorneys who think they can do anything for him." He also noted that it was evident to him that Jin Fuey "has rather influential friends and powerful enemies."

Smith responded through an assistant that although he doubted there was much material assistance he could provide Jin Fuey, he was willing to look into the matter, but only upon payment of a $1,000 retainer fee. This proposition did not sit well with the prisoner. Perhaps the fee was too high, or perhaps Jin Fuey recognized that it would not be money well spent, but in any event that seems to have been the end of the matter, as there was no further correspondence on this subject and no indication Smith was ever retained in the case.

The indefatigable Hattie was back at the Justice Department in mid-January, this time railing that Jin Fuey had lost nearly 50 lbs. since his imprisonment, that he was suffering from a lesion on his heart, mold in his urine and gravel in his bladder, and that unless he received a special diet, further imprisonment would endanger his life. Again, the Justice Department requested a physical exam. This time the physician responded that Mrs. Moy was "very much mistaken" in her representation, because Jin Fuey had actually gained weight during his time in the penitentiary; he weighed 161 lbs., five pounds more than he had when he was admitted. "He is active and is up at work every day, and there is nothing to indicate that his confinement here is endangering his health to the least degree." And he added that, to the contrary, "I am inclined to think that the regularity of a life and a diet are calculated to be of help to him instead of an injury."

The process was repeated several more times, with Hattie upping the ante on symptoms each time she visited Washington. In early March she complained again about weight loss; by late March failing eyesight had been added to the list. By May he was alleged to have "taken a turn for the worse," and she predicted he "will not long survive." Why the Justice Department allowed this charade to continue is a mystery. Each time, Jin Fuey was hauled before a doctor for another examination, and each time the doctor failed to find any symptoms remotely comparable to those being alleged in Washington, which got more extreme and further from the truth at each round. A final report issued on May 14 did allow that Jin Fuey's health had deteriorated marginally, but the doctor was quick to add, "the information furnished you that the prisoner will not long survive is, in my opinion, far from correct."

Jin Fuey did survive prison, and he actually stayed a month longer than his expected term. Allowing for good behavior, his sentence was to expire on September 4, 1922, but there was the matter of the $1,000 fine. "On account of inability to pay," he served 30 additional days and was finally released on October 22, 1922, having served one year, eight months and two days in total. Since it is doubtful, in light of the $100-per-day income he had earned from drug sales before his arrest, that he really lacked the ability to pay a $1,000 fine, one can only conclude that, having sat in prison for more than a year and a half, Jin Fuey calculated that another 30 days was not going to be that much of a hardship, and that it was worth the savings.

He returned to Pittsburgh after his release, but lived only another year and a half before succumbing to cancer of the tonsils that had spread to the sternum and elsewhere. These symptoms were not associated with either of the illnesses that

Jin Fuey Moy's death certificate, listing his place of birth as California and his cause of death as cancer. He is buried in an unmarked grave at Pittsburgh's Uniondale Cemetery. Source: Pennsylvania State Archives.

had plagued him in prison, although cardiac failure, listed on his death certificate as a contributory cause of death, could certainly have been exacerbated by his diabetes and kidney problems.

Jin Fuey's remains lie in an unmarked grave in Pittsburgh's Uniondale Cemetery. "Elaborate funeral services began today for Dr. Jin Fuey Moy, one of the most widely known Chinese physicians in the United States," noted the *Charleroi Mail* in a brief obituary. He had, indeed, been widely known. And perhaps it was for the best that the newspaper did not mention precisely why.

Chapter XXI
Peacemaker

The "Six Companies," the national association based in San Francisco, was unrivaled in its influence over Chinese Americans. An umbrella organization, it represented America's six most important regional Chinese-American mutual aid societies. Organized according to the Chinese county of origin of the immigrants, these groups collected dues and saw to the social, cultural, charitable, economic and political needs of their constituents. Their leaders came together as the Six Companies – later renamed the Chinese Consolidated Benevolent Association. It served as the supreme authority in Chinatowns throughout America, and the voice of the Chinese community on matters relating to their welfare and rights. Jin Mun had been part of it from the very beginning, and was said to have helped in its establishment in 1882.

The Six Companies had a long history of activism. In the early 1890s, it had lobbied against the Geary Act, collecting a dollar per head from nearly all of America's Chinese to fight it. It counseled its constituents to resist the law and threatened to retaliate against those who did not. By the second decade of the 20th century, however, having failed in its effort to have the exclusion laws repealed, the organization was focusing on other issues that affected its constituents.

For many years, according to the Moy family narrative, Jin Mun's "voice was heard in the assembly room as he worked for the benefit of his countrymen." By February 1916, that voice had become the pre-eminent one; Jin Mun became the president of the organization, which claimed 80,000 members throughout North and South America. His term of office was short, because it was a rotating presidency, filled at intervals by the heads of each of the six constituent associations, and another man was identified in the lead position by October 1917. But in the year and half or so that Jin Mun served, the Six Companies was actively involved in several initiatives.

It protested the treatment of Chinese merchants by Immigration inspectors at San Francisco's Angel Island to President Woodrow Wilson. It held political meetings opposing the regime of President Yuan Shih-kai (*Yuan Shikai*) in China. It forced the recall of the local Chinese Consul-General by accusing him of playing politics. It initiated an embargo against Japanese goods in retaliation against the "Twenty-One Demands" the Japanese government had made of China to secure political and economic domination there and urged a tribunal in the Hague to investigate the Japanese-Chinese crisis. It sent an offer to the National Council of Defense in Washington to replace American farm workers who had gone to war with temporary Chinese workers. And, of course, it mediated battles among the triads in Chinatown. The Six Companies, in short, had its hands full.

As president, Jin Mun was certainly heavily involved in all of these efforts, but the last was the one with which his name would be most closely associated. Violence among the tongs was a constant complaint of Chinatown merchants, since it was very bad for business. The tongs were involved in all sorts of enterprises, many of them illegal, like gambling, drugs and prostitution. They sold "protection" to merchants and battled, seemingly endlessly, over profits, franchises and territory. Triad conflict had plagued Chinatowns across America for years, and despite repeated efforts by government officials and Chinatown groups to broker peace, it stubbornly persisted.

In 1908, the Six Companies, working with the Chinese Consulate and the San Francisco police, mediated a war between the local Hip Sing (*Xiesheng*) and Ping Kung (*Binggong*) tongs, resulting in a peace agreement between the feuding parties that

The General Peace Association, meeting with the Hip Sing and Ping Kung tongs and the members of the San Francisco Police Department, February, 1921. Jin Mun is standing in the back at the far left. Courtesy of The Bancroft Library, University of California, Berkeley.

explicitly permitted members of other tongs to give their names to the police if violence should erupt. But while such agreements were often effective for short periods, they did not, ultimately, address the systemic problem in any permanent way.

To this end, a new organization called the General Peace Association was established on May 15, 1913 by 27 Chinese societies – fraternal groups, surname groups and regional groups – with the goal of promoting harmony and stopping violence. Jin Mun was a charter member of the new association. Its first chairman, Li Bao Chan (*Li Baozhan*), drafted a credo for the group, which translates:

> There are frequent battles among we overseas Chinese living in America. We are the laughingstock of foreigners and harmful to ourselves. The founders of this organization have all along been considering how to maintain peace, but the time was not ripe and

so it has not happened until now. The Chinese Republic has just been established, and we now have a legislature. Our five main ethnic groups have become one big family, and all citizens are equal. Since our motherland is becoming a republic, we should not retain the bad habit of fighting amongst ourselves. Therefore, all of these organizations have come together to establish this peace organization. Our purpose is peace and public security, and maintaining our blood relations and fellowship. In times of peace, we will love and help one another. In times of emergency, we will unite and solve our problems. Our aim is to wipe out hostilities among ourselves and to unite as one family.

Jin Mun traveled up and down the Pacific coast for several years soliciting funds to support the new organization. During one such trip to San Luis Obispo, an Immigration officer stopped him and demanded his "chak chee." This term was used by the Chinese to describe the identity papers they were required to carry under the Geary Act. It was an interesting blend of English and Chinese, "chak" being a corruption of the English word "check," and "chee" (*zhi*) the Chinese word for "paper." Jin Mun didn't have his document with him, and so he was detained for several hours. Eventually, he prevailed on one of the officers to contact a San Francisco judge he knew personally from his long tenure as a court interpreter, and the judge confirmed his right to be in the United States, securing his freedom. Jin Mun was fortunate in being so well-connected; most Chinese in similar circumstances would not have been able to get off so easily.

One of the General Peace Association's early challenges was to mediate a war between the local Hip Sing and Ping Kung organizations in Portland, Oregon. Open conflict had erupted in early 1916, and had alarmed local authorities because it been played out just a few blocks from the center of the business district. A member of Ping Kung had been shot, and on his deathbed had identified a Hip Sing man as his assailant, but the latter had disappeared and the war appeared to be escalating.

Then the throat of a laundryman in Roseburg, Oregon, had been slashed and his head crushed. Such conflicts, which played out locally, were often symptomatic of the wider rivalries that spread across the country. In Portland, the situation had clearly gotten out of hand, and peacemakers from Chinatowns in San Francisco and Seattle were summoned, joining those on the scene in an attempt to broker a truce. Jin Mun, as head of the Six Companies, was first among them.

On February 22, a cease fire was declared after a negotiating session in the Hip Sing headquarters at 385½ Everett Street, but it was not formalized until the following day, because trust was so low that several local delegates did not feel safe enough to attend the meeting. After the District Attorney issued all the delegates "passports" and surrounded the venue with a squadron of police, the process continued. A 30-day truce was arranged, though its prospects for holding much beyond that time were seen as dubious. The captain of the police detectives, interviewed by the *Oregonian*, asserted that Chinese "would lie low for a short time, and when the opportunity came again would make an attempt to pay off old scores against the rival tong." The cynical statement, unfortunately, proved prophetic. In 1917, Portland would experience another outbreak of hostilities, as the truce collapsed and violence resumed.

Nowhere were secret society rivalries as intense as they were in San Francisco. Jin Mun helped end months of fighting among four of them by negotiating a creative deal. At Six Companies headquarters, the tongs signed a permanent cease fire agreement on August 6, 1922. The document was then given to the police department with the understanding that the police were to arrest the signatories in the event peace was broken. Jin Mun continued his work with the Peace Association throughout the 1920s, traveling throughout the West and offering mediation where needed. He also continued his work with other organizations. In 1921, he was elected English secretary of the local Chee Kung Tong, the Masonic-like order to which his brother Jin Kee had

THREE TOUGH CHINAMEN

also belonged before his death, and one with which Jin Mun had been affiliated since he was a young man.

Then, at the close of the decade, Jin Mun, like many others, lost much of his wealth when the stock market crashed. A family story suggests that it was Leland Stanford who had introduced him to the San Francisco Stock and Bond Exchange and that he had been the first Chinese to do business there. This may have been true, and if he had been heavily invested on the eve of the crash, he surely would have lost a great deal. But he didn't lose everything. In 1930, when he was nearly 80 years of age, he was still enumerated in the census as a merchant, and still at 886 Washington Street. His household that year consisted of himself and his wife, three sons, one daughter and one daughter-in-law, two granddaughters, a grandson, a brother-in-law and a godson. And those were only the ones who were living with him; many other descendants lived in San Francisco, and a few lived elsewhere at the time.

Moy Jin Mun family, 1930. Top row, from left: Steven, Daniel, Dip Tso, Dip Wing and Edison. Front row, from left: Lillian, Violet, Wong Shee, Jin Mun, Loy Yee and Lydia. Photo courtesy of Roberta Gee.

SCOTT D. SELIGMAN

Peking Opera star Mei Lan-fang was photographed at the Shanghai Low in San Francisco on April 29, 1930 with several members of the Moy family. Jin Mun owned an interest in this night club. In the front row, from left, are Moy Dip Wing, Wong Mee Hee (brother of Jin Mun's wife, Wong Shee) holding Daniel's daughter Marian Moy, Mei Lan-fang, Jin Mun holding Daniel's daughter Lora Moy, Wong Shee and an unidentified person. Standing second from left is Loy Yee Moy, between Mei and Jin Mun is Violet Moy, immediately behind Jin Mun is Daniel Moy, and between Jin Mun and Wong Shee is Lydia Moy. Steven Moy is visible over his mother's shoulder, and Edison Moy is standing at far right. Photo: May's Studio, San Francisco. From the Collection of Chinese Theater Images in California, Museum of Performance and Design, Pefforming Arts Library. Used with permission.

Jin Mun also worked as an insurance broker and, together with his son-in-law D. W. Lowe, owned an interest in the Shanghai Low, a San Francisco night club that years later would serve as the set for many scenes in the 1948 Orson Welles film, *The Lady from Shanghai*. In 1930, Beijing Opera star and Chinese theatrical idol Mei Lan Fang visited the United States with a troupe of 27 players and dancers to present a repertory of classical and modern Chinese plays. They visited at least five major American cities, including New York, Los Angeles and San Francisco, and played to packed houses. On April 29, 1930, Mei, 36 years old, appeared in San Francisco, and a banquet was held in his honor at the Shanghai Low. Jin Mun, a host, who shared Mei's surname (Mei being the Mandarin pronunciation of the character for Moy), was seated in a prominent position at

THREE TOUGH CHINAMEN

A photo taken on May 20, 1936 shows members of Moy Jin Mun's family setting out offerings to prepare him for his final journey. Collection of the author.

the head table, and later, together with members of his extended family, was photographed with the singer. The photos survive as testimony to Jin Mun's high-ranking position in Chinatown. Not long afterward, he retired and left his business interests to his sons.

On May 1, 1936, Jin Mun died of a paralyazing stroke in the Chinese Hospital in San Francisco. The *Oakland Tribune* hailed him as "unofficially the 'mayor' of Chinatown," a designation his brother Jin Kee had enjoyed in Indianapolis. To others, he was "the sage of Chinatown," venerated and sought out often for his counsel. Press reports around the country carried a quote about him attributed to Moy's countrymen in Chinatown: "What Moy Jin Mun does not know, is not beneath the moon."

Friends and relatives of the 87 year-old gathered at the Chapel of Wing Sun, 17 Brenham Place, to pay their last respects as incense burned and banners inscribed in Chinese decorated the walls. Among the mourners were five sons, eight daughters, 40 grandchildren and 50 great-grandchildren. Finally, "to the rhythmic clang of brass cymbals and the monotonous chant of

Chinese priests," a procession accompanied the old man to the Hoy Sun Ning Yung Cemetery (*Taishan Ningyang Yuqingtang Gongmu*) in Daly City, California, where he was interred.

Jin Mun died without a will. He left an estate valued at less than $2,000 after hospital fees and funeral expenses were paid. His portfolio consisted of 25 shares of General Motors common stock and two shares of the Borden Milk Company, all in his own name. He also had a joint savings account with Wong Shee at the Bank of America in the amount of $102.40. But he owed the bank $1,300, the balance due on a son-in-law's promissory note of which he was guarantor.

In October of that year, his youngest daughter Lillian filed a petition with the court to award the entire estate to Wong Shee, which involved notification of all other potential heirs, her nine living siblings and half-siblings, to that effect. None raised any objection, and the money went to Wong Shee, although she had to wait three years for it. She lived another 17 years, and died in San Francisco in 1953.

Jin Mun died a beloved and revered figure in San Francisco's Chinatown, the last of the three brothers to join his ancestors, and the only one to leave behind a long line of descendants.

Moy Jin Mun's tombstone (left) is in the Hoy Sun Ning Yung Cemetery in Daly City, California. The plot also includes a stone for both of his wives (not shown), even though Gong Shee, his first wife, died in China and is almost assuredly not buried there. In between the tombstones is an extensive genealogy carved in stone that names Jin Mun's ancestors (right). Photos courtesy of David Abelmann.

Epilogue

Did the Moy brothers "elevate humanity," as their family motto had commanded so many generations earlier? Each did contribute, in his own way, to the advancement of Chinese in their adopted land. But each was also capable of selfishness and greed.

That they deeply resented the restrictions and humiliations imposed on them by the Chinese Exclusion Act and its successor legislation is understandable and justifiable. All Chinese did. That they used what means they had at their disposal to circumvent the rules is nearly equally so. With their race singled out for discriminatory treatment as it was, they could scarcely be expected to show fealty to the very laws that sought so assiduously to ostracize and sideline them. Jin Fuey was very possibly complicit in smuggling Chinese into the United States, even while employed by the U.S. government, and Jin Kee vouched for two young men who were not the blood sons he claimed they were. Jin Mun probably did the same for two or three "paper sons" of his own.

Less morally defensible were some of their other crimes. By any measure, Jin Fuey's prescribing of opiates in lethal quantities to drug addicts he did not even examine was a monstrous act for a physician. While opium did not carry the same social stigma in 1915 that it does today, even the court that convicted Jin Fuey could not help remarking on the wickedness of what he had done, and the ethical equation appears essentially unchanged a century later.

What of Jin Kee's stealing from his employer in New York, or the allegation that he had locked the two "paper sons" in his basement for several weeks pending receipt of a smuggling fee from their real relatives? Or Jin Mun's opium dealings, or his apparent attempt to extort money from his cousin? None of these can be excused as an act of desperation; profit was the clear motive in each case, and the Moy brothers were not above exploiting such opportunities when they presented themselves – even at the expense of other Chinese, or, for that matter, of blood relatives.

They were also certainly not above stretching the truth. When investigators zeroed in on the questions of Jin Fuey's birthplace, the disposition of Jin Kee's restaurant and Jin Mun's alleged attempt to extort money from a cousin, denials came swiftly and easily. This habit was one that they – and, for that matter, most other Chinese in America – had no doubt imported wholesale from China, where government officials were generally corrupt, were seldom honest brokers and were typically anything but disinterested in the ways in which they dispensed justice. There had never been a premium on honesty when dealing with the authorities in the old country; indeed, it was often the worst policy.

But if the Moys were capable of misdeeds, they were also capable of altruism, primarily to the benefit of their fellow Chinese. Jin Kee and Jin Fuey had been trained as preachers and ran missions to reach out to, and educate, the residents of the New York and Philadelphia Chinatowns. Jin Fuey published a newspaper to keep his compatriots informed and tried to stop violence against New York's Chinese, while Jin Kee worked on several occasions to raise money to help people in need, whether flood victims in China or earthquake survivors in San Francisco. And Jin Mun extended himself for a friend who asked protection for his fiancée and, on a larger canvas, tried to stop Chinese-on-Chinese violence and keep the peace in Chinatowns in San Francisco, Portland and elsewhere in the West.

Unlike most Chinese in America, the Moy brothers were activists, speaking out against injustices imposed on their countrymen. Jin Kee decried the Exclusion Act, created the

Chicago Chinese Club to benefit local residents and spearheaded a lobbying effort to improve the treatment of Chinese nationwide. Jin Fuey railed against the Geary Act and publicly decried a bill aimed at destroying the livelihood of New York's Chinese laundrymen. And Jin Mun pursued multiple agendas as head of the Six Companies and worked to promote Chinese unity through the General Peace Association. These evinced not only altruism, but also leadership.

At a time when most Chinese in America were content to keep their heads down, put away some money to provide for their families in China and return there toward the end of their lives or even posthumously, the three Moy brothers had made a clear commitment to live in the United States, and it is worthwhile to ponder why. Here the experience of the fourth Moy brother – Kye Hin – may be instructive. The third eldest, behind Jin Kee and Jin Mun but several years older than Jin Fuey, Kye Hin came to America with his wife in 1876, if a story he told an Immigration inspector in 1914 is true. He allegedly fathered two American-born sons and worked for many years at the Quong Yick Wah Company, his brother Jin Mun's establishment in San Francisco. Eventually, he relocated to Philadelphia, where he was employed by the Kwon Wo Lung Company, a Moy clan-owned business specializing in oriental goods located in the heart of Chinatown. But Kye Hin was not an investor in this company; he was, rather, an assistant bookkeeper and salesman. For his efforts, he received a salary of $50 per month.

Unlike his more prominent brothers, Kye Hin made little mark in the United States, and while it is unquestionable that he lived and worked in America, there is scant corroborating evidence for it. If he landed in San Francisco in 1878, he ought to have been listed in the 1880 census, but there is no record of him there. Nor is there a record for him in San Francisco or Philadelphia – or anywhere else – in either the 1900 or 1910 censuses, the only other extant enumerations that took place during his tenure in the U.S. Neither does he appear in the city directories for either location, although as a practical matter, many Chinese were never listed. In short, Kye Hin was a marginal figure in America. His entire Immigration file consists of two documents, which were concerned only with cancelling his residence certificate when he went back to China for good in 1918, lest someone else attempt to gain entry in his name.

Men like Kye Hin were far more likely to return to China to live out their lives than were his brothers. Kye Hin did not master English – he was interviewed through an interpreter when he met with Immigration officials. Nor does he appear to have established much of a foundation or created much of an enterprise, as the Moy family poem had urged. He eked out a living as an employee in a family business in which he had no financial stake, probably banked as much of a meager salary as he could, and then quietly returned to his native land to enjoy what he surely hoped would be a comfortable retirement. It was a story that could have been told of countless other men of Taishan who had made the journey to America and, eventually, the return trip to China.

Not so Jin Kee, Jin Mun or Jin Fuey, or their cousin Gop Jung. All worked as interpreters and their language acumen enabled them to mix easily among white Americans – probably the first predictor of success in their adopted country. Jin Mun's command of English got him work in the courts and with the railroad; Jin Kee's grasp of the language earned him prominence as a preacher and a community leader and Jin Fuey's skills helped him get a medical education. Jin Kee, Jin Mun and Gop Jung all brought their wives over from China, something only a small minority of Chinese men ever did, and Jin Fuey married an American and left New York City for an affluent New Jersey suburb in which he was certainly the only Chinese resident. He had a vast network of American friends who outnumbered Chinese on the list of those with whom he corresponded while he was incarcerated.

Then too, the Moys became Christians, which only a minority of early Chinese immigrants did. Whether they were "rice

Christians," more in search of material than spiritual benefit, isn't clear, but at various points in their lives they did appeal to the Almighty and discuss their beliefs in ways that suggest more than a mere utilitarian approach to religion. Even Jin Fuey, certainly the least moral of the brothers, evinced a belief that appears quite genuine when he wrote his wife Hattie from prison that "each of us must place our confidence in God relative to our tribulation and trial, like Job of old. He knows what is best for us all, so we must be submissive, and endure the trial in which he places us, until he sees fit to relieve us the burden." Since the vast majority of their contemporaries did not abandon the religious beliefs they had brought with them from China, one can take the brothers' interest in embracing Christ as something else that set them apart and that drew them further into mainstream American culture.

The ability of all three brothers to bridge the chasm between the Chinese and white communities opened doors for them, and that, coupled with their intelligence and ingenuity, permitted them to become players on the national stage. The three Moy brothers' names appeared often in the press, which was by no means the norm for Chinese in America; by contrast, brother Kye Hin left almost no paper trail. Jin Kee, Jin Mun and Jin Fuey had each amassed a significant amount of capital and attained a certain social status and even a measure of fame. In short, they were successes in their adopted land.

The opportunity to realize the American dream, taken for granted in the case of people like my grandfather who came from Byelorussia in 1905 or members of most other ethnic groups, was largely denied to the Chinese by racial prejudice and discriminatory laws. But having at least partially surmounted these obstacles, the Moys were able to achieve considerable success in America, and with one exception never seriously considered returning permanently to their native land. To be sure, Taishan always remained part of the Moys' lives. Jin Kee went back three times in all and Jin Mun went back twice; each chose a wife from home. Even Jin Fuey flirted with a trip home but never actually made one. Jin Kee came closest to a permanent return when he and Chin Fung went back in 1908, but in a year's time he was back, having concluded that life would be better in America, and perhaps that America had changed him so much that a happy and comfortable existence in China was no longer even a possibility for him.

Had the Moys stayed home and never sought their fortunes in America, their future would most likely have been played out in the rice fields of impoverished Duanfen. Instead, one graduated from medical school and became a wealthy physician. Another became a successful merchant and presided over a powerful national organization. And the third befriended a Manchu Prince, was granted an imperial title and hobnobbed with the President of the United States. These were no mean feats for the sons of a Cantonese peasant, and would have been quite impossible in their native land.

In the end, America offered the Moy brothers a measure of the upward mobility it extended to most other immigrant groups. That it did so grudgingly meant merely that they had to work harder, and surmount more obstacles in order to succeed. What set the Moys apart from the Chinese who made their way home to China was that they were intelligent, talented, nimble and resourceful enough to seize and exploit what opportunities presented themselves. And in so doing they were able, as their ancestor had exhorted so many years earlier, to establish a foundation and create an enterprise – albeit in a foreign land.

Moy Family Tree (Abridged)

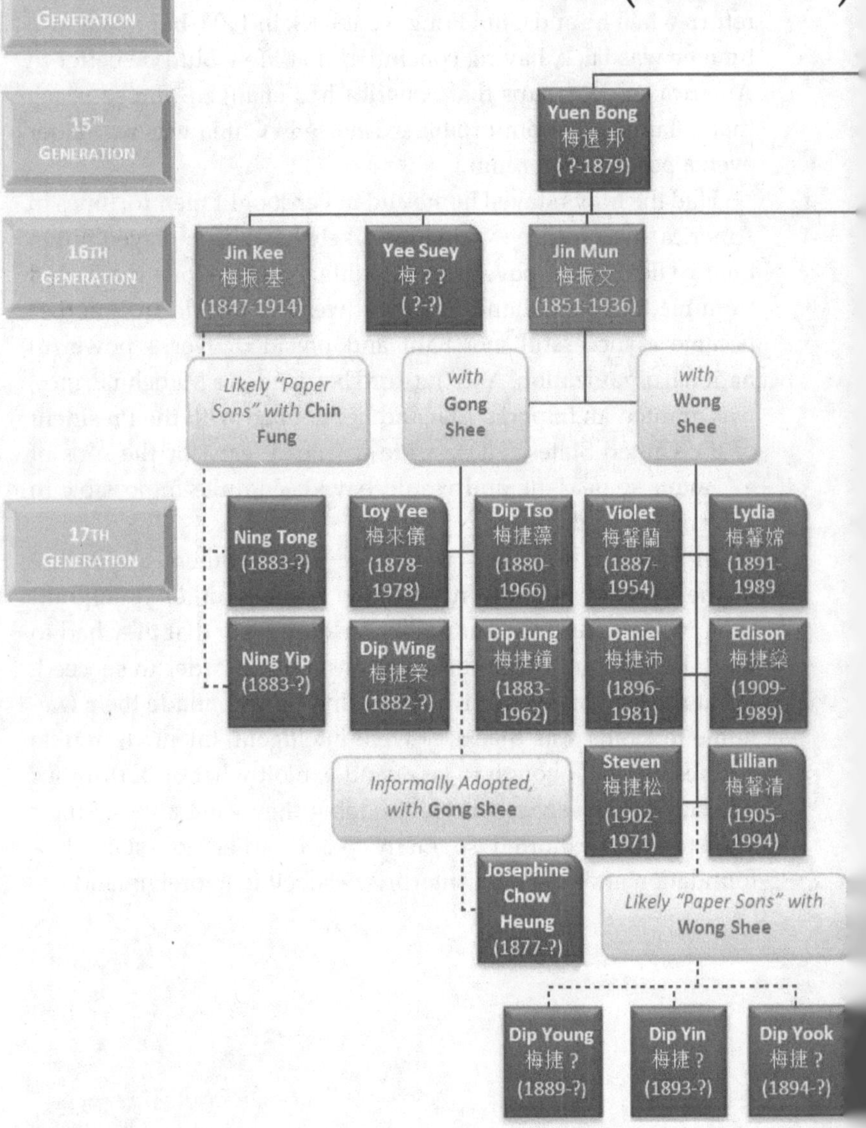

14th Generation

15th Generation
- Yuen Bong 梅遠邦 (?-1879)

16th Generation
- Jin Kee 梅振基 (1847-1914)
- Yee Suey 梅?? (?-?)
- Jin Mun 梅振文 (1851-1936)

17th Generation

Likely "Paper Sons" with Chin Fung:
- Ning Tong (1883-?)
- Ning Yip (1883-?)

with Gong Shee:
- Loy Yee 梅來儀 (1878-1978)
- Dip Wing 梅捷榮 (1882-?)
- Dip Tso 梅捷藻 (1880-1966)
- Dip Jung 梅捷鐘 (1883-1962)

with Wong Shee:
- Violet 梅馨蘭 (1887-1954)
- Daniel 梅捷沛 (1896-1981)
- Steven 梅捷松 (1902-1971)
- Lydia 梅馨嬌 (1891-1989)
- Edison 梅捷榮 (1909-1989)
- Lillian 梅馨清 (1905-1994)

Informally Adopted, with Gong Shee:
- Josephine Chow Heung (1877-?)

Likely "Paper Sons" with Wong Shee:
- Dip Young 梅捷? (1889-?)
- Dip Yin 梅捷? (1893-?)
- Dip Yook 梅捷? (1894-?)

18th Generation

Compiled by the author, with special thanks to Roberta Gee, a member of the 19th generation. Females are indicated by boxes with a rounded upper right-hand corner. Blood relations are depicted with a solid line.

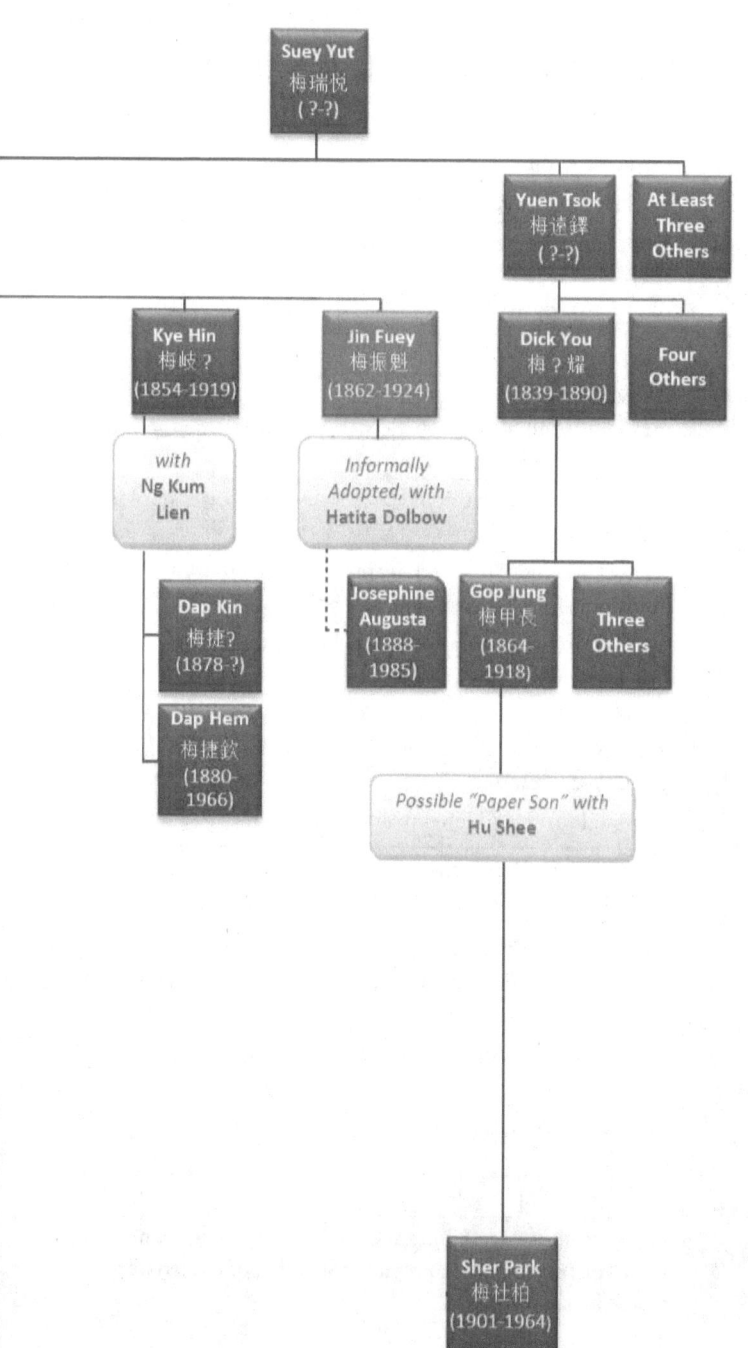

Moy Jin Kee Chronology

1847	Born in Hai Yang Village, Xinning County, Guangdong Province, China.
ca. 1859	Leaves China with an uncle and arrives in California.
1864	Finds work as a cook for the family of Leland Stanford in Sacramento.
ca. 1869	Returns to China.
1873	Marries Chin Fung.
1875	Arrives in San Francisco aboard S.S. *City of Pekin* with younger brother Jin Fuey. Remains in California for three years.
1878	Converts to Christianity at Methodist Mission School in San Francisco.
	Arrives in New York and is employed by Henry C. Parke, an importer of Chinese and Japanese goods.
1879	Speaks out against anti-Chinese legislation before Congress in the *New York Tribune*.
	Opens a Christian Chinese mission at 14 Mott Street, New York, New York, under the auspices of the Methodist Episcopal Church.
	Arrested for grand larceny and jailed.
1880	Files Declaration of Intention to become a U.S. citizen with the Superior Court of New York City.
ca. 1881	Returns to China.
1883	Arrives in San Francisco from Hong Kong with wife Chin Fung aboard the S.S. *Oceanic*.
1885	Opens Chinese hotel and restaurant in Newark, New Jersey.
1886	Relocates to Chicago and enters laundry business on State Street.
1890	Opens tea shop in Chicago.
1894	Organizes Chicago Chinese Club for "benevolent and social purposes" and to agitate for rights of citizenship for Chinese.

1897	Relocates to Indianapolis, Indiana.
	Obtains certificate of U.S. citizenship from Marion County Court.
1901	Receives gift of 100 "hundred-year eggs" from Viceroy Li Hung Chang, a member of the Chinese Imperial Court.
1904	Attends St. Louis World's Fair as a local Chinese exhibitor.
	Hosts Manchu Prince Pu Lun in his Indianapolis restaurant.
	Elevated to rank of "Mandarin of the Fifth Degree."
1905	Named in the press as leader in the fight against the Chinese Exclusion Act.
1906	Meets President Theodore Roosevelt, Vice President Charles W. Fairbanks, Rep. Jesse Overstreet and Chinese Legation officials in Washington.
1907	Stripped of his Mandarin rank and deposed as "mayor" of Indianapolis Chinatown by the Chinese Legation in Washington.
1908	Turns over restaurant to partners and returns to China with wife Chin Fung.
1909	Lands in Tacoma, Washington with Chin Fung. Detained for several weeks while their right to enter the United States is investigated.
	Couple is admitted to the United States. Proceeds to Indianapolis.
1911	Citizenship revoked by Federal Court, which concludes it was granted erroneously after Federal law forbade naturalization of Chinese.
1914	Dies suddenly of heart failure at restaurant in Indianapolis. Funeral service conducted by members of Chinese Masonic Lodge.
	Wife sells home and restaurant and departs for China with his remains.

Moy Jin Mun Chronology

1851	Born in Hai Yang Village, Xinning County, Guangdong Province, China.
ca. 1861	Arrives in San Francisco. Lives with relatives and studies English.
1865	Joins elder brother Jin Kee in Sacramento and works for the family of Leland Stanford, Sr., whose wife Jane offers adoption.
ca. 1866	Departs Sacramento.
1866–1869	Mines gold in California, prospecting old claims.
ca. 1869	Returns to China. Weds Gong Shee in arranged marriage.
ca. 1870	Returns to the United States alone. Travels across California and Nevada reworking old mines.
1874	Caught in anti-Chinese riot in Truckee, California, but is saved from injury.
ca. 1875	Visits China and returns to San Francisco with Gong Shee.
1876	Leases land on Andrus Island in the Sacramento River delta and plants eucalyptus trees. Also is said to work for the Central Pacific Railroad.
1878–1883	Gong Shee bears four children.
1879	Becomes official Chinese interpreter for the U.S. District Court in California.
1882	Helps establish the "Six Companies," the umbrella organization that governs Chinatown.
1886	Gong Shee returns to China with her children.
	Marries Wong Shee.
1887–1905	Wong Shee bears six children.
1891–1892	Informs authorities of a forthcoming shipment of opium and secures agreement to split reward. Cohorts renege on agreement.

1892	Translates warning that all Chinese must register with government, ostensibly earning repeated death threats from Chinatown "highbinders."
1895	Called as expert in an opium smuggling case and samples drug in open court to determine its origin.
1906	Loses his establishment in the San Francisco earthquake and subsequent fire.
	Returns to mining, and reworks old claims in gold mines of northern California.
1910	Purchases 92-acre parcel of placer claims near Applegate, Oregon. Returns to San Francisco.
1913	Helps found the General Peace Association, an organization formed to stem triad violence.
1914	Allegedly attempts to extort money from cousin Gop Jung, spurring an investigation by the U.S. Immigration Bureau. Complaint is eventually withdrawn.
1916-1917	Becomes president of the Six Companies, a.k.a. the Chinese Consolidated Benevolent Association.
1920s	Travels to west coast cities mediating triad disputes.
1929	Ruined financially in the stock market crash.
1930	Hosts Beijing Opera star Mei Lan Fang at Shanghai Low, a Chinese restaurant in which he holds a share.
1936	Dies in San Francisco. Buried in Chinese Cemetery, Daly City, California.

Jin Fuey Moy Chronology

1862	Born in Hai Yang Village, Xinning County, Guangdong Province, China.
1875	Arrives in San Francisco aboard the S.S. *City of Pekin* with brother Jin Kee. Engaged as a servant by George Washington Reed, publisher of the *Brooklyn Daily Eagle*. Relocates to Brooklyn, New York.
1880	Baptized a Methodist. Enrolls in New Jersey's Pennington Seminary.
1883	Joins Methodist Episcopal Chinese Mission in New York's Chinatown.
1884	Becomes superintendent of the Chinese-American Union in Philadelphia, Pennsylvania.
1886	Enters Philadelphia's Jefferson Medical College.
1889	Elopes to Camden, New Jersey with 19 year-old Hatita Alice Dolbow. Both are arrested in Philadelphia the following day.
1890	Earns M.D. degree. Opens medical office in Philadelphia.
1891	Informally adopts Josephine Augusta Moy, 31-month-old daughter of Philadelphia laundryman Moy Shoo Chong.
1892	Publishes the *Chinese-American Advocate*.
	Returns to New York and works briefly for a Chinese Hospital in Brooklyn, but the institution fails.
1893	Becomes superintendent of the Chinese Guild at St. Bartholomew's Protestant Episcopal Church in New York City.
1897	Appointed official interpreter for the New York criminal courts.
1898	Employed by the U.S. Immigration Bureau as investigator and Chinese interpreter.
1901	Purchases farm in Woodcliff Lake, New Jersey.
1902	Accused of smuggling Chinese immigrants into the United States from Canada. Discharged from the Immigration Bureau.

1908	Applies to U.S. and Canadian governments for patent on a nutcracker, possibly making him the first Chinese in America ever to apply to the U.S. government for patent protection.
1911	Arrested in New Jersey for conspiracy to smuggle Chinese into the United States from Jamaica. Acquitted of charges in Boston trial.
1912	Relocates to Pittsburgh. Arrested for using the U.S. mail to promote illegal medical practices or the sale of drugs and instruments for illegal purposes.
1915	Charged with violating the Harrison Narcotics Tax Act by writing illegal prescriptions for heroin and morphine.
	District Court rules Harrison Act applies only to manufacturers, importers and dealers; prosecution halted. Case appealed to Supreme Court.
	United States v. *Jin Fuey Moy* is argued before U.S. Supreme Court.
1916	Supreme Court affirms District Court decision in *United States* v. *Jin Fuey Moy*. Indictment is nullified.
1917	Indicted again for conspiracy to violate the Harrison Narcotics Tax Act.
1918	Convicted and sentenced to two years in the Federal penitentiary. Appeals case to U.S. Supreme Court on constitutional grounds.
1920	*Jin Fuey Moy* v. *United States* is argued before U.S. Supreme Court, which sustains conviction.
1921	Begins incarceration at United States Penitentiary, Atlanta, Georgia.
1922	Released from prison.
1924	Dies in Pittsburgh. Buried in Uniondale Cemetery.

Glossary of Chinese Terms and Place Names

Note: Chinese place names employed throughout this book are spelled according to the pinyin romanization system. Other names are spelled as they appeared in the contemporary documents consulted in the book's preparation. These are defined below, together with their corresponding standard Chinese characters. Where older or non-standard spellings are employed, pinyin equivalents are provided.

Anhui (安徽). A province in eastern China said to be the ancestral home of the Moy clan.

Beijing (北京). The capital city of China until 1911, and again beginning in 1949.

chak chee ("check" 紙, *zhi*). Identity papers Chinese in America were required to carry under the terms of the Geary Act of 1892. A blend of the English word "check," and the Chinese word "chee," meaning "paper."

Chee Kung Tong (致公堂, *Zhigong Tang*). A Chinese organization with some ties to the Freemasons, but stemming from a very different tradition. Literally, "Hall of Universal Justice."

Chinese-American Advocate (華美字報, *Huamei Zibao*). A newspaper published briefly by Jin Fuey Moy in Philadelphia in 1892.

Dai Fow (大埠, *Dafu*). Colloquial Cantonese term for San Francisco. Literally, "big city."

Duanfen (端芬). District in Taishan County to which nearly all overseas Moy clan members can trace their ancestry.

Fuzhou (福州). The capital city of Fujian Province.

General Peace Association (美洲華僑和平總會, *Meizhou Huaqiao*

Heping Zonghui). An organization established in San Francisco in 1913 by 27 Chinese fraternal organizations to put an end to violence among the triads.

Guangdong (廣東). A coastal province in southeast China that includes the Pearl River delta county of Taishan, where the Moy brothers were born.

Guangxi (廣西). A province in southern China immediately west of Guangdong.

Guangzhou (廣州). The capital city of Guangdong Province.

haer-mai (蝦米, *xiami*). Dried shrimp.

Hakka (客家, *Kejia*). Migrants from northern China who settled in Guangdong and Fujian provinces in the early years of the Qing dynasty. The term translates literally as "guest people."

Hoy Sun Ning Yung Cemetery (臺山寧陽餘慶堂公墓, *Taishan Ningyang Yuqingtang Gongmu*). Chinese cemetery in Daly City, California.

Hai Yang (海陽). Village in Taishan in which the three Moy brothers and their cousin Moy Gop Jung were born. Alternately spelled Hoy Yeung, Hey Yin, Whey Young, Hoy Hong and Hey Young.

Hip Sing Tong (協勝堂, *Xiesheng Tang*). A Chinese triad organization engaged in criminal activities in Chinatowns across America.

lai chee (荔枝, *lizhi*). Lychee, a tropical and subtropical fruit native to southern China and Southeast Asia.

lap chong (臘腸, *la chang*). A dried, smoked variety of Chinese pork sausage.

low-wee (魷魚, *youyu*). Squid.

Ming (明). The last native Chinese dynasty, which ruled China from 1368-1644.

Moy Family Association (梅氏公所, *Mei Shi Gongsuo*). Chicago-based organization of members of the Moy clan with branches in many other cities.

mu (亩, *mu*). A unit of measurement equivalent to about 1/6 acre.

Ping Kung Tong (秉公堂, *Binggong Tang*). A San Francisco-based triad organization engaged in criminal activities in Chinatowns across America.

Qing (清). The Manchu dynasty, which ruled China from 1644-1911.

shee (氏, *shi*). Title used for married and unmarried females outside of their families in place of their given names. Can be translated as "née" or "Ms."

Six Companies (六大公司, *Liu Da Gongsi*). Umbrella organization established in 1882 that governed Chinatowns throughout the United States and served as the voice of America's Chinese. Eventually renamed the Chinese Consolidated Benevolent Association.

Xinning (新寧). An earlier name for Taishan that ceased to be used in 1914 following the establishment of the Republic of China.

Taishan (臺山). One of four counties in Guangdong Province's Pearl River delta. Source of most Chinese emigration to the United States during the late 19th and early 20th centuries.

tong (堂, *tang*). A Chinatown secret society or triad, formed for mutual protection, often associated with violence and criminal enterprises.

Yee Fow (二埠, *Erfu*). Colloquial Cantonese term for Sacramento. Literally, "second city."

yin wa (燕窩, *yanwo*). A swallow's nest, used in making a variety of Chinese soup.

Notes

ABBREVIATIONS

BS	Baltimore Sun
BP	Binghamton Press
BJ	Boston Journal
BG	Boston Globe
BDE	Brooklyn Daily Eagle
BE	Buffalo Express
CIO	Chicago Inter Ocean
CT	Chicago Tribune
CPD	Cleveland Plain Dealer
GL	The Gleaner
IN	Indianapolis News
IS	Indianapolis Star
KG	Kalamazoo Gazette
KCS	Kansas City Star
LAT	Los Angeles Times
LS	Lowell Sun
NHR	New Haven Register
NYDT	New York Daily Tribune
NYET	New York Evening Telegram
NYH	New York Herald
NYMT	New York Morning Telegraph
NYS	New York Sun
NYST	New York Sunday Tribune
NYT	New York Times
OT	Oakland Tribune
ODT	Owego Daily Times
PI	Philadelphia Inquirer
SDRU	Sacramento Daily Record Union

SDT	Seattle Daily Times
SFB	San Francisco Bulletin
SFC	San Francisco Chronicle
SFMC	San Francisco Morning Call
SR	Springfield Republican
TDT	Tipton Daily Tribune
TT	Trenton Times
WP	Washington Post

ENDNOTES

Author's Preface
Page ix: *I happened on the story:* Three *WP* articles recount the story of Moy Gop Jung: "How Moy Gop Helped Run Down Notorious Highbinders," 6 Sep 1908; "Moy Gop Yahn, Chinese Detective, Marries American Woman," 16 Jan 1900; and "Chinaman as Sleuth" 14 Jan 1900.

Chapter I: Tangled in a Snarl
Page 3: *has excited attention in this country and China:* Untitled, *SDT*, 12 Apr 1909 and "Moy Kee Says He is Victim of Fraud," *SDT*, 11 Apr 1909.
Page 3: *my wife and I allowed:* Ibid., 11 Apr 1909.

Chapter II: The Road to Exclusion
Page 4: *several times the number:* Martin Stuart-Fox, *A Short History of China and Southeast Asia: Tribute, Trade and Influence* (Sydney, Australia: Allen & Unwin, 2003), 126 and Roger Daniels, *Asian America: Chinese and Japanese in the United States Since 1850* (Seattle, WA: University of Washington Press, 1990), 69.
Page 4: *a fraction of the estimated two million:* Lynn Pan, *Sons of the Yellow Emperor: The Story of the Overseas Chinese* (London: Mandarin Paperbacks, 1991), 43.
Page 5: *emigration was explicitly forbidden:* Shih-Shan Henry Tsai,

The Chinese Experience in America (Bloomington, IN: Indiana University Press, 1986), 2.

Page 5: *brought many thousands more:* Lucie Cheng and Liu Yuzhun with Zheng Dehua, "Chinese Emigration, the Sunning Railway and the Development of Toisan," *Amerasia*, Vol IX, No. 1, 59-74, 1982.

Page 5: *an estimated 25,000 Chinese:* "The Chinese in California, 1850-1925," *Library of Congress website*, [http://www.loc.gov/teachers/classroommaterials/connections/chinese-cal/history.html.]

Page 5: *just over 63,000 in 1870:* Charles McClain, *Chinese Immigrants and American Law* (Florence, KY: Routledge, 1994), 448.

Page 6: *as early as 1852 agitation began:* Frank Soulé, John H. Gihon, M.D. and James Nisbet, *Annals of San Francisco* (New York: D. Appleton & Company, 1855), 380-381.

Page 6: *where it would benefit Americans:* "Chinese Immigration: Letter from Senator Blaine," *NYDT*, 24 Feb 1879.

Page 7: *they should all be kept out entirely:* Eithne Luibhéid, *Entry Denied: Controlling Sexuality at the Border* (Minneapolis, MN: University of Minnesota Press, 2002), 32-36.

Page 8: *Chinese bureaus were set up:* Peggy Spitzer Christoff, *Tracking the Yellow Peril* (Rockport, ME: Picton Press, 2001), xi-xii.

Page 9: *citizenship under the Fourteenth Amendment: United States* v. *Wong Kim Ark*, 169 U.S. 649 (1898).

Page 9: *the overall Chinese population was declining:* Erika Lee, *At America's Gates* (Chapel Hill: University of North Carolina Press, 2003), 201.

Chapter III: Beginnings

Page 12: *it was truth that was in short supply:* The various versions appeared in "Moy Jin Kee," *BDE*, 24 Mar 1879; Untitled, *Skaneateles Free Press*, 4 May 1905; Deposition of Dr. Jin Fuey Moy before Inspector W.W. Sibray, 24 Oct 1916, Case Files of

Chinese Immigrants, File 2702-C, Record Group 85, National Archives, Philadelphia, PA; Dr. Jin Fuey Moy to Messrs. McLanhan and Burton, 7 Mar 1917, Entry 9, File 54180/334, Record Group 85, National Archives, Washington, DC; "Moy Kee as a Boy," *WP*, 1 Mar 1900 and "Moy Jin Kee in Prison," *NYDT*, 13 May 1879.

Page 13: *trace their origins to this 1,300 sq. mile county:* Renqiu Yu, "Educational Development of Toisan 1910-1940," in Don T. Nakanishi and Tina Yamano Nishida, eds., *The Asian American Educational Experience: A Sourcebook for Teachers and Students* (Florence, KY: Routledge, 1994), 42.

Page 13: *The name is associated with 123 different villages:* "Village Database Search Utility," *Chinese Cultural Center of San Francisco website*, 2009. [http://www.c-c-c.org/villagedb/search.cgi].

Page 14: *beautiful beaches and islands:* Moy Min Kui, *Clan Genealogy of the Moys of Duanfen* (端芬梅氏族譜) (Duanfen, China, 1664). In the collection of Tow H. Moy of the Moy Family Association, Washington, DC.

Page 14: *sufficient arable land to sustain its inhabitants:* Him Mark Lai, "Geographical and Historical Notes on the Wuyi Region," *Taishan Genealogy website*, 7 Apr 2002. [http://www.apex.net.au/~jgk/taishan/notes.html].

Page 15: *a bright future for your descendants:* Translation courtesy of Marc Abramson.

Page 17: *the moral teachings embodied in them:* William Hoy, "Moy Jin Mun – Pioneer," *Chinese Digest*, 15 May 1936, Vol. II, No. 20, 11. This source, which is the basis for virtually every extensive article published about Moy Jin Mun, is itself based in large part on the recollections of Steven C. Moy, Moy Jin Mun's son.

Page 17: *veneration of ancestors and the education of sons:* Moy Min Kui, *Clan Genealogy of the Moys of Duanfen.*

Page 17: *do not think it fun to hurt anyone:* "Moy Kee as a Boy," *WP*, 1 Mar 1900.

Page 18: *end of the string and make it jump: Ibid.*
Page 18: *then I decided to run away:* "How Moy Gop Helped Run Down Notorious Highbinders," *WP*, 6 Sep 1908.

Chapter IV: California Dreaming
Page 20: *capable of cutting the time in half:* "The Commerce of the East," *Charleston Daily News*, 27 Mar 1867.
Page 20: *was essentially rendered moot:* Guofu Liu, *The Right to Leave and Return and Chinese Migration Law* (Leiden, The Netherlands: Martins Nijhoff Publishers, 2007), 131-2.
Page 20: *their own bedding:* E. Mowbray Tate, *Transpacific Steam: The Story of Steam Navigation from the Pacific Coast of North America to the Far East and the Antipodes, 1867-1941* (Cranbury, NJ: Cornwall Books, 1986), 227.
Page 21: *accidentally caused a serious fire:* "Latest News By Telegraph to the Patriot," *Wisconsin Weekly Patriot*, 19 Nov 1859.
Page 21: *and taken to Honolulu:* "Interesting from California. Burning of the Clipper Ship Mastiff," *NYH*, 18 Nov 1859.
Page 21: *with a bag of gold dust:* "Moy Jin Mun, Liege Lord of Old Chinatown," *Westways*, Jan 1937.
Page 21: *just short of 150,000 by 1870:* "San Francisco Population," *SF Genealogy* website, [http://www.sfgenealogy.com/sf/history/hgpop.htm].
Page 22: *new wharves were constructed:* "Walking on Water - A History of Mission Bay," *University of California at San Francisco* website, [http://www.ucsf.edu/news/2007/11/7374/walking-water-history-mission-bay2].
Page 22: *every bit of space was utilized:* "The Chinese Quarter in San Francisco," *Pacific Rural Press*, 27 Sep 1873.
Page 22: *12 times that number in the rest of California:* 1860 United States Federal Census Online Database, *Ancestry.com*, [http://search.ancestry.com/search/db.aspx?dbid=7667&enc=1].
Page 22: *economic, social and political purposes:* Him Mark Lai, *Becoming Chinese American* (Lanham, MD: Altamira Press,

2002), 39.

Page 23: *to appease the spirits of their departed:* Frank Soulé, John H. Gihon, M.D. and James Nisbet, *Annals of San Francisco* (New York: D. Appleton & Company, 1855), 378-387.

Page 24: *Yerba Buena throughout the 20th century:* "Yerba Buena Cemetery Map," *San Francisco Cemeteries website,* [http://www.sanfranciscocemeteries.com/yrbamap.html].

Page 24: *enrolled in school to study English:* William Hoy, "Moy Jin Mun – Pioneer," *Chinese Digest,* 15 May 1936, Vol. II, No. 20, 11.

Page 24: *a social hall and a theater:* "1850 - The Beginnings of Sacramento's Chinatown at China Slough," *Sacramento's Chinatown Mall website,* [http://www.yeefow.com/past/1850.html].

Page 25: *the new transcontinental railroad:* "Encyclopedia of World Biography on Leland Stanford," *BookRags website,* 2009. [http://www.bookrags.com/biography/leland-stanford/].

Page 25: *had found the project enthralling: Memorial Addresses on the Life and Character of Leland Stanford* (Washington: U.S. Government Printing Office, 1894), 5-6.

Page 25: *would expand it substantially years later:* "More Stanford Mansion History," *Leland Stanford Mansion State Historic Park website,* 2009. [http://www.stanfordmansion.org/then_history.html].

Page 25: *and a coachman in residence:* 1860 U.S. Census, Sacramento City, Sacramento County, California, page 56, lines 32-40; National Archives, Washington, DC.

Page 25: *a solid English education:* "May Get His Final Papers," *CT,* 3 Feb 1893.

Page 25: *their household as a gardener:* Hoy, *Chinese Digest,* 11. Hoy's article is the principal source for all of the stories relating to Jin Mun's relationship with the Stanford family.

Page 26: *several of her Chinese servants as heirs:* Last Will and Testament, 1899, 1900 and 1901, Folders 5, 7 and 8, Series 4 - Death and Estate Matters 1894-1921, *Papers of Jane Lathrop*

Stanford, Stanford University Library, Stanford, CA.

Page 27: *deleterious influence upon the superior race:* "Leaves from California History – IV: Chinese Labor," *SFC,* 27 Aug 1911.

Page 27: *followed by an additional 50:* George Kraus, "Chinese Laborers and the Construction of the Central Pacific," in *Utah Historical Quarterly,* (Winter, 1969), Vol. 37, No. 1, 42-3.

Page 27: *work required in railroad building:* Alexander Saxton, *The Indispensable Enemy: Labor and the Anti-Chinese Movement in California* (Berkeley, CA: University of California Press, 1975), 62.

Page 28: *supporters of anti-Chinese bills:* Iris Chang, *The Chinese in America: A Narrative History* (New York: Viking Press, 2003), 56.

Page 28: *a device to drive out the Chinese:* "Negroes for California," *NYT,* 12 Aug 1891.

Page 28: *gold that might have been overlooked:* Hoy, *Chinese Digest,* 11.

Page 28: *return for labor expended:* David Valentine, "Chinese Placer Mining in the United States: An Example from American Canyon, Nevada," in Susie Lan Cassel, ed., *The Chinese in America: A History from Gold Mountain to the New Millennium* (Lanham, MD: Altamira Press, 2002), 37.

Page 29: *a woman, Chin Fung, for him:* "Moy Kee as a Boy," *WP,* 1 Mar 1900.

Page 29: *property at the landlord's expense:* Sucheng Chan, *This Bittersweet Soil: The Chinese in California Agriculture, 1860-1910.* (Berkeley, CA: University of California Press, 1989), 199-200.

Page 29: *head foreman for the railroad:* Wilson Chu, "The Chinese Railroad Men," *N.Y.C. Chinatown Reunion Newsletter,* 11 May 2006.

Page 30: *smaller only than that of San Francisco:* Jean Pfaelzer, *Driven Out: The Forgotten War Against Chinese-Americans* (Berkeley, CA: University of California Press, 2008), 167-168.

Page 30: *the few vocations open to them:* Joshua Alexander, "Chinese Immigration" in *The Banyan Quarterly* (Oregon City,

OR: Clackamas Community College, 2000), Volume 1, Issue 4, Fall, 2000.

Page 30: *union members went after the Chinese:* Hoy, *Chinese Digest,* 11.

Page 31: *organized until two years later:* "Herb Shop an Important Link to Truckee's Chinese History," *Sierra Sun,* 27 Feb 2004.

Page 31: *thieving millionaires, and scoundrelly officials:* Jerome A. Hart, "The Sand Lot and Kearneyism," *Virtual Museum of the City of San Francisco website.* Excerpt from 1931 book, *In Our Second Century,* [http://www.sfmuseum.org/hist2/kearneyism.html].

Page 31: *that employed Chinese workers:* "When Truckee Boycotted Chinese Workers," *Sierra Sun,* 28 Nov 2004.

Page 31: *with a torchlight parade:* Guy H. Coates, "Trout Creek Outrage," *Truckee-Donner Historical Society, Inc. website,* 2009. [http://truckeehistory.org/historyArticles/history6.html].

Chapter V: Another Good Man Gone Wrong

Page 32: *to sleep on comfortable bunks:* "The Chinese," *SFC,* 2 Apr 1876.

Page 32: *who was visiting California:* "Moy Jin Kee," *BDE,* 13 May 1879.

Page 32: *work as a servant in his home:* Arthur Bonner, *Alas! What Brought Thee Hither? The Chinese in New York, 1800-1950* (Madison, New Jersey: Fairleigh Dickinson University Press, 1997), 124.

Page 33: *lower Manhattan and Brooklyn:* 1870 and 1880 United States Federal Census Online Databases, *Ancestry.com,* [http://search.ancestry.com/search/db.aspx?dbid=7163] [http://search.ancestry.com/search/db.aspx?dbid=6742].

Page 33: *vice, disease and violence:* Taylor Anbinder, *Five Points* (New York: Penguin Putnam, Inc., 2002), 4.

Page 33: *part of Chinatown to this day:* Ibid., 396-397.

Page 33: *kitchen mantels of this Christian land:* "Chinese Servants in America," *NYT,* 28 Nov 1875.

Page 33: *Five Points Mission in lower Manhattan:* "A Mott Street Mission," NYH, 5 April 1880.

Page 33: *both the Fuzhou and Cantonese dialects:* O. Gibson, *The Chinese in America* (Cincinnati: Hitchcock & Walden, 1877), 172 and 177.

Page 34: *imported Chinese and Japanese goods:* "Moy Jin Kee," BDE, 13 May 1879.

Page 34: *porcelain and lacquer ware:* Moy Jin Kee in Prison," NYDT, 13 May 1879.

Page 34: *at a Sunday school in Harlem:* Jin Kee's various appearances were catalogued in "Marcy Avenue Baptist Church," BDE, 6 Oct 1878; "Two Curious Sunday Meetings," NYDT, 18 Mar 1879; "Grace Methodist Episcopal Church," BDE, 1 Mar 1879 and an untitled article in Warren, Pennsylvania's *Warren Ledger*, 9 May 1879.

Page 36: *on its way to passage in the Senate:* Andrew Gyory, "Chinese Exclusion Acts," in *Encyclopedia of U.S. Labor and Working-class History, Volume I,* Eric Arnesen, ed. (New York: Routledge, 2007), 240-241.

Page 36: *enjoyment of equal rights and privileges:* "Chinese Immigration: A Letter from William Lloyd Garrison," NYDT, 17 Feb 1879.

Page 37: *they would come in enormous numbers:* "Chinese Immigration: Letter from Senator Blaine," NYDT, 24 Feb 1879.

Page 38: *but they cannot bear everything:* "A Defence of the Chinese," NYDT, 27 Feb 1879.

Page 38: *are now being treated in California:* Ibid.

Page 39: *after Garfield was assassinated:* Gyory, *Encyclopedia of U.S. Labor,* 240-241.

Page 39: *a translator, a musician and a missionary:* "High-Toned Chinaman," NYMT, 13 Apr 1979.

Page 40: *a Chinese Methodist mission in New York:* Ibid.

Page 40: *a Bible class every Saturday evening:* The story of the opening of the mission appeared in "Opening a Chinese Mission," NYDT, 5 May 1879; "Chinese Mission in New

York," *NYH*, 12 Oct 1879; "A Chinese Mission in Mott Street," *NYT*, 25 Apr 1879; "Opening a Chinese Mission," *NYDT*, 5 May 1879; "School for Chinamen in New York," *SFB*, 30 Apr 1879; "Preaching to the Chinamen," *NYT*, 5 May 1879 and "A Mott Street Mission," *NYH*, 5 Apr 1880.

Page 40: *The grand opening on May 4, 1879:* The grand opening of the mission was covered in "Moy Jin Kee, the Christian Chinaman," *BDE*, 1 Mar 1879; "Preaching to the Chinamen," *NYT*, 5 May 1879; "A Chinese Mission," *NYH*, 5 May 1879 and "Opening a Chinese Mission," *NYDT*, 5 May 1879.

Page 42: *Black, yellow, white everybody:* "A Chinese Mission," *NYH*, 5 May 1879.

Page 42: *marvelous fluency and distinctness:* "Moy Jin Kee in Prison," *NYDT*, 13 May 1879.

Page 43: *many speakers cannot command:* "Moy Jin Kee," *BDE*, 24 May 1879.

Page 43: *others are allowed to do:* "A Defence of the Chinese," *NYDT*, 27 Feb 1879.

Page 43: *until the affair blew over:* Bonner, *Alas! What Brought Thee Hither*, 114.

Page 43: *to pacify the students:* "Moy Jin Kee in Prison," *NYS*, 13 May 1879.

Page 44: *$112 in bills and $30 in gold:* "Another Good Man Gone Wrong," *CT*, 17 May 1879 and "Moy Jin Kee, the Christian Missionary Committed for Grand Larceny," *NYH*, 13 May 1879.

Page 44: *as you will see by and by:* "Moy Jin Kee's Exploits," *NYH*, 12 May 1879.

Page 44: *that describes everything:* "Moy Jin Kee in Prison," *NYS*, 13 May 1879; "The Chinese in New York," *SDRU*, 14 May 1879 and "Moy Jin Kee, the Christian Missionary Committed for Grand Larceny," *NYH*, 13 May 1879.

Page 45: *held on $1,000 bail:* The court proceedings were chronicled in "Moy Jin Kee in Prison," *NYDT*, 13 May 1879 and "Missionary Moy's Fall," *NYET*, 12 May 1879.

Page 46: *the articles I picked up myself:* The quotations are from "Moy Jin Kee in Prison," *NYDT,* 13 May 1879.

Page 46: *liberate his brother from those circumstances:* "Moy Jin Kee, the Christian Missionary Committed for Grand Larceny," *NYH,* 13 May 1879.

Page 48: *until they have looked up his sleeves:* Jin Kee was judged harshly in several newspapers, including: "Moy Jin Kee," *NHR,* 13 May 1879; "A Word for Moy Jin Kee," *BDE,* 13 May 1879 and "Another Good Man Gone Wrong," *CT,* 17 May 1879.

Page 48: *24 jacks up his sleeve:* Francis Bret Harte, "Plain Language from Truthful James," *The Overland Monthly Magazine,* Sep 1870.

Page 48: *or a dismissed indictment exists:* Minutes of the Court of General Sessions, New York County, 19 May 1879.

Page 48: *meeting in Harlem the following month:* "Chinese Doctrine," *The Athens Messenger,* 12 Jun 1879.

Chapter VI: He Stands High Among His Countrymen

Page 49: *New Jersey's Pennington Seminary:* Mary Ting Yi Lui, *The Chinatown Trunk Mystery* (Princeton: Princeton University Press, 2005), 118.

Page 49: *whose ages ran from 13 to 27:* Pennington Methodist Episcopal Conference Seminary, 1880 U. S. Census, Hopewell Township, Mercer County, New Jersey, page 17, line 24; National Archives, Washington, DC.

Page 49: *rates moderate; catalogues free:* "Instruction," *NYT,* 25 Sep 1884.

Page 50: *missionaries in foreign countries:* Princeton, *Sixty-Three: Fortieth Yearbook of the Members of the Class of 1863, Collegio Neo Caesariensis, Nassau Hall, now Princeton University* (Albany, New York: Fort Orange Press, 1904), 57-59.

Page 50: *debates at its weekly meetings:* Thomas Hanlon, *A Concise History of Pennington Seminary of the New Jersey Conference* (Trenton, NJ: MacCrellish & Quigley, 1886), 4 and George

Preston Mains, *James Monroe Buckley* (New York and Cincinnati: The Methodist Book Concern, 1917), 122.

Page 51: *Church in nearby Trenton:* "Religious Notices," *Trenton State Gazette*, 18 Jun 1881.

Page 51: *his native land as a missionary:* "A Chinese Christmas Service," *NYS*, 1 Jan 1883.

Page 52: *and it costs them nothing:* "American Begins to Know Chinaman," *CPD*, 25 Feb 1906.

Page 52: *for whom Jin Fuey provided interpretation:* Sixty-Fifth Annual report of the Missionary Society of the Methodist Episcopal Church for the Year 1883 (New York: Missionary Society of the Methodist Episcopal Church, 1884), 212.

Page 52: *programs and non-sectarian worship:* Rev. Edwin W. Rice, D.D., ed., *The Sunday School World* (Philadelphia: American Sunday School Union, Jan 1887), 122.

Page 53: *assaulting and robbing another Chinese:* "Mongolian Robbers," *TT*, 22 Jul 1886.

Page 53: *course of study in the United States:* "Personal Mention," *PI*, 18 Nov 1886.

Page 53: *the first Chinese to enroll at Jefferson:* F. Michael Angelo, University Archivist and Special Collections Librarian, Thomas Jefferson University. Personal correspondence with the author, 21 Oct 2009.

Page 53: *looking for her for nine months:* "She Loved a Chinaman," *PI*, 4 Apr 1889 and "Off With a Chinese Laundryman," *BS*, 5 Apr 1889.

Page 54: *would, in fact, be legal:* "Moy Gop Yahn, Chinese Detective, Marries American Woman," *WP*, 16 Jan 1900.

Page 55: *Patton Makes a Queer Choice:* "Antwerp: Married a Chinaman," *Syracuse Evening Herald*, 17 Jan 1900.

Page 55: *marriage to Jin Fuey drew headlines, too:* "She Loved a Chinaman," *PI*, 4 Apr 1889 and "Off With a Chinese Laundryman," *BS*, 5 Apr 1889.

Page 55: *they seem to be contented:* "Live Like Melican Men," *CT*, 12 May 1889.

Page 55: *both Chinese and Caucasians:* Louis J. Beck, *New York's Chinatown: An Historical Presentation of Its People and Places* (New York: Bohemia Publishing Company, 1898) 268.

Page 56: *until returning in 1913:* Deposition of Moy Hand Fun before Inspector John F. Dunton, 3 Oct 1913, Case Files of Chinese Immigrants, File 2064-C, Record Group 85, National Archives, Philadelphia, PA.

Page 56: *procedures to formalize her adoption:* George W. Cliffe to Josephine Augusta Moy, 22 Oct 1913; Case Files of Chinese Immigrants, File 2702-C; Record Group 85, National Archives, Philadelphia, PA.

Page 56: *the circumstances of her birth:* Josephine Augusta Moy Passport Application, 13 Oct 1916, Record Group 59, National Archives, Washington, D.C.

Page 58: *under which he now is to live:* "Introduction," *The Chinese-American Advocate,* 20 Jun 1892.

Page 58: *iron and steel plant near Hankou:* Untitled, *The Chinese-American Advocate,* 20 Jun 1892.

Page 59: *a former American missionary in China:* Ibid.

Page 59: *from bodily injury or disease:* "A Chinese Hospital Association," *NYT,* 29 Dec 1890.

Page 60: *their surroundings are strange:* "Aid Asked for a Chinese Hospital," *NYT,* 22 Apr 1891.

Page 60: *the food at American hospitals:* "Noted in Their Day," *Arizona Republican,* 3 Aug 1892.

Page 60: *Washington Avenue Baptist Church:* Henry W. B. Howard, ed., *The Eagle and Brooklyn: The Record of the Progress of the Brooklyn Daily Eagle* (Brooklyn, NY: The Brooklyn Daily Eagle, 1893), Vol. II, 670.

Page 61: *because it violated the Exclusion Act:* "In and About the City," *NYT,* 19 Nov 1887 and Bonner, *Alas! What Brought Thee Hither,* 124.

Page 61: *the 15-20 herbalists in Chinatown:* "For Ill Chinamen," *Oswego Palladium,* 26 May 1891 and Bonner, *Alas! What Brought Thee Hither,* 124.

Page 62: *with a new pair of shoes:* The work of the Chinese Guild is discussed in Mary Ting Yi Lui, *The Chinatown Trunk Mystery* (Princeton: Princeton University Press, 2005), 125; "Notes from the United States," *The Church Weekly*, 25 Sep 1886; E. Clowes Chorley, *The Centennial History of St. Bartholomew's Church in the City of New York, 1835-1935* (New York: n.p., 1935), 221-2; Bonner, *Alas! What Brought Thee Hither*, 123 and "St. Bartholomew's Work," *NYT*, 13 Dec 1895.

Page 62: *secure a conviction to save your life:* Bonner, *Alas! What Brought Thee Hither*, 124.

Page 63: *the concept of the nearness of God:* "Sages of China," *BDE*, 7 Dec 1896.

Page 63: *their social and moral conditions:* "Ethics of the Chinese Sages," *BDE*, 2 Dec 1896.

Page 64: *less restive and more easy of control:* "Many Chinamen Approve," *NYT*, 12 Apr 1893.

Page 65: *his intention to leave his church:* "Chinamen are Downhearted," *NYT*, 7 Jul 1893.

Page 65: *to wave a red flag in his place: Ibid.*

Chapter VII: Moy Jin Mun Will Furnish The Corpse

Page 66: *every ten San Franciscans was Chinese:* "San Francisco Population," *SF Genealogy website*, [http://www.sfgenealogy.com/sf/history/hgpop.htm].

Page 66: *before the Exclusion Act took effect:* Charles George Herbermann, Edward Aloysius Pace, Condé Bénoist Pallen et al, *The Catholic Encyclopedia* (New York: The Universal Knowledge Foundation, 1911), Vol. X, 296.

Page 66: *having been born in California:* Jackson Street Chinese Lodging House, 1880 U. S. Census, San Francisco City, San Francisco County, California, page 6, lines 19-23; National Archives, Washington, DC.

Page 66: *two days after it occurred:* "Born," *Daily Alta California*, 16 Apr 1880.

Page 67: *packed like sardines in a box:* "The Chinese," *SFC*, 2 Apr

1876.

Page 67: *named by President Chester A. Arthur:* "Brief San Francisco Items," *SDRU*, 4 Apr 1882.

Page 67: *earned $75 per month in the job: Official Register of the United States*, Serial Set Vol. No. 2410, Session Vol. No.5 (Washington, DC: United States Government Printing Office, 1886), 638.

Page 68: *the State of California to his resumé:* Deposition of Moy Jin Mun before U.S. Immigration Bureau Inspector H. Schmoldt, 27 Nov 1931, Case Files of Chinese Immigrants, File 12017/43314, Record Group 85, National Archives, San Bruno, CA.

Page 68: *which meant a 30-day jail sentence:* "A Speedy Trial and Conviction," *SFB*, 2 Feb 1882.

Page 68: *the California State Circuit Court:* Erika Lee, *At America's Gates* (Chapel Hill: University of North Carolina Press, 2003), 43-4.

Page 69: *resulted in the payment of a fee:* "The Oceanic's Traders," *SFB*, 17 Dec 1883.

Page 70: *divide with a great many officials:* "Crooked Methods of a Chinese Interpreter," *SFC*, 28 Nov 1885.

Page 70: *prohibit the sale or use of the drug:* "125th Anniversary of the First U.S. Anti-Drug Law: San Francisco's Opium Den Ordinance (Nov. 15, 1875)," *DrugSense website,* [http://www.drugsense.org/dpfca/opiumlaw.html].

Page 71: *domestically produced opium as well:* "The History of the Drug Laws," *Schaffer Library of Drug Policy website,* 2009. [http://www.druglibrary.org/schaffer/LIBRARY/histdrug.htm].

Page 71: *that they would pay same:* "They Laughed at Mun," *SFMC*, 1 Sep 1892.

Page 72: *on the full $2,500 he was due:* "A Tender to Moy Jin Mun," *SFMC*, 2 Sep 1892.

Page 72: *eventually recovered $500 of it:* "Moy Jin Mun's Move," *SFC*, 13 Oct 1892.

Page 73: *he had received $1,500 to kill me:* "His Life is Threatened,"

SFMC, 19 Sep 1892.

Page 73: *had been raised to $1,800:* "Local News Notes," *SFC*, 21 Sep 1892.

Page 73: *a hatchet through his vitals:* "Pernicious Highbinders," *BE*, 20 Sep 1892.

Page 73: *by watching the store carefully:* "His Life is Threatened," *SFMC*, 19 Sep 1892.

Page 73: *Moy Jin Mun is a sneak:* "Highbinders Again Threaten Moy Jin Mun," *SFMC*, 29 Sep 1892.

Page 74: *always had more or less trouble:* Ibid.

Page 74: *less than two dollars per week:* "Chinese Boycott," *SFMC*, 2 Apr 1893.

Page 75: *failed to participate in the divide:* "Moy Jin Mun's Move," *SFC*, 13 Oct 1892.

Page 75: *as one of them:* "Shady Opium Deals," *SFC*, 24 Nov 1893.

Page 76: *an opium dealer as well as an interpreter:* "The Opium Dummies," *SFC*, 26 Nov 1893.

Page 76: *manufactured in Victoria, British Columbia:* "The Opium Ring," *SFMC*, 9 Jan 1894.

Page 76: *Him Victoria opium all light:* Ibid.

Page 76: *whiskey and salt water, he added:* "The Benica Smuggler," *SFC*, 16 Aug 1895.

Chapter VIII: A Thorough American

Page 77: *return to China for a while:* Bruce Hall, *Tea That Burns: A Family Memoir of Chinatown* (New York: Free Press, 2000), 65.

Page 78: *to a reporter the previous year:* "High-Toned Chinaman," *NYMT*, 13 Apr 1979.

Page 78: *a dozen Chinese in the city in 1880:* 1880 United States Federal Census Online Database, *Ancestry.com*, [http://search.ancestry.com/search/db.aspx?dbid=6742].

Page 78: *a laundry a decade earlier:* Wong Chin Foo, "The Chinese in the United States," *The Chautauquan*, Vol. IX, Jan 1889, 217.

Page 79: *as it was boarding house:* Taylor Anbinder, *Five Points* (New York: Penguin Putnam, Inc., 2002), 398.

Page 80: *the staple food with you Americans:* "A Chinese Hotel: Moy Jim Kee's New Venture in the Hotel Line," *TT,* 2 Feb 1885.

Page 81: *arranged for other supplies: Ibid.*

Page 81: *catered to Chinese customers:* Yolanda Skeete, "When Newark Had a Chinatown," *Newark Chinatown website,* 10 Oct 2008, [Defunct website, visible at [http://web.archive.org/web/20071008213800/www.newarkchinatown.org/history.html].

Page 81: *about 180 Chinese in the city in 1880:* 1880 United States Federal Census Online Database, *Ancestry.com.* [http://search.ancestry.com/search/db.aspx?dbid=6742].

Page 81: *in the heart of the vice district:* Chuimei Ho and Soo Lon Moy, eds., *Chinese in Chicago, 1870-1945* (Charleston, SC: Arcadia Publishing, 2005), 51.

Page 81: *there were 199 Chinese laundries:* Paul C. P. Siu, *The Chinese Laundryman: A Study of Social Isolation* (New York: New York University Press, 1987), 27.

Page 81: *would grow to 740:* Rand McNally & Co.'s New Pocket Atlas (Chicago and New York: Rand, McNally & Co., 1898), 80.

Page 81: *throughout the city's Chinese history:* Adam McKeown, *Chinese Migrant Networks and Cultural Change* (Chicago: University of Chicago Press, 2001), 199.

Page 82: *branches in many other Chinatowns:* Meishi Zongqin Zupu Mulu (梅氏宗親族譜目錄) (Taipei: Meishi Zongqin Hui [梅氏宗親會], 1991), 9.

Page 82: *go by the name Moy Ah Kee:* The "Ah" syllable, not a name *per se,* is a prefix added to one's personal name by those with whom one is familiar, not unlike suffixes in English that make "Bill" into "Billy" or "John" into "Johnny."

Page 82: *hair queue dangling down his back:* "No Chinese Need Apply," *NYT,* 19 Oct 1886.

Page 83: *every year to press his case:* "A New Chinese Club," *KCS,* 23 Jun 1894.

Page 83: *those of its Western counterpart:* "Chinese Secret Societies/Freemasons," *Chinese in Northwest America Research Committee website,* [http://www.cinarc.org/Freemasons.html] and Huping Ling, *Chinese Chicago: Race, Transnational Migration, and Community Since 1870* (Stanford, CA: Stanford University Press, 2012), 149-150.

Page 83: *something to do with this, it speculated:* "By Blade and Board: Cigarmakers Marched to Victory," *Chicago Herald,* 24 May 1891.

Page 83: *Moy Kee, the well-known Chinaman:* "In the Social World," *CIO,* 22 Sep 1891.

Page 84: *nearly always covered with a veil:* "Live Like Melican Men," *CT,* 12 May 1889.

Page 84: *pale as rice and graceful as the bamboo:* "Chinese in Chicago: Where They Congregate, How They Live," *CIO,* 11 Sep 1892.

Page 85: *an American hen-pecked husband:* Ibid.

Page 85: *declined to grant naturalization:* "Moy Kee is Half a Citizen," *CIO,* 24 Feb 1893.

Page 86: *initially promised he would do so:* "Refuses to Naturalize Moy Ah Kee," *CT,* 25 Oct 1894.

Page 86: *chicken, fruit and rose wine:* "A New Chinese Club," *KCS,* 23 Jun 1894.

Page 88: *members have not the power to vote:* "Chinese in Politics: A Movement Begun in Chicago to Make the Celestials a Factor in Elections," *NHR,* 16 Jun 1894.

Page 88: *making this county their permanent home:* "A New Chinese Club," *KCS,* 23 Jun 1894.

Page 88: *as their first president:* "Chinese Clubs Being Organized," *NYT,* 20 Jun 1894.

Page 88: *his first papers for naturalization:* "Chinese Naturalization Party," *SR,* 20 Jun 1894.

Page 89: *to prosecute the suit vigorously:* "Moy Kee Claims He is Slandered," *CT,* 24 Jun 1894.

Page 89: *and prosecute the proprietors:* "Chinese Form a Club: Chicago Celestials Will Strive for Citizenship," *SFC,* 10 Nov 1894.

Page 89: *on several occasions, threatened his life:* "Moy Kee Claims

He is Slandered," *CT*, 24 Jun 1894.

Page 90: *Harrison Street district, the Tribune crowed:* "Odd Chinese Fight," *CT*, 27 Jan 1895.

Page 90: *a small Chinese army to capture that flag: Ibid.*

Page 91: *a hit man to assassinate the laundryman:* "Say it is a Trap for Moy Ah Kee," *CT*, 19 Feb 1895.

Chapter IX: "I Created Enmity Among Our Own Countrymen"

Page 92: *and use Arabic numerals:* "Against Chinese Laundries," *NYT*, 2 Feb 1898.

Page 92: *his patrons and their wares:* "A Blow at Chinese Laundries," *BDE*, 11 Feb 1898.

Page 93: *driving white women out of work:* "News of the Labor World," *NYT*, 7 Feb 1898.

Page 93: *His only clue is his own ticket:* "Fighting the Eagan Bill," *NYT*, 11 Feb 1898.

Page 94: *had left the city:* "Six Chinamen Without Certificates," *Naugatuck (CT) Daily News*, 29 Dec 1898.

Page 94: *unlucky Chinese to await trial:* "Chinamen Shaken Up," *North Adams Transcript*, 29 Dec 1898.

Page 94: *also had a Caucasian wife: Ibid.*

Page 94: *must have shut down for the day:* "Question of Chinese Identity," *SR*, 27 Jan 1899.

Page 95: *still room for improvement:* "One Chinaman Must Go," *SR*, 28 Jan 1899.

Page 95: *back of the counterfeiting ring:* "Girl Passes Bad Pennies," *NYDT*, 10 Feb 1901.

Page 95: *Kelly Street in the Bronx:* 1900 U. S. Census, Bronx Borough, New York County, New York, Supervisor's District 1, Enumeration District 1006, page 24, lines 79-81; National Archives, Washington, DC.

Page 96: *manner with Chinese laborers:* "Chinaman Buys a Country Home," *NYT*, 8 Nov 1901.

Page 97: *his salary of $100 per month:* Moy Gop Jung to the Commissioner-General of Immigration, 9 Oct 1911, Case Files of Chinese Immigrants, File 669C, Record Group 85, National Archives, Philadelphia, PA.

Page 97: *into the United States from Canada:* Deposition of Dr. Jin Fuey Moy before U.S. Immigration Bureau Inspector Charles V. Mallet, 19 Jan 1917, Case Files of Chinese Immigrants, File 669C, Record Group 85, National Archives, Philadelphia, PA.

Page 97: *taking bribes and selling government information:* "Boston Behind," *BG*, 25 Feb 1901.

Page 98: *this late date to expose it:* W.H. Ottis to Frank H. Larned, 6 Apr 1901, Entry 9, File 52730/53, Record Group 85, National Archives, Washington, DC.

Page 98: *my connection with the U.S. government:* Jin Fuey Moy to Moy Gop Jung, 8 Sep 1909, Case Files of Chinese Immigrants, File 669C, Record Group 85, National Archives, Philadelphia, PA.

Chapter X: Disaster and Rebuilding

Page 99: *to break up the incipient riot:* "Boys Create a Riot," *SFC*, 22 Apr 1898.

Page 99: *arrest and trial of the offenders:* Arthur Bonner, *Alas! What Brought Thee Hither? The Chinese in New York, 1800-1950* (Madison, New Jersey: Fairleigh Dickinson University Press, 1997), 124.

Page 99: *California Street police station:* "Boys Create a Riot," *SFC*, 22 Apr 1898.

Page 100: *after the General's death:* "Moy Jim [sic] Mun in a Lawsuit," *SFC*, 20 May 1899.

Page 100: *the case went to court: Ibid.*

Page 100: *for "rents" and "damages":* W. S. Keyes et al., Respondents, v. Moy Jin Mun, Appellant, 136 Cal. 129; 68 P. 476 (1902).

Page 100: *a judgment for that sum of money: Ibid.*

Page 101: *paths of truth and usefulness:* "Methodist Oriental Home is Dedicated by the Bishop," *SFMC*, 18 Jul 1901.

Page 101: *if she would permit it:* Moy Jin Mun to Kate Burton Lake, 20 May 1899. Burton/Lake/Garton Family Papers, Special

Collections and University Archives, University of Oregon Libraries, Eugene, OR.

Page 103: *having been married for 14 years:* The two records can be found in the 1900 U. S. Census, San Francisco, San Francisco County, California, Enumeration District 272, page 1, lines 48-50 and page 3, lines 48-54, National Archives, Washington, DC.

Page 103: *but not until 1906:* Deposition of Moy Jin Mun before U.S. Immigration Bureau Inspector W.W. Thiess, 17 Mar 1913, Case Files of Chinese Immigrants, File 12017/528, Record Group 85, National Archives, San Bruno, CA.

Page 103: *to replace her:* Deposition of Moy Jin Mun before U.S. Immigration Bureau Inspector H. Schmoldt, 27 Nov 1931, Case Files of Chinese Immigrants, File 12017/43314, Record Group 85, National Archives, San Bruno, CA.

Page 103: *when they were married:* William Hoy, "Moy Jin Mun – Pioneer," *Chinese Digest,* 15 May 1936. Vol. II, No. 20, 14.

Page 104: *each other during that period:* Wilson Chu, "The Chinese Railroad Men," *N.Y.C. Chinatown Reunion Newsletter,* 11 May 2006.

Page 104: *his first wife was no longer living:* Deposition of Wong Shee before U.S. Immigration Bureau Inspector W.W. Thiess, 17 Mar 1913, Case Files of Chinese Immigrants, File 12017/528, Record Group 85, National Archives, San Bruno, CA.

Page 104: *I never told her:* Re-Examination of Moy Jin Mun before U.S. Immigration Bureau Inspector W.W. Thiess, 17 Mar 1913, Case Files of Chinese Immigrants, File 12017/528, Record Group 85, National Archives, San Bruno, CA.

Page 104: *according to Chinese custom only:* Deposition of Wong Shee before U.S. Immigration Bureau Inspector H. Schmoldt, 27 Nov 1931, Case Files of Chinese Immigrants, File 12017/43314, Record Group 85, National Archives, San Bruno, CA.

Page 105: *near Volcano in Amador County:* "Legal and Official," *SFC,* 4 Mar 1895.

THREE TOUGH CHINAMEN

Page 105: *to prevent the discharge of debris:* "Abandoned Claims," *SFMC*, 16 May 1985.

Page 105: *Howland Flat, Sierra County:* "Business Changes," *SFC*, 20 Oct 1901.

Page 105: *in Oregon as late as 1910:* "Oregon," *Salt Lake Mining Review*, 15 May 1910.

Page 106: *quite near to San Francisco:* "The Great 1906 San Francisco Earthquake," *U.S. Geological Survey website*, 29 Jan 2009, [http://earthquake.usgs.gov/regional/nca/1906/18april/index.php].

Page 106: *threw many from their beds: The California Earthquake of April 18, 1906: Report of the State Earthquake Investigation Commission* (Washington: Carnegie Institute of Washington, 1908), Vol. I, 1-3.

Page 106: *Chinese quarter was completely destroyed:* "Details of the Relief," *NYT*, 20 Apr 1906.

Page 106: *black tunnels open on every side:* "Dens Like Ratholes," *WP*, 22 Apr 1906.

Page 107: *and died the death of rats: Ibid.*

Page 107: *ruined by the disaster, were among them:* Hoy, *Chinese Digest*, 14.

Page 107: *had headed for the ferries:* "Army of Homeless Fleeing from the Devastated City," *New York Times*, 20 Apr 1906.

Page 107: *across the bay to Oakland:* "1906 Earthquake: Chinese Displacement," *U.S. Department of the Interior National Park Service website*, 10 Feb 2007, [http://www.nps.gov/prsf/historyculture/1906-earthquake-chinese-treatment.htm].

Page 107: *famine and disease loomed:* "Famine Follows in the Wake of the Flames," *WP*, 21 Apr 1906.

Page 108: *about recording their deaths:* "100 Years Later, Quake's Dead Still Being Counted," *MSNBC website*, 14 Apr 2006, [http://www.msnbc.msn.com/id/12301877/ns/us_news-san_francisco_earthquake_1906/].

Page 108: *they will apply for native papers:* Inspector W.E. Walsh to the Commissioner, 1 Apr 1913, Case Files of Chinese

Immigrants, File 12017/528, Record Group 85, National Archives, San Bruno, CA.

Page 109: *the eastern United States somewhere:* Deposition of Wong Shee before U.S. Immigration Bureau Inspector H. Schmoldt, 19 Nov 1936, Case Files of Chinese Immigrants, File 12017/51154, Record Group 85, National Archives, San Bruno, CA.

Page 109: *had destroyed all of his records:* Deposition of Moy Jin Mun before U.S. Immigration Bureau Inspector W.W. Theiss, 19 Mar 1913, Case Files of Chinese Immigrants, File 12016/86, Record Group 85, National Archives, San Bruno, CA.

Page 109: *in the heart of San Francisco:* "Rebuilding of San Francisco," *WP*, 21 Apr 1906.

Page 110: *would be permitted to rebuild there:* "Looking for a Chinatown Site," *SFC*, 23 May 1906.

Page 110: *where it had stood before:* "1906 Earthquake: Chinese Displacement," *U.S. Department of the Interior National Park Service website,* 10 Feb 2007, [http://www.nps.gov/prsf/historyculture/1906-earthquake-chinese-treatment.htm].

Page 110: *this time in northern California:* Hoy, *Chinese Digest,* 14.

Page 110: *to purchase additional property:* "Chinese Buys Claims," *St. John's Review,* 13 May 1910.

Page 110: *with a modern hydraulic system:* Ibid.

Page 110: *back in the mining business:* "Oregon," *Salt Lake Mining Review,* 15 May 1910.

Chapter XI: Meet Me At the Fair

Page 111: *a dozen were listed a decade later:* 1870 and 1880 United States Federal Census Online Databases, *Ancestry.com*, [http://search.ancestry.com/search/db.aspx?dbid=7163] and [http://search.ancestry.com/search/db.aspx?dbid=6742].

Page 111: *and nearly all laundrymen:* R. Keith Schoppa, "Chinese," in Robert M. Taylor, Jr., *Peopling Indiana: The Ethnic Experience* (Indianapolis, IN: Indiana Historical Society, 1996), 87.

Page 111: *Chinese men living in the city:* 1900 United States Federal

Census Online Databases, *Ancestry.com,* [http://search.ancestry.com/search/db.aspx?dbid=7602&enc=1].

Page 111: *subsequently gravitated to Indiana:* Schoppa, in *Peopling Indiana,* 87.

Page 111: *for the purchase of a laundry:* "Moy Kee in Town," *Logansport Pharos,* 30 Mar 1894.

Page 112: *who has the accomplishment:* "News and Views," *BE,* 7 Aug 1899.

Page 112: *the only one there in 1900:* "Moy Kee as a Boy," *WP,* 1 Mar 1900.

Page 112 – 113: *though not with their parents:* 1900 U. S. Census, Centre Township, Indianapolis, Marion County, Indiana, Supervisor's District 7, Enumeration District 104, page 6, lines 63-65; National Archives and Records Administration.

Page 113: *the couple was childless:* "Live Like Melican Men," *CT,* 12 May 1889.

Page 113: *wealth and caste in that land:* "Journey's End Life's as Well," *LAT,* 28 Jan 1914.

Page 113: *506 E. Washington Street:* Schoppa, in *Peopling Indiana,* 88.

Page 113: *an interpreter or a secret agent:* "Chinaman Passes Civil Service Exam," *ODT,* 9 Mar 1901.

Page 113: *effect of the Chinese Exclusion Act:* "Chinaman Wants Office," *Ft. Wayne Evening Sentinel,* 9 Mar 1901.

Page 113: *anything further was ever done about it:* "Chinaman Passes Civil Service Exam," *ODT,* 9 Mar 1901.

Page 114: *known only to the cooks of China:* "Ancient Eggs from Li Hung Chang," *Rochester Democrat and Chronicle,* 15 Jun 1901.

Page 114: *sent a fresh batch from Beijing:* "The Li Hung Chang Chop Suey Affair," (李鴻章雜碎胡搞)," *Taiwan United News website (Taiwan Lianhe Xinwen Wangzhan*臺灣聯合新聞網站), 9 Jun 2009, [http://mag.udn.com/mag/newsstand/storypage.jsp?f_ART_ID=197112].

Page 115: *head up China's delegation to the Fair:* Charles M. Kurtz, *The Saint Louis World's Fair of 1904* (St. Louis, MO: Gottschalk

Printing Company, 1903), 100.

Page 115: *pursuits that filled 20 albums:* Mark Bennitt and Frank Parker Stockbridge, eds., *History of the Louisiana Purchase Exposition Compiled From Official Sources* (St. Louis, MO: Universal Exposition Publishing Company, 1905), 289, 292-294.

Page 116: *for his highness from the Orient:* "Friendly Cannon Greets the Prince," *IN*, 18 May 1904.

Page 116: *his business card attached:* Schoppa, in *Peopling Indiana*, 90.

Page 116: *amounted to at most 100 men:* "Educated Chinese," *OT*, 8 Mar 1907.

Page 117: *at the Claypool Hotel:* Schoppa, in *Peopling Indiana*, 90.

Page 117: *a banquet was arranged for May 27:* "Pu Lun Calls On His New Friends," *IN*, 26 May 1904.

Page 117: *festooned with colorful tissue ribbons:* Ibid.

Page 118: *Charles Jones and William Fortune:* "Farewell Waved to Prince Pu Lun's Train," *IN*, 28 May 1904.

Page 118: *as well as preserved eggs:* "Eggs 100 Years Old at a Chinese Banquet," *Augusta Chronicle*, 9 Apr 1904.

Page 118: *that Jin Kee be granted a title:* "Farewell Waved to Prince Pu Lun's Train," *IN*, 28 May 1904.

Page 118 – 119: *the brass button of dignity was presented him:* Ibid.

Page 119: *the rank of Mandarin of the Fifth Degree:* "Indianapolis Chinaman Made a Noble," *NYT*, 20 Jul 1904.

Page 119: *vacancy in the upper house of Congress:* Untitled, *Piqua Leader-Dispatch*, 23 Jul 1904.

Chapter XII: Leading the Fight

Page 120: *because it needed capital:* Lynn Pan, *The Encyclopedia of the Chinese Overseas* (Cambridge, MA: Harvard University Press, 1999), 99.

Page 120: *who by this time was dead:* "Popular Chinese Woman," *SFMC*, 18 Apr 1905.

Page 120: *a cousin of Prince Pu Lun:* "China Lady in Society," *SR*,

13 Sep 1905.

Page 121: *a Chinese* habeas corpus *petitioner: United States* v. *Ju Toy*, 198 U.S. 253 (1905).

Page 121: *suspected of being a laborer:* Wong Sin-Kiong, "Mobilizing a Social Movement in China: Propaganda of the 1905 Boycott Campaign," in *Chinese Studies*, Vol. XIX, No. 1, 381.

Page 121: *abuses of the exclusion policy:* "Wu Ting Urges Boycott," *CPD*, 17 May 1905.

Page 121: *none other than Moy Kee of Indianapolis:* "Chinamen United to Gain Protection from Law," *Janesville Daily Gazette*, 19 May 1905.

Page 121: *was decorated by the Mikado:* "To Lead the Fight to Let Chinese In," *Fort Worth Star-Telegram*, 26 May 1905.

Page 123: *as all the people may understand:* Ibid.

Page 123: *in the direction of our rights:* "Chinese Are Pleased," *CPD*, 21 May 1905.

Page 124: *all but impossible in most cases:* "The Chinese Must Go," *CPD*, 11 Nov 1904.

Page 124: *the Chinese exclusion laws, at least temporarily:* "To Try Chinese Case," *CPD*, 29 Sep 1904.

Page 124: *such a writ against a Federal judge:* "Government Versus Judge," *NYT*, 15 Mar 1904.

Page 124: *a census of all the Chinese in the district:* "Use Photograph of Dead Man," *CPD*, 27 Jan 1905.

Page 124: *Chinese quarter for this purpose:* "Midnight Trips in Chinatown," *CPD*, 21 Jan 1905.

Page 124: *nine Chinese men had been arrested:* "Will Fight to the End," *CPD*, 20 May 1905.

Page 125: *as the original Act required:* "Cases Watched in Far Peking," *CPD*, 7 Jul 1905.

Page 125: *filed an appeal with the Supreme Court:* "Goes to Supreme Court," *CPD*, 26 Jan 1906.

Page 125: *and ending the matter:* "Appeal Was Vain; Chinese Must Go," *CPD*, 6 Mar 1906.

Page 125: *taken part in the discussions:* "High Chinese Arrive," *WP*,

13 Jan 1906.

Page 126: *between rival tongs of Indianapolis:* "Small Talk of Washington," *NYT*, 3 Feb 1906.

Page 126: *took them to the White House:* "Chinamen Meet President," *WP*, 2 Feb 1906.

Page 126: *the presidential audience took place there:* "At the White House," *NYDT*, 2 Feb 1906.

Page 126: *in conjunction with that event*: Desk Diaries of President Theodore Roosevelt, 1906. Entry for 1 Feb. *Theodore Roosevelt Papers,* Manuscript Division, Library of Congress.

Page 127: *tends to the peace of the world*: President Theodore Roosevelt, *State of the Union Address to the U.S. Congress,* 5 Dec 1905. Infoplease website [http://www.infoplease.com/t/hist/state-of-the-union/117.html].

Page 127: *audience in the first place*: Guanghua Wang, *In Search of Justice: 1905-1906: Chinese Anti-American Boycott* (Cambridge, MA: Harvard University Press, 2002), 15.

Chapter XIII: I Deem It To Be A Lesson For Him

Page 129: *the heart of the Chinese quarter:* "Census in Chinatown," *WP*, 7 Jun 1900.

Page 129: *$50 one year and $200 another year:* Deposition of Moy Bak Kwai before U.S. Immigration Bureau Inspector Robert F. Davis, 6 Mar 1916, Case Files of Chinese Immigrants, File 669C, Record Group 85, National Archives, Philadelphia, PA.

Page 130: *government service a decade earlier:* Affidavit of Moy Gop Jung, 27 Feb 1913, Case Files of Chinese Immigrants, File 669C, Record Group 85, National Archives, Philadelphia, PA.

Page 130: *permitted to bring in families:* Moy Gop Jung to Bertram N. Stump, 23 Mar 1913, Case Files of Chinese Immigrants, File 669C, Record Group 85, National Archives, Philadelphia, PA.

Page 131: *the Immigration officer who examined them:* Office of Immigrant Inspector, Pittsburgh, PA to Commission of Immigration, San Francisco, CA, 21 Jun 1913, Case Files of

Chinese Immigrants, File 669C, Record Group 85, National Archives, Philadelphia, PA.

Page 132: *as nephew and uncle very unpleasant:* Moy Gop Jung to Moy Nai Gun and Moy Nai Dung, 15 Mar 1914 [but probably not dated correctly], Case Files of Chinese Immigrants, File 669C, Record Group 85, National Archives, Philadelphia, PA.

Page 134: *such untruth against myself or my family:* Moy Jin Mun to Samuel W. Backus, 10 April 1914, Case Files of Chinese Immigrants, File 13330/2-2, Record Group 85, National Archives, San Bruno, CA.

Page 136: *I deem it to be a lesson for him:* Moy Gop Jung to Samuel W. Backus, 21 May 1914, Case Files of Chinese Immigrants, File 13330/2-7, Record Group 85, National Archives, San Bruno, CA.

Chapter XIV: Less Than Savory Characters

Page 137: *arrested by a United States Marshal:* "Dr. Jin Moy Arrested," *NYT,* 3 May 1911.

Page 137: *charging each $400 to $500:* "Marshal Arrests Wealthy Chinese," *OT,* 3 May 1911.

Page 137: *might one day become a point of contention:* Ibid.

Page 139: *someone he knew through the church:* City Directories for Newark, New Jersey (New Haven, CT: Price and Lee Company, 1912), 598.

Page 139: *transferred to Boston to stand trial:* "Snowden Takes Chinaman to Hub," *TT,* 13 May 1911.

Page 139: *China's first overseas patent filer:* Jin Fuey Moy, Inventor; Attachment for Nutcrackers. U.S. Patent 883,558, 31 Mar 1908.

Page 139: *accused of swindling and forgery:* "Chinatown Plot Thickens," *BS,* 22 Sep 1905.

Page 140: *and a merchant in Mott Street:* "Wealthy Chinaman is Brought Here for Trial," *BJ,* 14 May 1911.

Page 141: *you will not see me here long:* Jin Fuey Moy to Moy Gop Jung, 25 Jun 1910, Case Files of Chinese Immigrants, File 669C, Record Group 85, National Archives, Philadelphia, PA.

Page 141: *in the event of a trip back:* "He'll Stay at Home," *SDRU,* 11 Jul 1889.

Page 141: *his smile and his pearl stickpin:* "How Chinamen are Smuggled," *Turtle Mountain Star,* 1 Jun 1911.

Page 143: *letters of introduction to Chinese in Jamaica:* "The Chinese Smuggling Case," *GL* (Kingston, Jamaica), 27 May 1911.

Page 143: *Daley was arrested later:* "Clyde Ambrose Makes Known Plot of Chinese Gang," *LS,* 17 May 1911.

Page 143: *but actually to hire a boat:* "Woman Tells of Loan During Smuggling Trial," *BJ,* 17 May 1911.

Page 143: *to smuggle Chinese into the United States:* "Smuggling Case," *Daily Kennebec Journal,* 19 May 1911.

Page 143: *denied any complicity in the plot:* "Denies Offering Smuggling Fee," *BG,* 19 May 1911.

Page 143: *he told him to leave the shop:* "Two Are Guilty," *LS,* 20 May 1911 and "The Chinese Smuggling Case," *GL* (Kingston, Jamaica), 27 May 1911.

Page 144: *from Liverpool to Canada:* "Denies Offering Smuggling Fee," *BG,* 19 May 1911.

Page 144: *as exhibits in the trial:* Jin Fuey Moy to Moy Gop Jung, 12 Jun 1911, Case Files of Chinese Immigrants, File 669C, Record Group 85, National Archives, Philadelphia, PA.

Page 145: *when they arrested me:* "Chinese Case," *GL* (Kingston Jamaica), 30 May 1911.

Chapter XV: Reversal of Fortune I

Page 146: *stripped of his rank as a Mandarin:* "Moy Kee is Indignant," *IS,* 19 Oct 1907.

Page 147: *the decision was handed down:* "Chinatown Mayor Ousted," *WP,* 19 Oct 1907.

Page 147: *seeking cadavers for dissection:* "Many Murders Traced At Last to Bold Gang," *PI,* 10 Aug 1903.

Page 147: *the action of the Chinese minister:* "Moy Kee is Indignant," *IS,* 19 Oct 1907.

Page 148: *said he would reduce my rank:* Deposition of Moy Jin Kee before U.S. Immigration Bureau Examining Inspector H. A. Monroe, 14 Apr 1909, Case Files of Chinese Immigrants, File 602, Record Group 85, National Archives, Chicago, IL.

Page 148: *defrauding some of the local Chinese:* "Moy Ah Kee Dies Suddenly," IS, 7 Jan 1914.

Page 148: *to reverse the order: Ibid.*

Page 149: *live out his remaining years in China: Ibid.*

Page 149: *applications for return certificates:* Depositions of Moy Jin Kee, Chin Fung, Moy Bing Hee, Moy Hun and Dong Gum Hong before U.S. Immigration Bureau Examining Inspector L. T. Plummer, 15 Oct 1907, Case Files of Chinese Immigrants, File 602, Record Group 85, National Archives, Chicago, IL.

Page 151: *recently acquired full title to them:* L.T. Plummer to John H. Sargent, 18 Oct 1907, Case Files of Chinese Immigrants, File 602, Record Group 85, National Archives, Chicago, IL.

Page 151: *set sail for China on October 26:* Deposition of Moy Jin Kee before U.S. Immigration Bureau Examining Inspector H. A. Monroe, 14 Apr 1909, Case Files of Chinese Immigrants, File 602, Record Group 85, National Archives, Chicago, IL.

Page 151: *at the Port of Tacoma, Washington:* S.S. *Suveric* Passenger Manifest, 11 Mar 1909, Passenger and Crew Lists of Vessels Arriving at Seattle, Washington, Record Group 85, National Archives, Washington, DC.

Page 151: *since their departure in 1907:* U.S. Immigration Bureau Seattle Office to Chicago Office, 13 Mar 1909, Case Files of Chinese Immigrants, File 602, Record Group 85, National Archives, Chicago, IL.

Page 151: *Find property transferred:* U.S. Immigration Bureau Chicago Office to Seattle Office, 19 Mar 1909, Case Files of Chinese Immigrants, File 602, Record Group 85, National Archives, Chicago, IL.

Page 152: *most unsanitary structures in the city:* John R. Litz, "Seattle's 'Angel Island' Reaches Century Mark," *North American Post*, Vol. 63, 1 and 2 (1 Jan 2008).

Page 153: *proof of it along as an enclosure:* Charles W. Moores to L.

T. Plummer, 22 Mar 1909, Case Files of Chinese Immigrants, File 602, Record Group 85, National Archives, Chicago, IL.

Page 153: *that they were their sons:* L. T. Plummer to Charles W. Moores, 23 Mar 1909, Case Files of Chinese Immigrants, File 602, Record Group 85, National Archives, Chicago, IL.

Page 154: *returned and repaid the loan:* Deposition of Moy Bing Hee before U.S. Immigration Bureau Examining Inspector H. E. Tippett, 1 Apr 1909, Case Files of Chinese Immigrants, File 602, Record Group 85, National Archives, Chicago, IL.

Page 154: *who had handled the transaction:* Deposition of Dong Gum Hong before U.S. Immigration Bureau Examining Inspector H. E. Tippett, 1 Apr 1909, Case Files of Chinese Immigrants, File 602, Record Group 85, National Archives, Chicago, IL.

Page 155: *it had been a* bona fide *sale:* Deposition of Cass Conaway before U.S. Immigration Bureau Examining Inspector H. E. Tippett, 2 Apr 1909, Case Files of Chinese Immigrants, File 602, Record Group 85, National Archives, Chicago, IL.

Page 155: *whether she had ever borne children:* Deposition of Moy Hun before U.S. Immigration Bureau Examining Inspector H. E. Tippett, 1 Apr 1909, Case Files of Chinese Immigrants, File 602, Record Group 85, National Archives, Chicago, IL.

Page 156: *with a $750 payment: Ibid.* Also Deposition of Cass Conaway before U.S. Immigration Bureau Examining Inspector H. E. Tippett, 2 Apr 1909, Case Files of Chinese Immigrants, File 602, Record Group 85, National Archives, Chicago, IL.

Page 157: *Moy Dung Hoy and Hip Lung:* Deposition of Moy Jin Kee before U.S. Immigration Bureau Examining Inspector H. A. Monroe, 14 Apr 1909, Case Files of Chinese Immigrants, File 602, Record Group 85, National Archives, Chicago, IL.

Page 157: *unlikely all of them were lying:* Deposition of Moy Dung Hoy before U.S. Immigration Bureau Examining Inspector H. E. Tippett, 5 Apr 1909, Case Files of Chinese Immigrants, File 602, Record Group 85, National Archives, Chicago, IL, and Deposition of Moy Tong Chew before U.S. Immigration

THREE TOUGH CHINAMEN

Bureau Examining Inspector H. E. Tippett, 5 Apr 1909, Case Files of Chinese Immigrants, File 602, Record Group 85, National Archives, Chicago, IL.

Page 158: *Moy Kee and his wife, the applicants:* H. E. Tippett to L. T. Plummer, 7 Apr 1909, Case Files of Chinese Immigrants, File 602, Record Group 85, National Archives, Chicago, IL.

Page 159: *admitted at Port Huron in 1904 as their sons:* Deposition of Chin Fung Kee before U.S. Immigration Bureau Examining Inspector H. A. Monroe, 17 Apr 1909, Case Files of Chinese Immigrants, File 602, Record Group 85, National Archives, Chicago, IL. and Deposition of Moy Jin Kee before U.S. Immigration Bureau Examining Inspector H. A. Monroe, 14 Apr 1909, Case Files of Chinese Immigrants, File 602, Record Group 85, National Archives, Chicago, IL.

Page 159: *never heard of your ever having any children:* Ibid.

Page 160: *they were therefore eligible for re-entry:* Harry A. Monroe to L. T. Plummer, 22 Apr 1909, Case Files of Chinese Immigrants, File 602, Record Group 85, National Archives, Chicago, IL.

Page 161: *manager of the show's commissary department:* "Circus Roster," *Billboard*, March 20, 1909.

Page 161: *on display in the Lambrigger show:* "Moy Kee: Chinese Mayor of America," *KG*, 23 Jul 1909 and "Girl's Slayer is Dead, Says Chinese Mayor," *KG*, 24 Jul 1909.

Chapter XVI: Reversal of Fortune II

Page 162: *the American military system:* "Chinese Prince Coming," *NYT*, 21 Mar 1910.

Page 162: *caused much comment:* "Chinese Prince in Hawaii," *NYT*, 17 Apr 1910.

Page 162: *from China's army and navy:* "Taft Dines Chinese Prince," *NYT*, 29 Apr 1910.

Page 162: *the Washington Navy Yard:* "China Seeks Naval Hints," *NYT*, 30 Apr 1910.

Page 162: *shorn of their pigtails:* "Prince Tsai Visits West Point Academy," *NYT*, 3 May 1910.

Page 163: *against the weakening dynasty:* "Grave Signs in China," *NYT*, 18 May 1910.

Page 163: *apparently agreed with him:* "To Cut Off Queues," *Hopkinsville Kentuckian*, 27 Aug 1910.

Page 164: *the first time on November 4:* "Their Queues Cut Off," *NYT*, 4 Nov 1910.

Page 164: *victims to the operators' shears:* "Chinese Hasten to Remove Their Queues," *SFC*, 7 Nov 1910.

Page 164: *the report went on to say:* "Moy Kee Denounces Ukase," *IS*, 14 Nov 1910.

Page 164: *with long braids of hair:* "Approves Queue Cutting," *IS*, 16 Jan 1911.

Page 165: *appeared in the* Kalamazoo Gazette: "Moy Kee: Chinese Mayor of America," *KG*, 23 Jul 1909.

Page 166: *for appropriate action:* The Department of State to the Secretary of Commerce and Labor, 17 Feb 1909, File 1506/451, Entry 26, Record Group 85, National Archives, Washington, DC.

Page 166: *rendered ineligible for citizenship:* The Secretary of Commerce and Labor to the Department of State, 24 Feb 1909, File 1506/451, Entry 26, Record Group 85, National Archives, Washington, DC.

Page 166: *section 14 of the Chinese Exclusion Act:* Chief of the Division of Naturalization, Commerce and Labor to the Department of Justice, 24 Feb 1909, File 1506/451, Entry 26, Record Group 85, National Archives, Washington, DC.

Page 166: *the saddest moments of his life:* "Uncle Sam is After Moy Kee," *IS*, 5 Aug 1911.

Page 166: *It's too bad: Ibid.*

Page 167: *the best city in the country:* "Moy Ah Kee," *IS*, 6 Aug 1911.

Page 167: *one of Indianapolis' best citizens:* "Shank Intercedes for Chinese," *IS*, 24 Aug 1911.

Page 167: *subject to the same ruling:* "Moy Kee Case is Settled," *IS*, 19 Oct 1911.

Page 169: *surpass all others in the past:* "Celebrate Chinese New Year Last Time," *IS*, 18 Feb 1912.
Page 169: *the new Chinese Republic:* "Moy Kee, 64, Is Host at Elaborate Chinese Dinner," *IS*, 27 Jun 1912.
Page 170: *given over to a funeral home:* "Moy Ah Kee Dies Suddenly," *IS*, 7 Jan 1914.
Page 170: *questions relating to Chinese affairs:* Ibid.
Page 170: *among all classes of people:* "Moy Ah Kee is Dead," *TDT*, 7 Jan 1914.
Page 170: *and chanted a death song:* "Moy Ah Kee Dies Suddenly," *IS*, 7 Jan 1914.
Page 170: *rekindle the fire of life:* "Moy Ah Kee is Dead," *TDT*, 7 Jan 1914.
Page 170: *his journey into the hereafter:* "Widow of Moy Ah Kee Pays Tribute to Dead Spouse at Vigils at His Bier," *IS*, 15 Jan 1914.
Page 171: *to return to the United States:* Ibid.
Page 171: *peculiar to a Chinese funeral service:* "Widow Sings Chant of Grief at Funeral of Moy Ah Kee," *IS*, 16 Jan 1914.
Page 171: *no sorrow for the widow:* Ibid.
Page 172: *a chain of Chinese laundries:* R. Keith Schoppa, "Chinese," in Robert M. Taylor, Jr., *Peopling Indiana: The Ethnic Experience* (Indianapolis, IN: Indiana Historical Society, 1996), 89.
Page 172: *keep the business open:* "Notices," *IS*, 17 Jan 1914.
Page 172: *on or before January 22:* "Legal Notices," *IS*, 21 Jan 1914.
Page 172: *January 22 edition of the Star:* "Chinese Widow Honored by Ralston," *IS*, 22 Jan 1914.
Page 172: *self-slain, on his grave:* "Journey's End Life's as Well," *LAT*, 28 Jan 1914.

Chapter XVII: Many Impeachable Practices
Page 174: *very truly, Moy Ling:* Moy Ling [pseudonym] to Immigration Office, Washington, DC, 21 Jan 1913, Case Files of Chinese Immigrants, File 669C, Record Group 85, National Archives, Philadelphia, PA.

Page 175: *office of Moy Gop Jung:* Commissioner of Immigration, Philadelphia Station to Commissioner-General of Immigration, Washington, DC, 31 Jan 1916, Case Files of Chinese Immigrants, File 669C, Record Group 85, National Archives, Philadelphia, PA.

Page 177: *worldly wise Jin Fuey:* Jin Fuey Moy to Moy Gop Jung, 8 Sep 1909, 19 Feb 1910, 25 Jul 1910, 17 Oct 1910, 15 Dec 1910, 24 Dec 1910, and 12 Jun 1911, Case Files of Chinese Immigrants, File 669C, Record Group 85, National Archives, Philadelphia, PA.

Page 178: *except to one party in New York:* Deposition of Dr. Jin Fuey Moy before U.S. Immigration Bureau Inspector Charles V. Mallet, 16 Feb 1916, Case Files of Chinese Immigrants, File 669C, Record Group 85, National Archives, Philadelphia, PA.

Page 179: *put anything in black and white:* Ibid.

Page 179: *own dismissal from the Bureau:* "Inspector Charged with Blackmail," *House Documents, 59th Congress, First Session* (Washington: Government Printing Office, 1906), 133-4.

Page 181: *commit anything to paper:* Elmer E. Greenawalt to Jin Fuey Moy, 11 Jul 1916, Case Files of Chinese Immigrants, File 2652-C, Record Group 85, National Archives, Philadelphia, PA.

Page 181: *It will only create animosity:* Jin Fuey Moy to Elmer E. Greenawalt, 13 Aug 1916, Case Files of Chinese Immigrants, File 2652-C, Record Group 85, National Archives, Philadelphia, PA.

Chapter XVIII: The Chinese Nightingale

Page 183: *take part in the world's affairs:* "Lady Tsen Mei Thinks U.S. Wonderful Place," *San Antonio Light,* 29 Dec 1918 and "On Stage and Screen," *Grand Rapids Press,* 15 Sep 1922.

Page 183: *strongly suggested American teaching:* "The Bushwick," *BDE,* 9 May 1920 and "Palace – Vaudeville," *IS,* 31 Jul 1923.

Page 183: *imitations of birds and animals:* "Colonial Bill O.K.," *Utica Herald-Dispatch,* 4 Jan 1921.

Page 183: *to rise to stellar fame:* "Big Oriental Film at Regent," *Auburn Citizen*, 10 Apr 1919.

Page 183: *between 1912 and 1921:* "Remembering Betzwood Studio -- Hollywood on the Schuylkill," *Main Line Media News*, 4 Apr 2004.

Page 183: *the* New York Sunday Tribune *declared:* "Movie Notes," *NYST*, 9 Jun 1918.

Page 183: *Germans out of the Orient:* "Stone Opera House," *BP*, 22 Jan 1919.

Page 183 – 184: *history of the cinema industry:* "A Chinese-Made Film," *OT*, 7 Aug 1921.

Page 184: *to portray exotic characters:* The only known surviving print of "The Letter" is on deposit in the AFI/Paramount Collection at the Library of Congress, Washington, DC.

Page 185: *S.S.* Ventura *on November 7:* Josephine Augusta Moy Passport Application, 13 Oct 1916, Record Group 59, National Archives, Washington, D.C.

Page 185: *that she was American-born:* Assistant Commissioner-General, Bureau of Immigration, Washington, to Commissioner of Immigration, Philadelphia, 20 Oct 1916, Case Files of Chinese Immigrants, File 2702C, Record Group 85, National Archives, Philadelphia, PA.

Page 185: *my arrival 41 years ago:* Deposition of Dr. Jin Fuey Moy before Inspector William W. Sibray, Pittsburgh, PA, 24 Oct 1916, Case Files of Chinese Immigrants, File 2702C, Record Group 85, National Archives, Philadelphia, PA.

Page 187: *the circumstances of her birth:* Ibid.

Page 187: *actually born in San Francisco Bay:* Inspector William W. Sibray, Pittsburgh to Commissioner of Immigration, Philadelphia, 24 Oct 1916, Case Files of Chinese Immigrants, File 2702C, Record Group 85, National Archives, Philadelphia, PA.

Page 187: *refused to say any more:* Charles V. Mallet to Commissioner of Immigration, Philadelphia, 27 Oct 1916, Case Files of Chinese Immigrants, File 2702C, Record Group

85, National Archives, Philadelphia, PA.

Page 188: *been born in Wilmington:* A. M. Benkhart to Commissioner of Immigration, Philadelphia, 28 Oct 1916, Case Files of Chinese Immigrants, File 2702C, Record Group 85, National Archives, Philadelphia, PA.

Page 188: *the location of her birth:* A. Warner Parker Note to the File, 1 Nov 1916, Case Files of Chinese Immigrants, File 2702C, Record Group 85, National Archives, Philadelphia, PA.

Page 188: *been born in San Francisco Bay:* Charles V. Mallet to Commissioner of Immigration, Philadelphia, 27 Oct 1916, Case Files of Chinese Immigrants, File 2702C, Record Group 85, National Archives, Philadelphia, PA.

Page 188: *a Chinese who is not a citizen:* A. Warner Parker Note to the File, 1 Nov 1916, Entry 9, File 54180/334, Record Group 85, National Archives, Washington, DC.

Page 189: *the record shown until I objected:* Jin Fuey Moy to Charles F. Baker, 7 Mar 1917, Entry 9, File 54180/334, Record Group 85, National Archives, Washington, DC.

Page 189: *January 10, 1917 letter to Parker:* Charles F. Baker to A. Warner Parker, 8 Jan 1917, Entry 9, File 54180/334, Record Group 85, National Archives, Washington, DC.

Page 189: *Gop Jung there as a little boy:* Alfred Hampton to Charles F. Baker, 25 Jan 1917, Entry 9, File 54180/334, Record Group 85, National Archives, Washington, DC.

Page 190: *San Francisco, Cal. in the year 1875:* Jin Fuey Moy to Charles F. Baker, 7 Mar 1917, Entry 9, File 54180/334, Record Group 85, National Archives, Washington, DC.

Page 190: *will now be very difficult:* Alfred Hampton to Charles F. Baker, 21 Mar 1917, Entry 9, File 54180/334, Record Group 85, National Archives, Washington, DC.

Chapter XIX: The Man Who Took the Teeth Out of the Drug Act

Page 192: *a quarter of a million in 1900:* Steven Yale Sussman and Susan L. Ames, *Drug Abuse: Etiology, Prevention, and Cessation* (Cambridge: Cambridge University Press, 2008), 47.

THREE TOUGH CHINAMEN

Page 192: *ways to regulate the substance:* Humberto Fernandez, *Heroin* (Center City, MN: Hazelden Publishing, 1998), 26.

Page 192: *for making numberless 'dope fiends':* "Uncle Sam is the Worst Drug Fiend in the World," *NYT*, 12 Mar 1911.

Page 193: *for smoking and consumption:* Fernandez, *Heroin*, 26.

Page 193: *control domestic drug distribution:* David F. Musto, "Background to the Harrison Act," in Steven R. Belenko, *Drugs and Drug Policy in America: A Documentary History* (Westport, CT: Greenwood Press, 2000), 47.

Page 194: *in its 1910-11 session:* Fernandez, *Heroin*, 27.

Page 194: *and so he was released:* "Five Arrests Were Made," *NYDT*, 21 Nov 1912.

Page 194: *go into effect on March 1, 1915:* David F. Musto, *The American Disease: Origins of Narcotic Control* (New Haven, CT: Yale University Press, 1973), 121.

Page 194: *under the Hague Convention:* Edward M. Brecher and the Editors of *Consumer Reports Magazine*, "The Consumers Union Report on Licit and Illicit Drugs," *Schaffer Library of Drug Policy website*, 1972, [http://www.druglibrary.org/Schaffer/library/studies/cu/cu8.html].

Page 195: *a perfectly legitimate medical practice:* Musto, *American Disease*, 124.

Page 195: *was given before one was made:* Ibid., 123.

Page 196: *$100 per day from this enterprise:* "Chinese Physician Arrested," *BS*, 16 Apr 1915.

Page 196: *Drug Profit Causes His Arrest:* "Chink Doctor Gets Rich But His $100 a Day Drug Profit Causes His Arrest," *Macon Weekly Telegraph*, 16 Apr 1915.

Page 197: *to have prescribed it for him:* United States v. Jin Fuey Moy, 225 Fed. Rep. 1003 (W. D. Pa. 1915).

Page 198: *and did not extend more broadly:* "Law Which Forbids Drug Traffic May be Practically Useless," *BP*, 7 Dec 1915.

Page 198: *commitments under the Opium Convention:* Gail Winger, James H. Woods and Frederick G. Hofmann, *A Handbook on Drug and Alcohol Abuse: The Biomedical Aspects* (Oxford:

Oxford University Press, 2004), 156.

Page 198: *subject to criminal punishment:* United States v. Jin Fuey Moy, 241 U.S. 394 (1916).

Page 198: *the measure to a large extent:* "Draws Grinders of the Drug Law in Supreme Court," *Hagerstown Daily Mail*, 6 Jun 1916.

Page 198: *obtain the drugs from public dealers:* "The Harrison Drug Law," *Ft. Wayne News*, 12 Jun 1916.

Page 198: *teeth out of the Harrison Drug Act:* "Persons and Things," *Daily Northwestern*, 7 Feb 1918.

Page 199: *conspiracy to violate the Harrison Act:* "Pittsburgh Druggists Indicted," *PI*, 12 May 1917.

Page 199: *written by Jin Fuey himself:* "Charge Wide Drug Plot," *WP*, 13 May 1917.

Page 201: *becomes painfully and alarmingly apparent:* United States v. Jin Fuey Moy, 253 Fed. 213 (W. D. Pa. 1918).

Page 201: *no discussion of the subject is required:* Fernandez, Heroin, 28.

Page 202: *evidence rejected by the trial court:* Jin Fuey Moy v. United States, 254 U.S. 189 (1920).

Page 203: *and not given, to the jury: Ibid.*

Page 203: *kind of testimony she might give: Ibid.*

Page 203: *necessity of cracking down on them:* Kurt Hohenstein, "Just What the Doctor Ordered: The Harrison Anti-Narcotic Act, the Supreme Court, and the Federal Regulation of Medical Practice, 1915–1919," in *Journal of Supreme Court History*, Vol. 26, 234-236 (2001).

Page 203: *to which group Dr. Jin Fuey Moy belonged: Ibid.*, 252-254.

Chapter XX: Prisoner #11990

Page 204: *could be used in an escape:* "Uncle Sam's Model Prison," *NYS*, 16 May 1909.

Page 204: *who also served as librarian: Ibid.*

Page 205: *which presumably meant pornography: Ibid.*

Page 207: *ample opportunity for meditation: Ibid.*

Page 207: *Jin Fuey entered in 1921:* Anne Diestel, Federal Bureau of Prisons, to the author, 27 Jul 2009.

Page 207: *resistance to the military draft:* "Personal History," *Eugene Victor Debs (1855-1926) website,* 1 Sep 2009. [http://www.debsfoundation.org/pacifism.html].

Page 207: *inmates was Charles Ponzi:* Mitchell Zuckoff, *Ponzi's Scheme: The True Story of a Financial Legend* (New York: Random House, 2006), 46-49.

Page 207: *until his discharge:* Jin Fuey Moy, Certification of Belongings, 9 Feb 1921, Inmate No. 11990 File, Record Group 129, National Archives, Atlanta, GA.

Page 207: *gentlemanly and orderly manner:* Jin Fuey Moy, Petition to the Warden, 9 Feb 1921, Inmate No. 11990 File, Record Group 129, National Archives, Atlanta, GA.

Page 208: *the Assistant Attorney General:* Annette Abbott Adams to Fred G. Zerbst, 11 Mar 1921, Inmate No. 11990 File, Record Group 129, National Archives, Atlanta, GA.

Page 209: *my experience with him:* Jin Fuey Moy to Hatita Moy, 18 Jul 1921, Inmate No. 11990 File, Record Group 129, National Archives, Atlanta, GA.

Page 209: *as comfortable as [possible] for him:* Scott Ferris to Warden J. E. Dyche, 1 Jun 1921, Inmate No. 11990 File, Record Group 129, National Archives, Atlanta, GA.

Page 209: *in any way be life-threatening:* J. Calvin Weaver to the Warden, 10 Jul 1921, Inmate No. 11990 File, Record Group 129, National Archives, Atlanta, GA.

Page 210: *statements made to the contrary:* Jin Fuey Moy to Hatita Moy, 18 Jul 1921, Inmate No. 11990 File, Record Group 129, National Archives, Atlanta, GA.

Page 210: *demanded a medical report:* Heber Votaw to Warden J. E. Dyche, 1 Aug 1921, Inmate No. 11990 File, Record Group 129, National Archives, Atlanta, GA.

Page 210: *would jeopardize his life:* J. Calvin Weaver to the Warden, 8 Aug 1921, Inmate No. 11990 File, Record Group 129, National Archives, Atlanta, GA.

Page 210: *against Asiatic immigration:* "Hoke Smith Tells of Work in Senate, "*Marietta Journal,* 8 Aug 1913.

Page 211: *occurred in late December:* Ronald Sansom to Hon. Hoke Smith, 29 Dec 1921, Folder 13, Box 19, Subject Files 1891-1929, Hoke Smith Papers, 1879-1931, Richard B. Russell Library for Political Research and Studies, University of Georgia Library, Athens, GA.

Page 211: *parole the previous October:* Hatita Moy to Hon. Hoke Smith, 6 Jan 1922, Folder 13, Box 19, Subject Files 1891-1929, Hoke Smith Papers, 1879-1931, Richard B. Russell Library for Political Research and Studies, University of Georgia Library, Athens, GA.

Page 211: *legal issues surrounding his case:* Jin Fuey Moy to Ronald Sansom, 23 Feb 1922, Folder 13, Box 19, Subject Files 1891-1929, Hoke Smith Papers, 1879-1931, Richard B. Russell Library for Political Research and Studies, University of Georgia Library, Athens, GA.

Page 211: *influential friends and powerful enemies:* Ronald Sansom to Hon. Hoke Smith, 27 Feb 1922, Folder 13, Box 19, Subject Files 1891-1929, Hoke Smith Papers, 1879-1931, Richard B. Russell Library for Political Research and Studies, University of Georgia Library, Athens, GA.

Page 211: *payment of a $1,000 retainer fee:* Hon. Hoke Smith to Ronald Sansom, 27 Feb 1922, Folder 13, Box 19, Subject Files 1891-1929, Hoke Smith Papers, 1879-1931, Richard B. Russell Library for Political Research and Studies, University of Georgia Library, Athens, GA.

Page 212: *imprisonment would endanger his life:* James A. Finch to Warden J. E. Dyche, 18 Jan 1922, Inmate No. 11990 File, Record Group 129, National Archives, Atlanta, GA.

Page 212: *instead of an injury:* J. Calvin Weaver to the Warden, 22 Jan 1922, Inmate No. 11990 File, Record Group 129, National Archives, Atlanta, GA.

Page 212: *in my opinion, far from correct:* Dr. A. L. Fowler to the Warden, 14 May 1922, Inmate No. 11990 File, Record Group

129, National Archives, Atlanta, GA.

Page 214: *in a brief obituary:* "Funeral Services for a Noted Chinese Doctor," *Charleroi Mail*, 5 May 1924.

Chapter XXI: Peacemaker

Page 215: *political needs of their constituents:* Him Mark Lai, *Becoming Chinese American* (Lanham, MD: Altamira Press, 2002), 39.

Page 215: *for the benefit of his countrymen:* William Hoy, "Moy Jin Mun – Pioneer," *Chinese Digest*, 15 May 1936. Vol. II, No. 20, 14.

Page 215: *president of the organization:* "Chinese Tongs Holding Peace Conference," *Idaho Statesman*, 23 Feb 1916.

Page 215 – 216: *North and South America:* "Japan's Demands to Hague," *NYT*, 25 Apr 1915.

Page 216: *each of the six constituent associations:* "Chinese Consolidated Benevolent Association, 'Chinese Six Companies,' A Strong Organization," *SFC*, 12 Jan 1916.

Page 216: *lead position by October 1917:* "Historic Chinatown," *SFC*, 15 Oct 1917.

Page 216: *President Woodrow Wilson:* "Chinese to Carry Protest to Wilson," *Ogden Examiner*, 4 Apr 1914.

Page 216: *President Yuan Shih-kai:* "Chinese Troops Revolt in Four Big Districts," *SFC*, 28 Jul 1914.

Page 216: *accusing him of playing politics:* "Abducted by Tramps," *LS*, 26 May 1914.

Page 216: *economic domination there:* "Chinese Boycott on Japanese Growing on the Coast," *Nevada State Journal*, 1 Mar 1915.

Page 216: *the Japanese-Chinese crisis:* "Diplomacy Cause of Embargo," *OT*, 26 Feb 1915.

Page 216: *the triads in Chinatown:* "Halt is Called on Tong Battle," *OT*, 26 Mar 1916.

Page 217: *if violence should erupt:* "Tong War Ends in Strong Peace Pact," *SFMC*, 29 Jan 1908.

Page 217: *charter member of the new association:* Hoy, *Chinese Digest*,

14.

Page 218: *to unite as one family:* "Chinatown Organizations of Overseas Chinese from the Five Counties," (唐人街中的邑橋團), *JMN News Website* (*Zhongguo Jiangmen Wang,* 中國江門網), 29 Sep 2004, [http://www.jmnews.com.cn/c/2004/09/29/17/c_398547.shtml].

Page 218: *securing his freedom:* "The Chinese in American Courts," *Bulletin of Concerned Asian Scholars,* Vol. 4, No. 3, Fall, 1972.

Page 219: *was first among them:* "Chinese Tongs Holding Peace Conference," *Idaho Statesman,* 23 Feb 1916.

Page 219: *headquarters at 385½ Everett Street:* "Chinese Tong Men Are Holding Peace Convention in Portland," *SFC,* 23 Feb 1916.

Page 219: *old scores against the rival tong:* "Truce is Arranged by Chinese Tongs," *The Oregonian,* 23 Feb 1916.

Page 219: *in the event peace was broken:* "Tong Peace Pact Terminates Strife in S.F. Chinatown," *SFC,* 7 Aug 1922.

Page 220: *belonged before his death:* "List of Leaders Chosen by San Francisco Freemasons" (金門致公總堂選舉職員表), Ta Kung Pao (大公報), 6 Dec 1921.

Page 220: *affiliated since he was a young man:* Hoy, *Chinese Digest,* 14.

Page 220: *lived elsewhere at the time:* 1930 U. S. Census, San Francisco, San Francisco County, California, Supervisor's District 6, Enumeration District 38-393, page 29A, lines 1-12; National Archives and Records Administration.

Page 221: *an interest in the Shanghai Low:* Deposition of Wong Shee before U.S. Immigration Bureau Inspector H. Schmoldt, 27 Nov 1931, Case Files of Chinese Immigrants, File 12017/43314, Record Group 85, National Archives, San Bruno, CA.

Page 222: *left his business interests to his sons:* Hoy, *Chinese Digest,* 14.

Page 222: *unofficially the 'mayor' of Chinatown:* "Rites Tomorrow for Chinatown 'Mayor,'" *OT,* 16 May 1936.

Page 222: *the sage of Chinatown:* "Sugar Eases Chinese Grief,"

Vidette Messenger, 5 Jun 1936.

Page 222: *is not beneath the moon:* "Mourn Death of Old S.F. Chinese," *Bakersfield Californian*, 4 May 1936.

Page 223: *where he was interred:* "S. F. Chinatown 'Mayor' Buried," *OT*, 18 May 1936 and "Moy Jin Mun Joins Fathers," *San Mateo Tribune*, 21 May 1936.

Page 223: *of which he was guarantor:* "Petition for Letters of Administration with Prayer to Set Aside Estate Under $2,500.00 to Widow in the Matter of the Estate of Moy Ki Choo, also known as Moy Jin Mun, Deceased." Superior Court of the State of California, 26 Oct 1936.

Page 223: *and half-siblings, to that effect:* Ibid.

Epilogue

Page 224: *stigma in 1915 that it does today:* Kurt Hohenstein, "Just What the Doctor Ordered: The Harrison Anti-Narcotic Act, the Supreme Court, and the Federal Regulation of Medical Practice, 1915–1919" in *Journal of Supreme Court History*, Vol. 26, 231-232 (2001).

Page 226: *a salary of $50 per month:* Deposition of Moy Kye Hin before U.S. Immigration Bureau Inspector F. S. Pierce, 13 Feb 1914, Case Files of Chinese Immigrants, File 6970, Box 24, Record Group 85, National Archives, New York, NY.

Page 227: *back to China for good in 1918:* Entry 9, File 5450916, Record Group 85, National Archives, Washington, DC.

Page 228: *to relieve us the burden:* Jin Fuey Moy to Hatita Moy, 18 Jul 1921, Inmate No. 11990 File, Record Group 129, National Archives, Atlanta, GA.

ACKNOWLEDGMENTS

Sasha Gong, who shared my daily discoveries and intimacies with the Moy brothers, helped me track down Chinese sources and decipher Chinese documents, and broadened my understanding of the period and of the Chinese immigrant population.

Debbie Strauss, Dan Metcalfe and Alice Thurston, my "legal dream team," who helped this non-attorney make sense of the various court cases and legal documents mentioned in the book, and especially the Supreme Court cases involving Jin Fuey Moy, which tax even the legal mind, let alone that of the layman.

Yoma Ullman, friend, neighbor and meticulous editor, who read the first draft of each chapter as soon as I finished it, and made me think more deeply about content even as she had me minding my punctuation and diction.

Marc Abramson, whose excellent writing skills, coupled with a scholar's command of classical Chinese, produced the elegant translation of the Moy family's generation poem introduced in the third chapter.

Roberta Gee, a great-granddaughter of Moy Jin Mun and a fellow genealogist, who shared my quest to confirm family legends, helped compile the Moy family tree and solve some of its mysteries and provided several vintage family photographs that appear in this book.

Raymond Lum of the Harvard-Yenching Library, who I met online when he fielded an inquiry from me, and who has become a good friend and a valuable source of counsel, reference materials and editorial advice.

ACKNOWLEDGMENTS

Marian L. Smith, surely the foremost authority on the Chinese Exclusion Act files on deposit in the National Archives, who gave generously of her time and counsel to help me locate relevant files from all over the United States.

Marsha Cohan, Marcia Ristaino, Howard Spendelow and **Judith Shapiro,** friends and fellow "China-hands", who read all or part of the manuscript and offered useful advice.

Don Chamblee, a voracious reader of history; the late **Howard J. Happ,** a historian of religion and **Margery Elfin,** a historian and political scientist; all friends who provided very useful comments and editing suggestions.

Jack (John Kuo Wei) Tchen of New York University, who gave the manuscript a scholar's review and urged me to think more about the contrast between American and Chinese core values that played out in the book in the context of the American political culture in which the Moys found themselves.

Soo Lon Moy and **Andrea Stamm,** historians of Chicago's Chinese community, who located additional information about Moy Jin Kee after I thought I had read all there was to read about him.

Peggy Spitzer Christoff, a China scholar who generously lent me her time, her books and her judgment. Her discussion of how the Immigration Bureau kept track of America's Chinese population in *Tracking the Yellow Peril* is first-rate and was especially helpful.

David Abelmann, a Mandarin-speaking friend who traveled to Daly City, California on my behalf and waded through two muddy Chinese cemeteries in a successful, "above and beyond the call of duty" search for Moy Jin Mun's gravesite.

ACKNOWLEDGMENTS

John K. Lem, who knows his way around Washington's Chinatown better than most, and who opened the door for me to local members of the Moy clan.

Tow H. Moy, who generously shared a copy of a document dating from 1664 about the origins of the Moys of Duanfen.

Kurt A. Hohenstein of Winona State University, who helped me fathom why the Supreme Court seemed to change its mind between its two very different decisions regarding Dr. Jin Fuey Moy and the Harrison Act.

F. Michael Angelo, University Archivist and Special Collections Librarian for Thomas Jefferson University, who helped retrieve records relating to the matriculation of Jin Fuey Moy.

Wilson Chu, a grandson of Moy Jin Mun, who shared family stories about his grandfather.

Henry Tom, who helped me pinpoint the town in Taishan from which the Moys emigrated, and **Tan Shicheng,** who visited the village for me in search of clues.

Lissa Kiser and **Justin Langlois** of the Pennington School, who tracked down an 1882 Jin Fuey Moy letter that survives in the school's archives.

Megan Rowe of Stanford University, who combed the Leland Stanford Papers and the Jane Lathrop Stanford Papers for references to Moy Jin Mun and who tracked down the two extant editions of Jin Fuey Moy's *Chinese-American Advocate*.

Trent Sindelar of the St. Louis Public Library, who helped find information about Moy Jin Kee in the *History of the Louisiana Purchase Exposition*.

Jan Levinson of the Richard B. Russell Library for Political Research and Studies, University of Georgia, who helped locate letters written on behalf of Jin Fuey Moy in the Hoke Smith (1879-1931) papers.

Nancy Peterson of the California Genealogical Society, who helped retrieve and interpret Moy Jin Mun's probate records.

Toru Matsubayashi, M.D., for helping decipher Jin Fuey Moy's cause of death.

Kathy Ramanauskas, who graciously provided me with an autograph of Jin Fuey Moy from his time at Pennington Seminary from her personal collection.

Douglas A. Bicknese (Chicago), **Gail Farr** (Philadelphia), **Bill Greene** (San Bruno), **Ken House** (Seattle), **Ashley Judy** (Atlanta), **Glenn V. Longacre** (Chicago) and **Angela Tudico** (New York) and other unsung heroes and heroines at the National Archives and Records Administration, who not only helped obtain relevant files, but also advised me on strategy for locating records housed in other repositories.

Graham Earnshaw, Derek Sandhaus and **Jessica Li** of Earnshaw Books, for helping to make this a better book in myriad ways.

ABOUT THE AUTHOR

Scott D. Seligman is a writer, a historian, a genealogist, a retired corporate executive and a career "China hand." He has an undergraduate degree in history from Princeton University with a concentration in American civilization and a master's degree from Harvard University. Fluent in Mandarin and conversant in Cantonese, he lived in Taiwan, Hong Kong and China for eight years and reads and writes Chinese. He has worked as a legislative assistant to a member of the U.S. Congress, lobbied the Chinese government on behalf of American business, managed a multinational public relations agency in China, served as communications director for a Fortune 50 company and taught English in Taiwan and Chinese in Washington, DC's Chinatown. He is the author of *Chinese Business Etiquette* (Hachette, 1999) and *Dealing With the Chinese* (Warner Books, 1989) and co-author of the best-selling *Cultural Revolution Cookbook* (Earnshaw Books, 2011), *Chinese at a Glance* (Barron's Educational Series, 1985 and 2001) and *Now You're Talking Mandarin Chinese* (Barron's, 2006). He has also published articles in the *Asian Wall Street Journal*, the *Washington Post*, the *China Business Review*, *China Heritage Quarterly*, the *Jewish Daily Forward*, *Traces* (the Journal of the Indiana Historical Society) and elsewhere, and has created websites on historical and genealogical topics. He lives in Washington, DC.

www.ingramcontent.com/pod-product-compliance
Lightning Source LLC
LaVergne TN
LVHW030317070526
838199LV00069B/6489